"*So We and Our Children [...]* ful book for our time. Sara[...] us tools for talking about [...] in today, but what it takes to place ourselves in a relationship of care with Mother Earth and one another along the way. In this refreshing book that melds faith and science, the research, stories, and world-wide Indigenous wisdom included will help readers find the courage to act in a time that feels overwhelming. For those who wish to use their spiritual lives to invest in a better future for all, this book is essential."

—**KAITLIN B. CURTICE**, bestselling author of *Native* and *Living Resistance*

"In this tour de force, Sarah Augustine and Sheri Hostetler empower readers to promote the kingdom of God by connecting the dots between cosmic shalom and Spirit-propelled decolonization. What a gift for us, our children, and our children's children."

—**NATHAN CARTAGENA**, assistant professor of philosophy at Wheaton College

"Sarah Augustine and Sheri Hostetler's book crackles with truth-telling born of their love for the earth and its inhabitants. It is a book that demands reading and rereading—not simply because it is important (though it is) or challenging (though it is), but because its message slices through illusion and awakens imagination. Those willing to receive the Reality they name will find themselves transformed and inspired for the work to come."

—**REV. AIMEE MOISO, PHD**, associate director of the Louisville Institute and an ordained minister in the Presbyterian Church (USA)

"This book is an invitation to imagine a world otherwise. It makes clear that to address the question of ecological injustice, it is necessary to expose the ideological superstructure behind current attempts at greening technology and economic growth. Though critical of Christianity's historical passive unwillingness to address the intertwined issues of colonization, global market capitalism, and ecological destruction, the authors draw on their own traditions to highlight the rich reservoirs from which Christians can address and respond to ecological justice today."

—REV. DR. NÉSTOR MEDINA, associate professor of religious ethics and culture at Emmanuel College, University of Toronto

"So We and Our Children May Live welcomes an unnerving yet essential dialogue examining the ways that growth-based, extractive impulses are not exclusive to the fossil fuel–driven economy, but are also present in some popular expressions of the green-growth, renewable energy revolution—in which society is placing so much hope. In a far-reaching and integrative manner, bringing together economics, biblical scholarship, social sciences, and Indigenous experiences and worldviews, Sarah Augustine and Sheri Hostetler invite all human systems (and we who design and shape them) to be collectively transformed by Creator's Spirit—toward living in balance with the community of life that holds us all. This book does not simplify the way forward into ten easy steps but lays the foundation for the deep shifts that are required of all of us."

—JONATHAN NEUFELD, Mennonite Church Canada Indigenous Relations coordinator

"Whether you're a Christian or not (me? no), you'll receive important insights from this book. Many of these insights are moral or ethical, centering on our responsibility to future generations and to other species; others have to do with understanding why environmental crises are tied to our current economic paradigm, which values growth over fairness or sustainability. The book benefits from Native American and Christian (Mennonite) perspectives on climate change and inequality—subjects too often discussed just in technical or political terms. Sarah Augustine and Sheri Hostetler will help you think more deeply and honestly about our future, our current societal choices, and perhaps even the way you yourself now live."

—RICHARD HEINBERG, senior fellow at Post Carbon Institute

SO WE & OUR CHILDREN MAY LIVE

Following Jesus in Confronting the Climate Crisis

SARAH AUGUSTINE & SHERI HOSTETLER

HERALD
P R E S S

Harrisonburg, Virginia

Herald Press
PO Box 866, Harrisonburg, Virginia 22803
www.HeraldPress.com

Library of Congress Cataloging-in-Publication Data
Names: Augustine, Sarah, author. | Hostetler, Sheri, author.
Title: So we and our children may live : following Jesus in confronting the
    climate crisis / Sarah Augustine and Sheri Hostetler.
Description: Harrisonburg, Virginia : Herald Press, [2023] | Includes
    bibliographical references.
Identifiers: LCCN 2023027147 (print) | LCCN 2023027148 (ebook) |
    ISBN 9781513812946 (paperback) | ISBN 9781513812953 (hardcover) |
    ISBN 9781513812960 (ebook)
Subjects: LCSH: Climatic changes—Religious aspects—Christianity. | Climatic
    changes—Moral and ethical aspects. | Human ecology—Religious aspects—
    Christianity. | Ecotheology. | BISAC: RELIGION / Christian Living / Social Issues
    | NATURE / Ecology
Classification: LCC BT695.5 .A95 2023 (print) | LCC BT695.5 (ebook) | DDC
    261.8/8—dc23/eng/20230726
LC record available at https://lccn.loc.gov/2023027147
LC ebook record available at https://lccn.loc.gov/2023027148

Study guides are available for many Herald Press titles at www.HeraldPress.com.

SO WE AND OUR CHILDREN MAY LIVE: FOLLOWING JESUS IN
CONFRONTING THE CLIMATE CRISIS
© 2023 by Herald Press, Harrisonburg, Virginia 22803. 800-245-7894.
    All rights reserved.
Library of Congress Control Number: 2023027147
International Standard Book Number: 978-1-5138-1294-6 (paperback);
    978-1-5138-1295-3 (hardcover); 978-1-5138-1296-0 (ebook)
Printed in United States of America
Cover and interior design by Merrill Miller
Cover image: pixelparticle/iStockphoto/Getty Images

Unless otherwise noted, scripture quotations are taken from the New Revised Standard
Version Updated Edition. Copyright © 2021 National Council of Churches of Christ
in the United States of America. Used by permission. All rights reserved worldwide.
Scripture quotations marked (CEB) from the COMMON ENGLISH BIBLE. Copyright © 2011 COMMON ENGLISH BIBLE. All rights reserved. Used by permission
(www.CommonEnglishBible.com). Scripture quotations marked (NIV) are taken from
the Holy Bible, New International Version®, NIV®. Copyright © 1973, 1978, 1984,
2011 by Biblica, Inc.® Used by permission of Zondervan. All rights reserved worldwide.
www.Zondervan.com. The "NIV" and "New International Version" are trademarks
registered in the United States Patent and Trademark Office by Biblica, Inc.®

27 26 25 24 23   10 9 8 7 6 5 4 3 2 1

For Micah, Oliver, Arlo, and Ziggy
—Sarah

For Patrick
—Sheri

CONTENTS

Foreword

WHY DID YOU *teach me to love this world?*

My oldest asked me this question one day while reflecting on his observations of climate change. Ben is a self-professed tree nerd who has worked with trees from planting to fires. This keeps him closely connected with the life cycles of forests and the landscapes that surround them, which means that he notices changes, and the consequences of those changes, long before I do. I watch Ben teach his son Charlie to love this world, and I see them teach each other to notice worlds beginning and ending all around them. They planted a garden together, the toddler carefully placing the seedlings offered by the father and patting them into place before ripping them back out again. The point of this garden, Ben says, is to teach Charlie to love the textures and smells of the living earth. To feel himself part of it.

We are Ojibwe Anishinaabe, and our wisdom contains a series of prophecies called fires. Each one refers to a particular confluence, with warnings and teachings to help us navigate the turbulence. Prophecy is a way of speaking truth into pivotal moments, and this book you are holding or hearing lays out the details of this particular confluence, this pivotal moment, in stark terms. Many Anishinaabeg believe that we are in the time of the seventh fire, a time when the latecomers will need to make a choice about how they will live. The fire following one constellation of choices will reveal a pathway lush and green, which we will follow together to the eighth fire, signifying a time of peace and friendship. Other choices unleash a fire that blackens the land, leaving a charred pathway that will cut our feet. I once thought these fires were metaphors or campfires, but Ben's friend Caleb assures him that these are wildfires.

The outcome of a wildfire depends on the environment, so the work of fighting them is largely about preparing and shaping the landscape to contain the fire, not simply dumping water on it. Like many peoples, the Anishinaabeg have worked with fire, using it to shape and maintain forests. For a healthy forest, the aftermath of a fire becomes a green path filled with grasses, fireweed, and berries in a cycle of reciprocal relationship of which people are an integral part, as Sarah Augustine and Sheri Hostetler remind us. But a clear-cut, with no vegetation to hold moisture, becomes a landscape so devastated by intense heat that nothing will grow. It is truly a charred path that will cut your feet. I cannot see these prophecies as metaphors any longer, not when early summer skies across Canada and the United States are filled with the smoke and haze of rampant fires.

Why did you teach me to love this world?

Ben asked me this question, but it would be just as true for me to ask it of him. Why did he, with his love of trees and gardening and the swamp behind our house, teach me to love this world? To notice the changes that might otherwise have gone unseen so that I must grieve the things that are surely passing, falling through our fingers while we grasp for "sustainable" consumer goods and the false promises of green energy that Sarah and Sheri unpack for us. How we shape the landscape will have a profound impact on the fires that are coming. The outcome is the responsibility of the latecomers, those whose terraforming and upheaval have created the conditions we are faced with today. It is your responsibility not only to make personal choices, but to confront the architects of death and to demand real change. In addition to laying out the stark realities of our circumstances, Sarah and Sheri have also laid out strategies for that confrontation. Things that we can and should do, things we can and should demand.

We teach each other to love this world. Parents and children. Indigenous people and latecomers. We teach each other and work together, that we may yet walk that green pathway, lush with life.

—Patty Krawec, Anishinaabe and Ukrainian writer and member of Lac Seul First Nation, cohost of the *Medicine for the Resistance* podcast, cofounder of the Nii'kinaaganaa Foundation, and author of *Becoming Kin*

Preface

IN 2014, ANITA Amstutz, Sarah (coauthor), and I (Sheri) founded the Coalition to Dismantle the Doctrine of Discovery. Katerina Gea joined our trio soon afterward. Our first years were spent educating people about the Doctrine of Discovery and how a five-hundred-year-old church doctrine justifying colonization and the slave trade forms the structures of our present society. Our coalition made a documentary. We created curriculum, a traveling exhibit, and worship resources, and assisted in developing a play. Sarah wrote a book based on her personal experience of the Doctrine of Discovery and her decades-long work trying to dismantle it. She logged many miles and Zoom hours preaching and speaking on dismantling the Doctrine of Discovery, as have many others. Together, she and I started a podcast called *The Dismantling the Doctrine of Discovery Podcast.* The goal of all this activity has been to educate people of faith about the Doctrine of Discovery so they can become change agents in dismantling it.

It has been amazing to watch this work bear fruit. More than thirty Christian congregations and communities have joined the coalition's Repair Network, which supports them in educating themselves and others about the Doctrine of Discovery and in taking concrete acts of solidarity and reparative action alongside Indigenous Peoples. Together, they have protested the dismantling of the Indian Child Welfare Act and stood in solidarity with members of the San Carlos Apache as they seek to save their sacred land of Chi'chil Biłdagoteel (Oak Flat). Others have worked alongside Maya people in the Yucatan Peninsula to oppose industrial agriculture and economic development projects that imperil their communities. Others are committing money and proceeds from the sale of property so Native tribes, like the Dakota, can buy back ancestral lands.

Our work as a coalition is grounded in decolonization. We will never stop trying to dismantle the laws and policies that remove Indigenous Peoples from their land. In this book, we'll dig into what colonization is and what it means to dismantle it. Along with others descended from white settlers, I participate in this work because I know I have benefitted from colonization and continue to do so. And like others who follow in the way of Jesus, I believe I am called to help build the kindom[1] of God on earth, the realm of right relationship and shalom that Jesus announced and enacted. Decolonization is a necessary part of that kindom-building.

There's nothing wrong with these motivations. But only in the past few years have I come to understand how my *survival* and that of my family's is bound up in this work. I am coming to a deeper understanding of the truth of what Aboriginal activists like Lilla Watson have said: "If you have come here to help me, you are wasting your time, but if you have come because your liberation is bound up with mine, then let us work together."[2] My liberation from systems of death is bound up with that of my Indigenous siblings.

I want to talk more about how I came to this understanding because it is key to what Sarah and I are trying to do in this book.

A decade ago, I realized I had to work on preventing climate change. My only child, Patrick, was eight at the time, and I kept imagining how I would justify myself to him decades from now. Would he be angry with me for my perceived inaction during those pivotal decades when we still had a chance to avert the worst catastrophes? Would my saying that we drove an electric car and used LED lighting cut it with future Patrick? Would he accept the excuse if I told him, "I was so busy with raising you and my job, and it all seemed so overwhelming, and I wasn't sure where to start"? I had a feeling he would not, nor should he.

As I was praying to find a way to engage in this work, I met Sarah Augustine through our mutual friend, Anita. Sarah was fighting for Indigenous sovereignty and land justice; she framed this work as "resisting extraction." Honestly, when I first met her, I wasn't sure what extraction was or why it mattered in the fight against climate change. But I trusted that the Spirit had brought us together and that working with Sarah on resisting extraction was exactly what I needed to be doing, despite my inability to articulate this connection to climate change.

I finally get it. We are fighting to dismantle structures designed to remove Indigenous Peoples from their land so that our economic system can continue to extract and consume resources at an ever-increasing pace. This growth-based system, designed to generate wealth and profits for individuals, is threatening the survival of all life on this planet. Climate change, I have realized, is only one symptom of the real threat, which is ecological overshoot. Ecological overshoot occurs when our demands on the planet are greater than what Earth's ecosystems can renew. Extraction and the pollution it causes are now pushing us past several planetary boundaries, including carbon dioxide emissions in the atmosphere. In short, extraction is devastating the life-support systems of our planet.

I'm now clear that I am *not only* fighting in solidarity with Indigenous Peoples. I am fighting for myself and for the life of my son and his friends. I am fighting for the life of Sarah's son and his friends. I am fighting for my home and neighborhood, which sit at sea level. I am fighting for the life of the persimmon tree in my backyard that provides bushels of fruit for us, as well as for the Eastern fox squirrels and scrub jays that eat there. I am fighting for coral reefs, some of the most beautiful and necessary ecosystems on earth. I am fighting for air, water, soils. I am fighting for the entire buzzing, bountiful beauty of life on this planet.

I think most of us in the dominant culture don't viscerally comprehend this direct connection between extraction and our own survival. When I mentioned this disconnect to Sarah recently, she said, "If you talk to Indigenous people around the world—from Africa and Asia to Norway to Central and South America to the United States—they will tell you the biggest threat to them is extraction. They know that climate change could get solved by electric vehicles and renewables, and brutal extraction will still occur." Indigenous people know that extraction is based on a worldview that sees the Earth as a resource to accumulate wealth and profit. It is an inherently unsustainable worldview because it is not congruent with ecological reality. Sarah told me that you could walk onto any reservation in the United States and ask the average Native person about this, and the response would be, "The dominant culture is not normal, and it makes no sense." In other words, the average Native person gets what it has taken me—a white settler working on Indigenous justice issues—years, if not decades, to really understand.

This book is structured to lead you through the process of discovering Reality, as I did. In part 1, we consider Reality versus reality. We contrast two systems of thought: systems of life ("Reality" with a capital R), which acknowledge that we live within a closed system of mutual dependence, and systems of death (or what is considered reality in our dominant culture), which are based on an extractive logic.

I come from a long line of Amish Mennonite farmers who fled religious persecution in Switzerland in the 1700s. About a century later, my family made their way to Holmes County, Ohio, where they became the first white settlers in that place. My family has lived there ever since. I feel a deep connection to and love for that land, an emotion complicated by the knowledge that my family displaced people even more deeply connected to it. My Mennonite faith instilled in me the belief that I was to be in the world but not of it.[3] For me, that means I am to constantly seek and see God's kindom, which is true Reality and often not synonymous with the world as it is.

The second part of this book scrutinizes the only consensus solution to climate change available today: decarbonizing the global economy through a green growth, renewable energy revolution. We argue that this solution alone will not heal creation, end climate change, or dismantle oppressive systems. Many renewable energy industries continue to follow an extractive, colonizing logic; accumulation and perpetual economic growth are still desired outcomes. We must look beyond green growth. We need ecological justice and right relationship—not more limited ends such as green growth.

In the final part, we begin to imagine how we can make first steps toward the necessary transformations for a decolonized future. This includes (1) recognizing the primacy of land and Indigenous sovereignty over that land; (2) dismantling the structures that are designed to remove Indigenous Peoples from their land so the system can continue to extract, consume, and grow; and (3) envisioning and building new economic and cultural systems that meet the needs of people and the planet.

WE MUST ENVISION NEW SOCIETAL STRUCTURES

We talk a lot in this book about how colonization and extraction characterize the structures of our present society. The concept of "societal structures" is rather abstract at first glance. I find it helpful to think of society as comprising three different but interrelated structural levels: infrastructure (material reality), structure (social reality), and superstructure (symbolic reality).[4]

A society's *infrastructure* is how people obtain the food, energy, and resources they need and desire. The difference in how societies provision themselves profoundly influences the other structural levels; some scholars believe a society's material reality is its defining characteristic. Note, for example, how we name different cultures according to infrastructural differences. We talk about hunting and gathering or agricultural societies. We talk about Bronze or Iron Age societies. We talk about preindustrial societies that use energy from humans, animals, and "biomass" (organic matter like wood or peat) or postindustrial societies that use fossil fuels.

When societies make changes in their infrastructure, revolutions ensue. The Agricultural Revolution, which started roughly twelve thousand years ago, led to large gains in food production as well as social inequality, male dominance over women, population growth, and slavery.[5] The curses God gives in Genesis 3:16–19 for Adam and Eve's disobedience may be an acknowledgment of the future negative consequences resulting from the Agricultural Revolution. In other words, the curses may be less a punishment than a diagnosis. Pastor and writer Grace Pritchard Burston wonders: "What if the man's hard agricultural labour and the woman's pain in childbearing are simply things that the writers of Genesis observed in the world around them, and decided that these things were, in fact, *not* the way the world should be, and therefore sought an explanation in the origin myth of their culture?"[6] In more recent history, the Industrial Revolution produced an incredible abundance of low-cost goods and led to increases in standards of living—as well as urbanization and environmental degradation. And the fossil fuels used to power this revolution resulted in human-caused, or anthropogenic, climate change.

Every society also has a *structure*, which determines how societies make decisions and distribute resources. This social reality includes a society's economy and political system. Specifically, the economy determines how a society allocates finite food, energy, and other resources; politics determines how decisions are made. The interrelationship of these two systems constitutes a society's political economy. Capitalism, socialism, and communism are all political economies, each with its own subcategories. For instance, both the New Deal political economy of post–World War II America and the neoliberalism that ascended during the Reagan era are capitalist, but large differences exist between them.

Finally, each society has a *superstructure*, which is reflected in the beliefs and rituals that supply the society with a sense of meaning. This symbolic reality includes the symbols and ideas from religion and philosophy, the arts and sciences, and even sports and games. The superstructure gives us ethics, as well as ideas about what is valuable or not and even what is real or not. The superstructure legitimates the structure of a society. For instance, the belief in the divine right of kings (superstructure) legitimates monarchies (structure). When monarchies are overthrown, the beliefs that legitimated them must also be cast aside.

Often, changes at one structural level lead to changes in other structural levels—or perhaps it is more accurate to say that these changes go hand in hand. The Black Death in Europe, for example, killed up to half of the population during the 1300s. This meant there were far fewer people left to work the land—a huge change in the infrastructure of that society. Those workers who survived started gaining power to change the structure of their society; they demanded better wages and benefits and wrested some decision-making power from landowners. The turmoil of this time contributed to the Reformation and Radical Reformation, changes in that society's superstructure.

Likewise, European colonization shaped all three levels of society. European people seized land and resources and enslaved and dominated certain peoples. This change in the infrastructure needed to be legitimated by the superstructure. Who was a full human being and who was not? Whose lands and bodies could legitimately be seized for resource needs? This domination also needed to be encoded into the structure, or social reality, of the political economy. Who had access to land and other resources (including their own labor), and how were decisions made about this access? A series of papal bulls issued in the fifteenth century—the seeds of the Doctrine of Discovery—provided the theological rationale for land seizure and enslavement (superstructure), which legitimated the laws and policies (structure) that govern our world to this day.

So when we say we want to dismantle colonization, we want to make changes at all three structural levels of society: how we provision ourselves (and what we think we need to do so), how we make decisions and allocate resources, and how we construct our beliefs and culture.

Although I have been talking rather dispassionately about how colonization was built into all three levels of society, allow me to be clear about the impact of this colonization. While the Black Death killed up to half of the European population, European colonization resulted in the deaths of almost 90 percent of Indigenous people of the Americas. People who had lived on this continent for thirty thousand to forty thousand years were decimated within the span of a century. Their deaths occurred on such a large scale that it led to an era of global cooling. With so many of the original stewards of the land gone, vegetation took over what had been, in many respects, a tended garden. The increase in vegetation led to decreases in carbon dioxide, and the planet's average temperature dropped by 0.15 degrees Celsius.[7]

It is hard to fathom the scale of such destruction. This destruction of Indigenous Peoples and their lifeways is ongoing, and it is now a threat to all people. It is no exaggeration to say that European colonization was a force that led to climate change—both at its beginning and still today.

"WHERE THERE IS NO VISION, THE PEOPLE PERISH"

For me (Sarah), this book is about vision. We must have the courage to imagine together a way of living consistent with Reality, a way of being that is more than the way we live now. I would like to ask you to join us in acknowledging Reality as it is. While we may believe in our twenty-first-century, post-industrial context that reality depends on perpetual growth in a market economy, the creation that we depend on holds a different Reality. This Reality dictates that we are mutually dependent in a finite world. When we discuss this Reality, we capitalize the word, acknowledging that actual Reality is not a matter of opinion. We must imagine together how we can live in this Reality.

This is not a metaphor. I really mean it. If we aren't willing to imagine a world beyond the death machine driving our nation and our world toward destruction, our days are numbered.

I am an Indigenous woman, and an assimilated one. I grew up in the mainstream, away from my land, language, people, and culture. Like many Indigenous people, I am displaced from the context of my people because my father was removed from his family when he was an infant. As an adult, I have explored my Indigenous identity and spirituality, learning how to be at ease in my own skin, and how to advocate for Indigenous people, my people. I am also a Christian, specifically a Mennonite. Mennonites and other Anabaptists are part of the Radical Reformation movement that emerged when Martin Luther was forming a way of understanding Christianity separate from the Holy Roman Empire. My Mennonite faith centers around active peacemaking, which includes simple living and a call to discipleship.

In 2013, I had a vision while I was in a sporting goods store parking lot. I was planning to buy a few things on my son's list of school supplies. As I began walking through the large asphalt parking lot, a vision occurred: *an explosion of sound, like a sonic boom, shakes the ground, and the black, oily surface of the parking lot splits beneath me. The sheet of asphalt where I am standing shoots up about ten feet, and another sheet that has broken off slides beneath it, blasting me and the ground under me further up. The parking lot fractures into islands of black asphalt floating on a liquified earth. My mind races—how will I get to my son? He is maybe twenty miles away. It is clear I won't be able to drive there. And then it hits me: I might not live through this. I might not be able to find a way out of this parking lot.*

This vision passed through my mind in a flash. The destructive surroundings enveloped me and then suddenly were gone, and once again I was walking through a perfectly mundane, flat parking lot. But in my mind and heart, I could feel the visceral truth of the experience. I could hear inside my head a truth I had not spoken: *catastrophic change is coming.*

I want to invite you to co-imagine with us what we might create together. To this end, I will share some of my visions with you in this book. Yes, visions plural, as in transformative spiritual experiences. It so happens that I am a Native woman, but as Bishop Steven Charleston instructs us, spiritual visions are for everyone. In *The Four Vision Quests of Jesus*, Charleston describes vision as "wild truth." He tells us, "Vision is not a private club for the initiated few, but a wide spiritual sea on which any person may set sail."[8]

While I have experienced visions since childhood, I have been reluctant to share them. I fear judgment where those from the dominant culture who hear my story decide that I am either untruthful or else silly. Will you take our ideas seriously if I acknowledge visions that have guided my thinking and my heart?

I am also protective of Indigenous cosmology. Among some tribes of the Pacific Northwest, it is traditionally taught that when you receive medicine, typically in vision space, it is possible to lose that medicine if you talk about it. Will I dishonor this teaching if I share my visions? But I am persuaded by Bishop Charleston, who says, "When we assert the validity of our visions, we acknowledge the power of God to change reality."[9] I am ready to share my visions, to reach out across time and space to others who may be willing to hear, to search, and to dream. Maybe vision can be amplified in this way, if we choose to embrace vision together. I know I am not the only one who has experienced visions. It is common, and human, to experience waking dreams. I encourage you to fully explore your visions, no matter how humble. Our visions release us from the false belief that we are alone. They help us to see and hear in a new way, and to experience transformation.

At the time I experienced the waking dream in the sporting goods store parking lot, it was clear to me that my life would change course. Big change was on the way, and I would need to be prepared for the earth to shake and for the very ground under my feet to become unstable. That was the start of my journey of laboring with the church to seek justice with Indigenous Peoples dehumanized by resource extraction. The waking dream also told of the distress of the earth itself, bearing witness to and protesting with the voices of the oppressed.

Charleston's writing has urged me that now is the time to share. "The experience God had as a human being is the same experience you and I have as human beings. . . . The borders of our sacred space are widened; we open up to an awareness of our existence. Vision does not take away the struggles of our existence, but it does show us how to cope with those struggles with confidence and hope."[10] My visions, along with Sheri's poems, form interludes at various places in the book. While Sheri does not experience visions in quite the same way I do, she experiences "wild truth" when writing poetry. We invite you to use these interludes to pause, to listen, and to dream.

WE MUST DECIDE TODAY

This morning, right before writing this preface, I (Sheri) read a front-page headline in the *New York Times*: "Earth Is Near the Tipping Point for a Hot Future." The subheads continued, "Alarm in UN Report" and "Calls for Drastic Action within This Decade to Avert Disaster." The article referred to the latest report from the Intergovernmental Panel on Climate Change, which warns that unless drastic changes are made, we will surpass the critical threshold of 1.5 Celsius degrees of warming by the beginning of the next decade.[11] We've diddled, we've dawdled, and we've been in denial. But the choice is clear, the report says. We are heading toward catastrophe, and we must choose to imagine and do something different. Now. Today.

As I contemplate our situation, I often think of Deuteronomy 30:15–20. The people of Israel had been freed from bondage in Egypt only to spend the next forty years wandering in the wilderness. During that time, they were schooled in what faithfulness to God required of them. Their imaginations—and daily lives—had to be transformed. And now, finally, they are about to enter the Promised Land.[12]

But Moses has one more word of truth to give them before this happens. He reminds them of the commandments they must follow if they are to walk in God's way. Lest they be overwhelmed by these commands, Moses says that they are neither difficult nor remote. "No, the word is very near to you; it is in your mouth and in your heart for you to observe" (Deuteronomy 30:14). If they follow those commandments, they will live and become numerous. They will experience life and prosperity as opposed to death and adversity. Just to make sure they get it, he says it one more time: "I call heaven and earth to witness against you today that I have set before you life and death, blessings and curses. Choose life so that you and your descendants may live" (30:19).

Moses wants to make it crystal clear: This is not the time for subtlety or more schooling or indecision. It's time to choose. Today is the day you will need to decide. And the choices are limited—simple, actually: life and death. Prosperity and adversity. Blessings and curses. Or, as the Common English Bible puts it in Deuteronomy 30:15, "life and what's good versus death and what's wrong." Your choice.

These words ring true down to us through the millennia. It's time to choose, and today is the day we need to decide. The choices are limited, even simple: We can imagine and choose a life-sustaining, just civilization, or we can continue business as usual. Life and death. What's good and what's wrong. That is our choice.

As the authors of this book, we pray that what we have written will help us choose life and what's good so that we and our children may live.

First Vision and Poem

The first vision happened when I (Sarah) was seven. When I came to my senses afterward, I was in my empty living room, with a feral cat that had never allowed me to touch it purring in my lap. The song was in me. If I quiet myself and listen carefully, I can still hear it unfolding.

Following

The song pulled me into the street. A part of me that I had not known was there leapt inside me; the cantor's song physically pulled me toward the song. A timid child, I was afraid, but the craving inside me was stronger. In the street, the song was strong and surrounding. Dark and deep down, rich brown notes, the heavy stillness of tree roots and black soil. Then lighter than air, soaring blue, high but mellow—morning sky. I was in it too. It was the first time I heard the single note that is my true name.

An empty streetcar moved slowly down the street, traveling absurdly on no tracks. I easily skipped onto it, sat on the cool floor at the feet of the cantor, a young old man.

He looked at me, and now the song was fierce, resonant notes vibrating in me, crashing, black and then fire—lightning exploded, notes deeper and then deeper still, too low to hear but, still, I heard. And then soft, gentle, barely-there-and-everywhere, bubbling now, and funny, I smiled and then laughed; I could hear creatures come to life in the song.

Behind the streetcar, animals followed, formed a strange procession of dogs and cats, birds and squirrels, more and more of them as we went along. We had moved away from the dark, low doorways of my neighborhood. Now on a broad and leafy street, as we ambled slowly along, doors were shut and bolted; others flew open and furtive faces looked out. Some people went about their business, hearing nothing. Others covered their ears in terror. Some paused and looked in our direction wistfully, as if trying to hear something far, far away. Only I rode the car.

Then my sister appeared, running hard to heft herself onto the streetcar. I was amazed to see her; I had forgotten her, my family, everything. Neither the cantor nor I spoke, but my sister yelled at me to get home. I was in trouble; I knew that I wasn't allowed to leave the house. She grabbed me by my hair, moved to jump off the back of the car as though she did not see or hear. I refused—braced myself, held fast to a handrail.

Still singing, the cantor gently fitted my sister with paper wings, carefully placing them on her back and fastening a harness across her chest. She jumped, floated to the street. I have never stopped following the singer; I still hear the song in my deepest heart.

Say Yes Quickly

Say yes quickly, before you think too hard
or the soles of your feet give out.
Say yes before you see the to-do list.
Saying maybe will only get you to the door,
but never past it.
Say yes before the dove departs for, yes,
she will depart and you will be left
alone with your yes,
your affirmation of what you
couldn't possibly know was coming.
Keep saying yes.
You might as well.
You're here in this wide space now,
no walls and certainly not a roof.
The door was always an illusion.

PART 1

Reality versus Reality

ONE

The Climate Crisis Is the Symptom—Not the Source— of the Problem

I (SARAH) BEGAN working with Indigenous communities in the Guyana Shield region of South America in 2004. Through this work, I learned a lot about how the dominant society I grew up in differs from the Indigenous communities where my friends and colleagues live.

While Indigenous Peoples in the United States face systemic inequity, many federally recognized tribes have treaties that define some rights. Indigenous Peoples in Suriname do not have rights to their traditional lands or treaty rights of any kind. Consequently, they are vulnerable to the impacts of economic development in their lands. National governments can provide concessions or leases to mining corporations, which are then free to mine in inhabited territories. Indigenous communities experience forced removal, militarization, violence, disease, and profound environmental contamination from extractive industries that are authorized to mine gold, bauxite, and oil from their traditional lands. In the process, mining industries leave behind huge quantities of toxic waste that contaminate the food web and the aquifer.

My friends in the rainforest also choose to live in a different way. They do not produce garbage. Their birth rate is stable. A primary goal of their existence is to live in balance with the community of life that surrounds them. As my work with Indigenous Peoples has led me around the world, I have been befriended by many Indigenous Peoples living in a variety of environments. This commitment to living in balance with nature is pervasive.

My friends and colleagues often live alongside the waste of extractive industry, dealing with contaminated water and food in their traditional homelands. Yet, despite the vulnerability this causes, they also tend to be the people in their societies who stand up as land and water protectors.

Several years ago, my husband Dan and I hosted a Locono leader from Suriname, whom we invited to Washington State, where we live, to participate in a speaking tour. He shared the plight of his people with any group that would listen.

He presented this plight with quiet dignity and passion in university lecture halls, church sanctuaries, and gatherings in the homes of supporters. On his circuit, we met with people from a well-known development organization. Project staff demonstrated a water filtration system they felt might be of use in Suriname rainforest communities. The staff explained that the clay filters they demonstrated could treat contaminated water easily and quickly. They then explained how our friend could go about purchasing them, using microcredit. Even better, they explained, he could sell them to entrepreneurs in the rainforest, one per village, who could treat water and sell it to those who desired clean water to drink. "If it is important to them to have clean water, they will pay for it," explained the presenters.

Note the double standard inherent in this thinking. We expect this rainforest community to pay, but if the situation involved Americans, we would not make the same assumption. If your property were damaged by eminent domain, if the water at your house were contaminated by the construction of a new freeway, would it be your responsibility to repair the damage, or the government's?

The pitch made to our friend was a common one—the solution to his problem was a technological and profit-making one. He buys the system from the development organization, which makes a profit; he, in turn, sells it to community entrepreneurs, who are poised to profit; and community members find a way to earn wages to pay for their own water. Everyone wins.

There is no space in this scenario to acknowledge that the same system that polluted his lands and waters now expects his people to pay for the cure. No one acknowledges that his people would have to travel away from their communities to work for the money to buy their own water, often leaving the most vulnerable people—children and elders—to fend for themselves, thereby further contributing to the erosion of community structure. In fact, making a community member pay another community member to meet a basic need is verboten in many traditional communities. It goes against a collective assumption that everyone has an equal right to live, and that those things required to live must be shared. From this perspective, the solution proposed by the development staff was hard-hearted at best, evil at worst.

I watched all this play across my friend's face as he sought to make a civil reply: disgust—fear—anger—resignation—despair. Looking through his eyes, I could see how unkind, how inhuman, this scenario truly is.

Let me lay it out.

The rivers and aquifers in rainforest communities are permanently damaged. There is no degree of remediation that could clean up the metric tons of mercury placed there by gold mining; it is now part of the environment. Since mercury bioaccumulates in organisms, where bacteria chemically change elemental mercury to make it available for incorporation into biological systems like bodies, mercury concentrates as it moves through the food web. So the bodies of bottom feeders who live in contaminated waters are also contaminated, and are consumed by small fish, which then become contaminated and then contaminate larger fish as they are consumed. By the time a child eats a top predator fish, mercury has been amplified up to ten times its initial concentration.[1] Neurological impact is a certainty in a community dependent upon fish as its primary source of protein.

These waters cannot be mended. They are altered, damaged. There is no technological solution that will fix them.

Yet a technological solution is offered: clay filters, and a plan for commercializing them. This is good, according to conventional wisdom, because the filters will turn a profit. This is considered a "sustainable solution," not because it works within the boundaries of the natural world or is renewable, but because it turns a profit. The term *sustainability* is often used in this context: if a solution can be sold, it can pay for itself and is therefore "sustainable." In this sense, sustainability is determined by what can earn money over time. Commercialization is built into the solution, with the idea that entrepreneurs will go into debt to assist their people, then enrich themselves in meting out shares of uncontaminated water. This will engage more people in the monied economy because it will drive more people away from villages to earn wages. So when it comes time to evaluate the health of the local economy, identifying more wage-earning workers will demonstrate that we have advanced a development goal: an increased gross domestic product and increased household buying power. It doesn't matter if life is worse for members of the community since we don't measure community well-being. Gross domestic product (GDP) only measures the monetary value of goods and services consumed.

The permanent damage to the river is ignored; it doesn't factor into the economic equation. In economic parlance, it is an "externality." There is no effort to slow or halt mining, the industry that caused the damage in the first place. The simple truth is that the well-being of shareholders is prioritized over the health of these communities. Stock in extractive industries like mining is considered "blue chip," or the most consistently profitable. Many middle-class Americans and Canadians hold these stocks in their retirement portfolios.

In short, there is no economic penalty for permanently damaging the rivers in Suriname's rainforest. And the onus for change falls to the individuals most impacted by the damage—Indigenous communities.

In the larger conversation about climate change, we see a similar process occurring. Our society invests in technology to provide a quick solution that will also turn a profit. Find a way to generate carbon-neutral energy and get rich doing it. Everyone wins. But the underlying problem—ecological overshoot—is ignored. Rather than slow or halt the processes that contaminate communities—namely, overconsumption and, by extension, overproduction—we focus on the end user to develop changes that focus on individual-level behavior: Recycle. Ride your bike. Buy a hybrid or electric car. There is no discussion about the ecological and social damage that will be caused by producing large quantities of solar panels or wind turbines or lithium batteries. Copper is the most widely used metal in renewable technologies, and demand is increasing exponentially. Predictions say that by 2030, copper demand will grow nearly six hundred percent![2] Yet there isn't a discussion about copper mining's impact on aquifers.

We believe that a system of thought is destroying the earth, or at least its ability to support human life. That system of thought is colonization and the assumption of perpetual growth and accumulation at its core. Colonization is the process by which some people seize land and resources, subjugating the Indigenous Peoples who live there. A technical solution to problems caused by this system of thought might offer a partial remedy. In the example I just shared, clay filters can produce drinking water. But they can do nothing to remediate damage to the river or the fish that swim in it. So-called green energy technology also addresses part of the problem: carbon load. But green energy does not offer a meaningful solution to the life-support systems that have already been damaged by a carbon-based economy and does not address the damage that will be caused by producing green energy, such as copper and lithium mining.

Green energy technologies also do not address our central challenge: the survival of human life on earth. If the problem is caused by colonization and the ecological overshoot that it has produced, then the solution to this problem is found in decolonization.

ABUNDANT LIFE BECOMES GREAT LOSS

Where I (Sheri) grew up, the world teemed with life. It was the 1960s, and I lived in a rural Amish-Mennonite community in Berlin, Ohio. My brothers would stand knee-deep in the bend of the Doughty Creek to catch crawdads, and when they got out, their calves would be covered with leeches. I was afraid of the leeches and wouldn't go near the creek except to watch my brothers from its banks.

At home I would watch my next-door neighbors, the purple martins, as they swooped in and out of the five-story birdhouse that my human neighbor had built for them. The martins seemed to be constantly redecorating the place or finding food for their brood. Our cat would crouch beneath the condo twelve feet below, looking up the pole like she had a chance of catching a martin, if only she could sprout wings. I think she dreamt of the martins and maybe the wings too.

Later that evening, after we had eaten the corn picked minutes before and the salted tomato slices that took up half the dinner plate, my family would go outside and watch dusk emerge from the day and disappear into night. Then the lightning bugs would emerge, and I would catch them and put them into a glass peanut butter jar, its tin lid poked full of holes. I would line the bottom of the jar with grass to make a nice home for the lightning bugs and make myself a magical lantern. Of course, they would not survive this capture. Lightning bugs don't eat grass. I eventually grew out of this childish cruelty and let them live. They must have forgiven me, because when I put out my arm, one would land and crawl up it, turning on its high beams as it tickled my skin with its tiny legs. This was better than a lantern anyway.

The next day, maybe, rain. Lightning, even, and thunder. We lived on the top of a hill, exposed. The green of the grass after the storm was almost hard to look at, a green so saturated it felt almost too bright to the eye.

And always, thrumming underneath everything, was the land. It bellowed out, like lungs full of breath, and made hills. It paused between breaths and made valleys. Occasionally, there would be a cleft, a vertical rupture in a landscape where everything else was rounded and gradual. I found out later that this cleft marked the boundary of glaciers from the previous Ice Age. One of those clefts was a place locals called the Doughty Valley, and it was a place set apart. Abrupt cliffs rising from the streambed cast shadows for much of the day. It felt dangerous and dark. The pit toilet near the Doughty Valley picnic area didn't help. I was sure it festered with snakes, maybe even leeches. The whole valley was enchanted—of that, I was sure.

There was so much I didn't know back then. I knew that Native Americans had lived there before us because my dad had arrowheads that he had found as a boy as he plowed the fields. But I didn't know what had happened to these people. I didn't know that my ancestors—my third and fourth great-grandparents—had been the first white people to come into that area and settle the land after the military had cleared it of its original inhabitants during the Ohio Indian Wars. I didn't know that my pacifist ancestors were the foot soldiers of the settler colonial project that is the United States.[3]

Nor did I know that I was living through what would come to be called the Great Acceleration, a time unique in human history. Starting in the 1950s, human economic activity accelerated sharply. Charts showing the rise in real gross domestic product from the 1750s onward look like a hockey stick. The line is mostly flat or climbs slowly until around 1950, when it begins climbing almost straight up. But it's not just GDP that follows the hockey stick pattern. So does world population, carbon dioxide concentration in the atmosphere, ocean acidification, water use, damning of rivers, biodiversity loss, fertilizer consumption, and even the number of McDonald's restaurants.[4] The Great Acceleration transformed nearly the entire globe into a Western industrial consumer society: More goods and services were produced and consumed from 1950 to 2000 than in all of human history before 1950.[5]

The Great Acceleration benefitted people like my family, at least in the short term.[6] My father, born in 1929 during the Great Depression, spent his later boyhood living on a small farm worked solely by his father. The house wasn't painted; there was no indoor toilet. He remembers getting an orange one year for Christmas and being delighted at receiving this "exotic" fruit all the way from Florida. (He was less delighted by his other gift—hand-knit socks.) His was the first generation in that family to graduate from high school. By the time he retired in 1991, he had a middle-class life and a healthy retirement fund, thanks to several decades of continuous stock market growth. He and my mother bought a mobile home in Florida surrounded by orange trees and spent several months there every winter.

While I was aware that my life had more material comforts and opportunities than my father and certainly my grandparents had, I didn't know that these things were possible because of neocolonial economic policies that extracted resources (like gold) from the Global South, or that other communities (like the Locono) were suffering because of my family's gains. I didn't know that our industrial growth civilization—built by colonization and powered by a one-time burst of cheap coal, natural gas, and oil—was on track to make the planet uninhabitable for all forms of life.

In 2004, at the age of forty-two, I had my first and only child. I had been living away from Berlin for decades. I longed to connect my son with the enchanted world I remembered from my youth. And so one day when Patrick was around six, we waded into the waters of Doughty Creek, which ran near my parents' home. There wasn't a lot of water in the creek, but it was hot, and the water that was there felt cool on our ankles and calves. Under the shade of maple trees, we found a pool with just enough water in it so Patrick could dog paddle.

When I got back to my parent's house and told my mother of our adventure, she said, with anxiety rising in her voice, that I should give Patrick a bath. "There's a lot of chemicals in the water due to fertilizer and pesticide runoff," she told me. By this point in my life, I was well aware of how agricultural runoff contaminated waterways, but somehow, I had thought my little corner of the world—where much of the county's population still used pre–fossil fuel technology—was immune from this problem.

It was a few years later when I learned that no place on earth is immune from the problems created by a global economic system demanding perpetual growth. We are consuming—and polluting—the earth faster than it can regenerate itself. The global economy uses more and more energy and resources and dumps more waste each year, and the hockey sticks keep rising. We are now overshooting what scientists have defined as safe planetary boundaries.

Here's the news that changed how I viewed the world: Climate change represents only *one* planetary boundary that we must not cross. To avoid catastrophic *ecological* change and potential tipping points, humanity must stay within nine planetary boundaries. In addition to climate change, these planetary boundaries include biodiversity integrity, ocean acidification, depletion of the ozone layer, atmospheric aerosol pollution, biogeochemical flows of nitrogen and phosphorus (due to fertilizer use in industrial agriculture), freshwater overuse, land-system change (particularly the conversion of tropical forests to farmland), and environmental pollutants (including heavy metals, radioactive materials, and plastics). We are already overshooting *six* of these areas: climate change, biodiversity integrity, biogeochemical flows of nitrogen and phosphorus, freshwater use, land-system change, and environmental pollutants.[7]

My mother had been correct: the creek my brothers played in as children was now unsafe for my son because of runoff from fertilizer use.

As for biodiversity loss, I couldn't show my son the purple martins I loved, because they don't come to my neighbor's bird condo anymore. Since 1966, there's been a 5 to 6 percent yearly decline in the purple martin population in Minnesota, a number that scientists think is consistent across the Midwest.[8] Scientists believe the decline could be due to deforestation in the martin's migratory grounds in South America, chemical use in the Midwest, or a decline in the insect population.[9]

I can't show my son the fireflies either. The last time I was in Berlin on a hot summer night, I saw one lonely firefly. No longer is the night sky lit with their gentle, blinking lights. Fireflies are disappearing around the world due to light pollution, pesticide use, and loss of habitat from development.[10]

The martins and fireflies are only part of the much bigger story of biodiversity loss. The 2022 Living Planet Index, which tracks almost thirty-two thousand species of mammals, birds, fish, reptiles, and amphibians, shows a 69 percent decrease in these populations since 1970.[11] In 2014, researchers found that insects or invertebrates have decreased by 45 percent on average over the past thirty-five years.[12] One-third of global insect species are now threatened with extinction.[13]

The lightning and thunderstorms I thrilled to as a child are becoming more commonplace. Climate change will bring more extreme rainfall and flooding to the Midwest, affecting infrastructure, health, agriculture, forestry, transportation, air and water quality, and more, according to an Environmental Defense Fund report. When it rains in the Midwest, it will more likely pour.[14]

I am a beneficiary of colonization and the Great Acceleration, and even my privileged, supposedly protected area of the world is not immune from environmental pollution, biodiversity loss, and climate change. No place is now immune from the problems created by colonization and an economic system demanding perpetual growth. While those who have been colonized—Indigenous communities, those enslaved during the African slave trade and their descendants, and people in the Global South—have suffered the most, colonization is coming for everyone, including those who have previously benefitted from it. This system of death is the source of the ecological overshoot that endangers all of us. Climate change is only a symptom of this larger problem.

CREATION HOLDS THE CREATOR'S STORY

As we described in the preface, in Deuteronomy 30, Moses speaks to the gathered Israelites as they prepare to enter the land of promise. Moses reminds the people that they face a choice:

> See, I have set before you today life and prosperity, death and adversity. If you obey the commandments of the LORD your God that I am commanding you today, by loving the LORD your God, walking in his ways, and observing his commandments, decrees, and ordinances, then you shall live and become numerous, and the LORD your God will bless you in the land that you are entering to possess. But if your heart turns away and you do not hear but are led astray to bow down to other gods and serve them, I declare to you today that you shall certainly perish; you shall not live long in the land that you are crossing the Jordan to enter and possess. I call heaven and earth to witness against you today that I have set before you life and death, blessings and curses. Choose life so that you and your descendants may live, loving the LORD your God, obeying him, and holding fast to him; for that means life to you and length of days, so that you may live in the land that the LORD swore to give to your ancestors, to Abraham, to Isaac, and to Jacob. (Deuteronomy 30:15–20)

I (Sarah) interpret this scripture through the lens of what I have learned from Indigenous elders. I look for what the apostle Paul calls God's invisible qualities—God's eternal power and divine nature—in creation (Romans 1:20). A complex ecosystem demonstrates interdependence: For top predators to thrive, herbivores must thrive, and for herbivores to thrive, plants must thrive, and for plants to thrive, soils must thrive. Soils are dependent upon microorganisms, and every part of the food web can crash if the tiny communities of microorganisms we don't fully understand can't prosper.[15]

I see that life is cyclical—that generation after generation is born and dies, and that life is a process that spans deep time. Each generation's actions affect the ones that come after it. While the dominant culture views "progress" as the accumulation of power, wealth, and security over time in a single direction, nature reveals a constant process of birth and death that spans far beyond a single lifetime.

I see God's faithfulness expressed in the cycle of the seasons, in the perpetual washing of the seas, or upwelling, by mechanisms most of us don't understand, in the cycles of pollination by wind and critters, in the waste disposal provided by insects, in the water cycle, in the many other cycles that ensure we have air to breathe, healthy soils, and clean water. We do nothing to earn these things—what grace!

At a recent Bible conference, I was shocked that a sanctuary of Bible scholars tasked with identifying truths across Scripture listed exactly one reference to nature; they stated creation is a "good gift from God to humanity." This token nod to the earth in Christian circles is common. God created nature, it is good, and it is a gift—full stop. Now let's move on to more important things . . .

For many Indigenous Peoples, creation holds the *entire* story of the Creator. The earth, as the Creator's full expression of Godself, is approached with reverence. We are dependent upon creation, we are a part of it, we are inextricably bound to it. We are not separate.

We are not separate.

The narrative of capitalism reduces this complex Reality to a symbiotic relationship between firms and households. Firms employ people in households and provide them wages; households, in turn, use wages to consume products made by firms. Firms need labor, and households need products. Labor has a value; products have a value. Education can provide training for labor, and therefore can be assigned an economic value. Health can create longevity for employees, and can even be sold to them in the form of healthcare, and therefore is assigned an economic value.

The problem is that so much is left out of this model, namely the ecosphere that we depend on for our life. Water, air, soil, and other resources related to nature have value only to the extent that they are commodified and given value in the economic system. Water has a value when it can be sold to firms or households. Soil has a value when it can be bought or sold as private property. The ecosystems of microbes in the soil have no inherent value unless they are assigned value in the marketplace. Nor do the insects that pollinate the plants that we depend on for our food. When things aren't assigned value, they don't exist in the system. With this narrow conception of reality that dominates Western culture, no wonder Bible scholars have such a stilted view of nature.

For many Indigenous cultures, nature *is* Reality, the only one. It is not an abstract good, a footnote in a conversation about important things, or a theological afterthought. It is the main event.

Viewed through an Indigenous cosmology, or way of describing the natural order of things, the exhortation to love the Lord your God and walk in obedience to God in Deuteronomy 30:20 takes on a different meaning. Acknowledging our interdependence with all of creation and the care and advocacy that we owe to the next generations *is* what it means to walk in obedience to the commandments of the Creator. This is what it means to love the Creator, the Lord our God: to live in a symbiotic relationship with the creation that God has made and to take our rightful place within this magnificent, complex web of life.

If we are obedient to the Creator's commandments—if we choose life—then we will live and prosper on the land. If we don't do this, if we choose to not live in Reality and instead choose systems of death, systems that reflect a limited reality, Deuteronomy is very clear: *You will certainly be destroyed. You will not live long in the land.*

Reality versus reality. Which one will we choose?

TWO

Reality and Systems of Life

EVERY MORNING WHEN I (Sarah) leave my house, I give thanks for the beauty that surrounds me, for the creation I walk on and am in relationship with. I have been taught to do this at dawn, but I acknowledge that it doesn't always happen for one reason or another! I am amazed, on the mornings when I can give thanks, to stand and witness that every morning is singular, unique. At dawn, creation is rediscovered, renegotiated. The early morning light reveals the robust and fragile world around me with a new lens—today's lens. The position of the earth relative to the sun changes. The cloud formations are unique each day. I see and hear different animals, depending on the season. But regardless of whether I make it outside in time to see the grand entry of the sun as it crests the horizon, I always give thanks when I step out onto my gravel drive. Every single day, warmth returns to my home, this hemisphere, and I am overwhelmed with gratitude. This practice—giving thanks first thing each morning—was taught to me in adulthood by

Indigenous elders who were patient and kind enough to help me discover the fullness of Reality.

My socialization as an American schoolchild and, later, my socialization through graduate school taught me to prioritize outcomes and to demonstrate my value by racking up accomplishments. These are the norms I learned in the dominant culture. I learned to be productive and to measure my value and the value of others in terms of individual performance. I was trained that I am only as good as my latest accomplishment—and so is everyone else. I learned to frame each relationship in terms of its usefulness to me.

The American Dream, broadly offered as the explanation for why the United States is a class-free society, states that if I am clever and work hard, I can rise to any level of achievement to which I set my mind. I can own my own home; I can own my own business; I can become a CEO at a Fortune 500 company. I can become a millionaire or even a billionaire if I am clever and hardworking enough. The reward for rising as high as I can is universal respect, admiration, and wealth for myself and my descendants. It is up to me, and I need not share success or financial gain with anyone unless I choose to do so.

When I taught sociology at the community college in the town near where I live, many of my students were low-income, first-generation college students. When we discussed the taxes exacted on estates valued at over $5 million after a person dies, the notorious "death tax," my students were universally against it. Although estate taxes help to balance economic inequality, the idea that a portion of personal earnings should be redistributed was anathema to my low-income students. Even though they would stand to benefit from it, they opposed it.

"But why?" I would ask them, term after term.

The answer was always the same: "We might earn more than $5 million dollars."

"But you would be dead," I would then argue, "so it wouldn't hurt you."

"But it would be our money," students told me. "We should get to decide what happens to it."

My students' responses are a clear expression of the cultural norm of self-interest: *I need not share with anyone, whether I am alive or dead; what is best for me is what is best.*

My elders gently instructed me in another way of seeing.

The very first practice I learned is the practice of giving thanks. It unfolds in two parts. First, observe Reality—what is happening in the environment around me: how the ground feels under my feet, how the breeze feels on my face, the sounds that surround me, the plants in my immediate view. I was taught to pay attention. Then, to give thanks.

Today, some people call this mindfulness—being here now, fully inhabiting this moment.

My elders taught me to first observe, then give thanks.

This was how I learned to see Reality.

On the two hundred acres of shrub steppe where I am fortunate to live, on the lands of the Yakama Nation, I have noticed many things about myself and my relationship to the Creator. I have lived in the same place for seventeen years, which equates to multiple generations among the animals that share this environment. The owl nest in our barn has been continuously inhabited for at least a decade, and every year, two owlets fledge. They are often unafraid of my husband, son, and me; we are regular fixtures, coming and going gently and causing no harm. Members of the family of crows that lives in the trees behind my house each have unique calls that I can identify and that my son imitates as he calls to them and they call back to him. We have walked the same trails by the wetland many times each day for years on our way to the horse barn. The red-winged blackbirds that carefully negotiate their territories in the wetland each spring often hop a few inches higher on their reed perches as we approach, rather than scattering. We are nothing new to them. Since we don't hunt in the land we tend, pheasant and quail flourish here, undisturbed. The mourning doves that live behind the calving sheds share the stand of golden currant, and each year we harvest just what we can reach from the ground, leaving the rest for the doves. Our rule of thumb: We don't use ladders to harvest. We eat what we can reach, and the birds eat what is within their reach.

I have learned this about myself: I am embedded in a food web. What is outside my house is Reality and is my reference, not what is inside. The natural world frames Reality, not the constructed world.

I have learned this about the Creator: the Creator is faithful regardless of what I do; They make rain to fall on the just and the unjust (Matthew 5:45); They have created a system of life that is complex, rooted in balance, complete, while simultaneously growing, expanding. And there are immutable rules, like gravity, that are not negotiable.

My family raises natural cattle. We depend on the deep-rooted native plants and grasses for our livelihood. Our herd depends on these plants to survive. Therefore, *we* depend on these plants. The microenvironment that includes the soil, microbes, and bacteria, depends on water, oxygen, and a cycle of organic material returning to the soil, such as animal waste (the remains of consumed grass returning to the soil). The native grasses and plants that our herd depends on in turn depend upon the microbes in the soils of this land. Therefore, we depend on the microenvironment. Our health depends on the health of the soils.

When I truly see the world around me every single morning, I see something larger and more complex than myself. I see a web of life. What does this tell me about Reality? When I step outside each day and *really see* the food web that surrounds me, what do I observe?

1. I am not the center. In fact, humans are not at the center. The web has no center, but rather interconnected, overlapping nodes.

2. There is a somewhat flexible balance, but it remains subject to the immutable rules of life. The grasses must have sunlight and water. Nothing I can do as a human will change that. The soils upon which the grasses depend need water but will be decimated by habitual overwatering. There is no amendment I can add to the soil that will change the devastating impact of overwatering, which leaches nutrients from the soil. Our herd requires a good mix of grasses and forbs, and in turn digests them and supplies partially broken-down organic matter as nutrients to the soil. Over-applying animal waste, more than can be broken down effectively, will contaminate the groundwater with nitrates, which endangers the health of the animals who live here, including humans.[1]

3. We live in an environment of mutual dependence. If we overwater, if we overgraze, if we apply too much animal waste, the outcomes will impact every life that abides here, from microbe to human. Our animals depend on healthy,

abundant, drought-resistant grasses and forbs. These plants depend on the groundwater and healthy soils. Soils depend on regular and disbursed application of organic matter, oxygen, and intermittent water. Soil health depends in part on rodents who live in the fields among the grass and aerate the soil, distributing oxygen beyond the surface, and who in turn provide an abundant and reliable source of food for raptors, who patrol the skies and return remains to the soil as a source of nutrients. We humans depend on all of these.

By extension, when our neighbors over-irrigate and use toxic herbicides and pesticides that seep into the groundwater and soils, this impacts us and all the life that thrives within our care.

4. The system in which we all live, our food web, is a closed system: matter cannot be transferred in or out. Groundwater provides a somewhat flexible range of self-cleaning and can dilute a concrete amount of contaminants via wetlands. However, that system cannot absorb infinite contaminants. Soils that have been over-irrigated can be rehabilitated; but at some point, they become inert, and their microbial environments can no longer sustain life. This immutable rule of a closed system applies to the whole earth. Just like in the microcosm of the ranch, there is no possibility of new water, air, or soil in the larger macrocosm—the life-support systems of earth are fixed. There is finite water, soil, clean air. The earth is all we have.

In teaching me about Reality, the elders have shown me grace and kindness by asking me to first observe—and then to give thanks. In this way, I have begun to see my place in the web of life, my place in the family of the universe. My place is not at the center, but it is important. It is as important as any other place in the universe. I have learned that *we live in a closed system of mutual dependence.* There is nothing I can do as a human to change this. No innovation or technology can change this fact.

I have learned from my elders that this shared mutual dependence allows us to grow in relations—to consider each other relatives. You are all my relations. Yet in the world today, every life-support system we depend on is in decline. I believe this is because our society is living in a way inconsistent with Reality.

MUTUAL DEPENDENCE, NOT INDIVIDUALISM AND SELF-RELIANCE

The reality of mutual dependence is in stark contrast to the message of the dominant culture: we are self-reliant individuals. When *my self* is at the center of my worldview, it is in my best interest to use every tool I can to enrich myself, since I am in competition for resources with every other person. Rather than cooperate with the world around me to thrive within a web of mutual dependence, I am encouraged to get what I can for myself and view all others as potential threats to my well-being. I may have time for a degree of generosity once I believe my needs are met, according to any standard I see fit. But sharing is not required of me. I am free to seek self-interest, and I will be rewarded with wealth and respect for my efforts.

In the same way, corporations are required to put the best financial interest of their shareholders above every other interest, including the public good. A posture of selfishness is a core assumption in our society and is regarded as not only justifiable but morally good (and legally good, in the instance of corporations).

Some of you may disagree that these are the values conveyed by the dominant culture. But we seem to be teaching these values to our children in the United States, regardless of our intentions.

A 2014 study from the Harvard Graduate School for Education surveyed ten thousand middle and high schoolers around the United States about their values. Nearly 80 percent of them named high achievement or happiness as their top choice over caring for others. What's more, they accurately predicted that this was what their parents most value for them as well: the youth were three times more likely to agree than disagree with the statement: "My parents are prouder if I get good grades in my classes than if I'm a caring community member in class and school." The researchers observe, "Our conversations with and observations of parents also suggest that the power and frequency of parents' daily messages about achievement and happiness are drowning out their messages about concern for others."[2]

They continue, "Some youth made it quite clear to us that their self-interest is paramount: 'If you are not happy, life is nothing. After that, you want to do well, and after that, expend any excess energy on others.'" I hear this theme frequently. Take care of yourself first, then what excess time, money, or energy you have left over can be shared and will be counted as "generosity."

While both parents and teachers claim to prioritize kindness, their behavior tells another story. Rick Weissbourd, the lead researcher in the Harvard study, calls this the "adult rhetoric/reality gap." Simply put, there is a gap between what adults *say* and what they prioritize in daily *action*.

In a follow-up to the Harvard study, National Public Radio interviewed members of the Barrera family. Parents Joel and

Mari both worked in the public sector, served their community as volunteers, and belonged to a church that highly values community service. But like the youth in the study, the Barrera children said their parents cared more about their success than about their being good to others. James, age thirteen, said his parents' rewards and nagging were related to his school achievement. Mila, age fifteen, said, "It's one of those things people say, I really want you to be a good person . . . but deep inside, I *really* want you to be successful."

Joel Barrera responded, "Our main job as parents is to launch them into the world." Mari Barrera said, "I worry all the time. I wonder what will happen down the road. . . . I hope I'm not condemning my kids to a life of poverty."[3]

This sentiment is common in the church. In conversations with Christians about financial holdings that harm Indigenous Peoples, I often hear, "But I have to put my kids through college. That has to be my first priority." I often wonder why these middle-class Christians don't see their own vulnerability in these sentiments. If they can turn aside from the suffering of the vulnerable, what prevents those more powerful than themselves from turning away from the concerns of the middle class, and even victimizing them? If all our morality boils down to self-interest and personal choice, doesn't that make all of us vulnerable?

In the 2008 financial crisis, American households lost an average of $100,000 in wealth.[4] Relaxed regulations made predatory housing loans commonplace, leading to a surge of investment in packaged mortgages on a secondary market, called the subprime market. Repackaged subprime loans were marketed as highly attractive, with high interest rates that promised high returns to investors. This market inevitably deflated in value when people began to default on mortgages they could not afford. Investors in the subprime market found themselves holding bad debt. Poor regulation around how much debt financial institutions could hold led many large financial institutions to overextend themselves. Banks, and then insurance companies, fell like dominoes. Unemployment doubled in just two years, and millions lost their jobs. Millions also lost their homes, and many retirement accounts were wiped out. Those that survived the stock market crash shrank by a third of their value on average.

This is a concrete example of prioritizing individualism over the common good, and how that leads to vulnerability for all. While low-income families were the original targets of predatory housing loans, nearly every American household was impacted by the recession that followed.

The Harvard study reported other troubling findings. Two-thirds of the youth in the study prioritized hard work as more important than fairness (a necessity for a healthy civil society), and over 60 percent ranked hard work above kindness. An earlier study validates this claim. In a 2012 study, a similar number of high school students agreed that "in the real world, successful people do what they have to do to win, even if others consider it cheating."[5] Over half admitted to cheating on a test or copying someone else's work. Notably, the Harvard study reported that ranking achievement first was associated with low levels of empathy.[6]

I have repeatedly seen such attitudes in church communities. In discussions about Mennonite Church investments in gold mining companies that harm Indigenous Peoples by contaminating their bodies and lands, one administrator told me, "Church employees have provided their labor to serve the church, often with modest compensation. Why should they have to give up the benefit of returns from their retirement funds [by divesting from mining]?"

According to the Harvard researchers, other studies of American values bear similar results. A social issues think tank investigated how American adults view moral development, focusing particularly on how their responsibilities contrast to their responsibilities to others and the common good. The findings show that adults had a weak commitment to larger collectives and the common good. While adults prioritized civility in their local communities, they did not necessarily prioritize the well-being of broader society.[7]

This notion—prioritizing self-interest and regarding the needs of others as a choice rather than a basic posture of survival—is fundamentally at odds with the reality of mutual dependence. The life-support systems of earth dictate that the decisions one entity makes impact every other entity. The business decisions of the boards of directors of oil and gas companies impact all life on earth. The investment decisions of financial management firms that normalize extractive logic impact all life on earth. International economic development schemes that endanger biomes in favor of increasing GDP harm all life on earth.

TAKING WHAT IS NEEDED, NOT TAKING EVERYTHING

The dominant culture is embedded in the logic of extraction, a logic with self-interest at the center. This logic says that progress is linear in time and is evidenced by accumulation. In other words, a successful life is one where an individual amasses as many resources as possible. When individual self-interest is at the center of one's worldview, everything else is a potential resource.

In this worldview, the earth is made up of raw resources to extract in service to "progress." Coal companies like Massey Energy, which is now owned by Alpha Natural Resources, are free to engage in mountaintop removal, a practice with documented environmental impacts like deforestation, soil erosion, and the contamination of vital water supplies with pollutants such as mercury, lead, and sulfur. Corporations like Massey are free to do this and consider it progress since the process produces two and a half times more coal per worker hour than other mining methods do.[8] This logic repeats itself in every sector. Success is measured by accumulating wealth, power, and security for individuals, households, companies, and nations. A successful life is one that amasses resources and takes more than one's share—extracting rather than gathering.

The dominant vision of progress is imbued with the logic of extraction: taking what is wanted from the earth to fulfill one's wishes or objectives. The earth is perceived as an object, a set of commodities. Extraction is rooted in the concept of domination and is justified by the notion of perpetual growth: for our economy to thrive, it must grow continuously. Since commodities extracted from the earth make up the engine of growth, we must habitually extract and consume more and more.

Extractive logic, the basis of our current economic system, threatens every life-support system on the earth by polluting air, water, and soil and depleting nonrenewable resources. This vision of progress is out of step with Reality, as I have learned it from my elders. I have been instructed as follows: Take just what you need. Leave plenty for future generations.

If we collectively choose to remain in a paradigm of extractive logic, we cannot effectively challenge climate change. Applying extractive logic to complex problems like climate change results in unviable solutions that are not consistent with the principles of life—with the principles of gathering carefully, leaving plenty, acknowledging our mutual dependence. Attempting to combat climate change without foregoing extractive logic results in strange dilemmas.

For example, a big part of what I do is advocate with Indigenous Peoples who are fighting mining operations that harm their bodies, communities, and environments. I recently asked a large, church-based financial advocacy organization about advocating alongside the Stronghold Apache, a group fighting the installation of the largest copper mine in US history in the Arizona desert. The organization shared with me that they are not at liberty to oppose mining investments that oppress Indigenous Peoples and threaten their lands. The Stronghold Apache are protecting sacred lands of Chi'chil Biłdagoteel (Oak Flat) where they have worshiped for untold generations, as well as the water supply of residents in large metropolitan areas like Phoenix and Tucson. The financial advocacy organization responded that because they support a carbon-neutral agenda, they acknowledge that more mineral extraction will be necessary in a carbon-free economy.

I had a similar conversation with a congregant at a church I visited recently. "We have to support mineral extraction, because it will provide us with sustainable energy solutions like solar panels and lithium batteries," he argued. "You may as well be speaking on behalf of the oil and gas industries. When you encourage churches to challenge mineral extraction, you are opposing the carbon-neutral economy."

When I proposed curtailing energy use as a solution, he responded, "This is a modern society based upon progress. You may be willing to go back to subsistence agriculture and hunting and gathering, but I'm not willing to."

MADE OF THE EARTH, NOT MADE TO DOMINATE

I believe that Christian acceptance of extractive logic is rooted in a common Christian narrative that places humanity in a position of "dominion" over creation. This idea comes from the first creation story in Genesis 1:26–29 (NIV, emphasis added):

> Then God said, "Let us make mankind in our image, in our likeness, so that they may *rule over* the fish in the sea and the birds in the sky, over the livestock and all the wild animals, and over all the creatures that move along the ground."
>
> So God created mankind *in his own image*,
> in the image of God he created them;
> male and female he created them.
>
> God blessed them and said to them, "Be fruitful and increase in number; fill the earth and subdue it. *Rule over* the fish in the sea and the birds in the sky and over every living creature that moves on the ground." Then God said, "*I give you* every seed-bearing plant on the face of the whole earth and every tree that has fruit with seed in it. *They will be yours* for food.

This story is widely interpreted as evidence that humanity is separate from a subordinate creation. However, there are actually two creation stories in Genesis: this one from Genesis 1, and another from Genesis 2.

In the first creation story, God creates most of the elements of the earth in the first five days and humanity on the sixth day. God places humankind in a position of supremacy in a hierarchy over other parts of creation. Humanity is thus poised to rule over the creatures of earth and hold dominion over creation. The story implies that this dominion is at least part of what it means to be made in the image of God.

I heard a sermon to this effect preached at the United Nations Church Center in New York City several years ago, where I happened to be attending a meeting of the UN Permanent Forum on Indigenous Issues. I was in the Church Center for services, waiting for the Permanent Forum to start. The sermon was preached by an Episcopal bishop, who used this creation story to justify humanity's dominance. The bishop explained that this dominance should be one of benevolence, where humanity—as rightful owner of a subordinate earth—must be kind and wise in our stewardship. It sounded very much like sermons in the early US church that legitimated slavery and sermons in the South African church that legitimated apartheid. The irony of this sermon preached in an Indigenous setting was not lost on me.

In the second creation story, found in Genesis 2:5–7 (NIV), humanity is made of the earth itself, not separate from it.

Now no shrub had yet appeared on the earth and no plant had yet sprung up, for the LORD God had not sent rain on the earth and there was no one to work the ground, but streams came up from the earth and watered the whole surface of the ground. Then the LORD God formed a man from the dust of the ground and breathed into his nostrils the breath of life, and the man became a living being.

In this version, being created in the image of God means that the first human is animated by God's breath. Chapter 2 goes on to say: "The LORD God took the man and put him in the Garden of Eden to work it and take care of it" (v. 15). This position, one of a caretaker, is quite different from one of dominion. In verses 19–20, God brings all the animals to the first human for naming. This implies that Adam had an interpersonal relationship, even friendship, with creation, given that he named each and every thing. Verse 19 explains that the animals were made from the ground, of the same substance as Adam.

Within Christian theology, a division exists between a vision of humanity's dominion over creation and a vision of humanity as part of creation. I want to be careful to note here that these interpretations are part of the Christian tradition and do not implicate other Abrahamic faiths in the formation of these theologies. In other words, I refer here only to my knowledge of Christian theology.

The first creation story has been used to justify empire and extractive logic. The second implies what theologian Wes Howard Brook calls the "religion of creation": a worldview grounded in nonviolent love, truth, justice, and peace. This theology is in alignment with the vision of Reality I have learned to see from my elders: a Reality of mutual dependence.

We also find the idea that creation is more than a set of resources to exploit and expend in the New Testament. John 3:16 states, "For God so loved *the world* that he gave his one and only Son, that whoever believes in him shall not perish but have eternal life" (emphasis added).

Not humanity alone, but the whole world: all of creation. Colossians 1:15–20 (NIV, emphasis added) says this:

The Son is the image of the invisible God, the firstborn over all creation. For in him all things were created: things in heaven and on earth, visible and invisible, whether thrones or powers or rulers or authorities; all things have been created through him and for him. He is before all things, and in him all things hold together. And he is the head of the body, the church; he is the beginning and the firstborn from among the dead, so that in everything he might have the supremacy. For God was pleased to have all his fullness dwell in him, and *through him to reconcile to himself all things, whether things on earth or things in heaven*, by making peace through his blood, shed on the cross.

Not humanity alone, but all things.

RETURNING TO EARTH, NOT SEPARATING FROM IT

In the beginning, says the creation story in Genesis 2, the Creator scooped up some dust (v. 7). It wasn't loamy, rich soil. It was dry, loose dust, the kind blown away by a brisk wind over bare ground. The Hebrew word for dust, *aphar*, is also translated as debris or ashes in the Bible. It is distinct from the word *adamah*, which refers to the loamy soil that contains humus. The Creator cupped this dust (*aphar*) of the ground (*adamah*) and formed it into . . . us. Into *adam*.[9] We are groundlings made of dust and ashes.

After my mom died, I (Sheri) was with my dad at his home in Ohio when the crematorium returned the box containing Mom's ashes, her *aphar*, to us. We planned to bury some of her ashes in the cemetery where the *aphar* of three generations of her ancestors lie. I purchased a biodegradable basket made of sustainable fibers for her ashes. My mom was a lifelong gardener, and I knew she would love being laid to rest in a basket that would quickly return her to the *adamah* into which she had dug her fingers so many times.

We needed to transfer her ashes from the box to this basket. And so my dad and I found ourselves outside his house on a sunny May morning. We opened the box on his patio table, and he poured while I held the basket. Of course, a slight wind blew at that precise moment, enough to blow some of the ashes onto the table and us. We laughed. Maybe Mom was playing a trick on us one last time. Afterward, we wondered how to clean the ash off the tabletop. It was so fine and dry. We tried to scoop it into our hands and put it in the basket, but it was difficult. To this day, the *aphar* of my mother is probably still in the cracks of that table.

When I read this passage from Genesis 2, I don't hear it as metaphor. We are literally *adam*, earth creatures, formed from the dust to which we return. We know this intuitively. The word for us in languages derived from Latin—*human, hombre, homem*—comes from the same root as *humus*, the word for earth, for soil. Our bodies and the body of the earth are formed from the same elements. We are made of the plants we eat, which are formed from the soil, air, and water, as are any animals we eat. We have almost the same water content in our bodies as the earth itself—60 to 70 percent. Our blood vessels and the earth's rivers and streams move life-giving liquids throughout our respective bodies, and photographs of both look strikingly similar. Like the earth, we consist of interconnected systems that support life. While we have nervous, musculoskeletal, cardiovascular, respiratory, and digestive systems, the earth has a hydrosphere (water system), biosphere (life system), lithosphere (land system), atmosphere (air system), and cryosphere (ice system). If any of these systems fails, our lives are threatened.[10]

It is true we are more than dust. The Creator breathed into us the *ruah*, the enlivening Spirit. In the creation story in Genesis 1, we are made in the image of the Creator. But lest we get too puffed up, the Jewish biblical scholar Avivah Gottlieb Zornberg reminds us that an image—*tselem* in Hebrew—is "less than and not identical to the model." At the root of *tselem* is the word for shadow or phantom. As Zornberg says, "There is the sense that the human being is a shadow that God casts in the world."[11]

I say all this because I believe now, more than ever, we desperately need a biblically based theological anthropology. Theological anthropology is a fancy phrase I learned in seminary that simply asks, Who are we? How does God see us? In light of our faith, what do we know about ourselves? And the answer is: We are earthen creatures, made of dust, in the shadowy likeness of the Creator. As Psalm 100:3 affirms, the Creator has made us, not we ourselves.

We are also made from the body of the earth, and our bodies are inextricably linked. We are not separate. We belong to earth's body; it is our home, our garden, our Eden. Together with all of creation, this earth is the realm of God as the Creator first imagined it into being. We can't survive on Mars or upload our consciousness to the cloud, and we won't fly away to heaven. A biblical understanding of heaven is not some realm "up there," but a restored earth. I still remember when theologian and activist Noel Moules said, animatedly, during a workshop at a Mennonite church convention in 2013, "You are not going to heaven! Our destiny is a resurrected community, a resurrected body on this earth." I had studied the Bible for years but hadn't realized that the biblical vision of the "afterlife" locates it squarely here on earth.

I believe many of us have forgotten this. We have fancied ourselves the crown of creation, the top of the evolutionary ladder, separate from and superior to nature, other animals, matter.[12]

We have fancied ourselves conquerors who have usurped the power of the Creator. Through our cleverness, we have become all-knowing or nearly so. We are in command, in control of the very building blocks of life. We are not the created—*we* create! We are masters of our own destinies. Rulers of nature.

And yet, here on Earth, we don't even understand soil, the substrate that supports life. A handful of healthy soil contains more living organisms than people on earth. That handful may contain billions of bacteria, millions of fungal cells, and thousands of arthropods, algae, protozoa, and nematodes. Soil scientists have not classified many of these species and don't understand how they function within the soil ecosystem.[13]

We pride ourselves on our ingenuity, how we have conquered the forces of nature. But so often, our cleverness comes back to bite us. In the mid-nineteenth century, Chicago grew so quickly that human waste polluted Lake Michigan, the source of the city's drinking water. An engineer proposed a bold scheme: Reverse the river so it flowed into the Mississippi River instead of the lake. The engineering marvel worked, saving many Chicagoans from waterborne illnesses. But the pollution didn't magically disappear. It just went down the new downstream, impacting other communities, some as far away as the Gulf of Mexico. Those same downstream communities also experienced flooding from the increased influx of water. And the reversal allowed invasive species, like the Asian carp, to take root in the Mississippi River system, drastically changing the river's ecology and damaging native fisheries.[14]

My daily newspaper is filled with stories of the unintended impacts of our technology, including an epidemic of depression, anxiety, and loneliness among teens attributed to social media; robots that have automated thousands of workers out of jobs and spew propaganda over the Internet; and fears over the brave, new world that artificial intelligence will create. We are called *Homo sapiens*—which means wise ones—but do we have the wisdom to impose limits on ourselves? Even now, as the carbon dioxide in our atmosphere increases each month, we don't stop ourselves. We've had three decades of climate conferences, but governments are still not doing what they have promised. Even if they did, we would still overshoot the total limit of 1.5 degrees Celsius of warming. Just how clever and in control are we?

I have long been thankful that I grew up in an Amish-Mennonite tradition that emphasized humility. I believe that those of us formed in the dominant culture must reclaim this inner orientation in order to survive. I realize that may be an objectionable statement, since many false or even toxic versions of humility exist. So let me say what humility is not. It is not low self-esteem or a sense of unworthiness. It is not hanging back, being unwilling to put ourselves forward. It is not allowing ourselves to be humiliated.

Humility is about knowing our proper place in the scheme of creation and regarding ourselves rightly. I once heard Benedictine sister Joan Chittister define humility as thinking either no more or no less of ourselves than we should. No more of ourselves—we are groundlings, made from dust, returning to dust, shadowy reflections of the One who made us. No less of ourselves—we are animated by the breath of God, made in the image of the One who created everything, possessing worth, beauty, and dignity. Jewish wisdom holds this tension by saying that every human must always have two pieces of paper with them. On one piece are the words "I am but dust and ashes." On the other is written "*Bishvili nivra ha'olam*": "For my sake, the universe was created."

As humans, we are most ourselves—we are most wise—when we are humble. The root for the word *human*, *humilis*, meaning "low," is the same as that for *humility* and *humus*. When we are humble, we are who God created us to be, people who are "low to the earth," connected to the interdependent web of life on this planet. To get back into alignment with God's intention for us, we must be truly humble, truly human Earth creatures.

THREE

Systems of Death, or What Is Taken for Reality

IT WAS A typical Saturday. I (Sheri) woke early, before my husband and son, fed the dog and cat, and sat down in the living room chair that allows me to catch the first rays of the sun as it rises over the sequoia trees that line my street. This is where I do my morning prayers. As usual, I prayed, "Open my eyes to your presence, O Christ, that I might glimpse you at the heart of each moment." Then I read the newspaper.

The front section featured a two-page spread about a South African town that was obliterated when a dam holding back mucky waste from a diamond mine collapsed. The collapse sent a "thunderous rush of gray sludge through the community that killed at least one person, destroyed 164 houses, and turned a six-mile stretch of neighborhoods and grassy fields into an ashen wasteland." The many photos accompanying the article showed Black and white residents trying to salvage whatever they could from their homes amid a lunar landscape.

When the mine reopened in 2010, the townspeople were initially glad that jobs were returning. But working conditions were bad, and dust from the mine soon had them coughing. Worst of all was the growing mountain of waste, which had doubled in height since the reopening. Despite warning the mine owners of the risk and asking them to take appropriate action, there was little the residents could do to stop it because, the article said, "it was big business."[1]

The front page of the business section read, "Where the New Climate Law Means More Drilling, Not Less." Under the recently enacted US Inflation Reduction Act, millions of acres of the Gulf of Mexico were now available for offshore oil and gas drilling. This drilling is a threat to the region's fishing industry. The Deepwater Horizon catastrophe of 2010 made national news. Still, dozens of lesser spills since then received far less attention, including one that ruined Louisiana's inshore shrimp season in August 2022.[2]

Justin Solet is a member of the United Houma Nation. "We are water people," he told the news reporter as he steered his boat past a web of pipelines and rusted storage tanks. "This is [our] livelihood. And it's right next to these tanks that I don't think have been fixed or serviced in years." Solet used to work on the oil rigs but became an activist against oil and gas expansion after the Deepwater disaster. In addition to the spills, his livelihood is threatened by coastal erosion and increasingly more devastating hurricanes. "I'm afraid that by the time my youngest one is sixteen years old, I won't be able to bring him here. It's going to be gone."[3]

Every day, I read about how the human economy is destroying the earth—gobbling it up, extracting resources from it, polluting its waters, soils, and air, and harming those who live within the sacrifice zones where this extraction occurs. Climate change is only one part of this larger story of ecological devastation:

- Human activity is so widespread that, according to one article, "in less than the lifespan of the US Constitution, the earth has gone from half-wild to a global farm. Domesticated animals now outweigh wildlife by a factor of twenty."[4] Over 95 percent of the mammal mass on earth now consists of humans and livestock.[5]

- Per- and poly-fluoroalkyl substances, or PFAs, comprise a group of "forever chemicals," toxic chemicals that essentially will never break down in our environment. PFAs are used to make Teflon pans, down jackets, burger and butter wrappers, dental floss, cosmetics, and ski wax. They are highly toxic, and they are everywhere: in our drinking water, in raindrops, in our food, and in our bodies.[6] They are linked to everything from cancer and compromised immune systems to low infant birth weights and hormone disruption.

- In Ghana, young people ages ten to twenty-five work in a ten-square-kilometer electronic graveyard filled with computers and electronic goods from Europe and North America. There, using their bare hands and without masks, they disassemble the equipment and burn plastic or rubber components to cull the copper, which is resold to make more computers and electronic goods. They are exposed to lead, mercury, cadmium, and PVC plastic. These same chemicals have seeped into the nearby canal and pastures.[7] This scene repeats itself many times over in the Global South.

I could just as easily mention articles referring to soil fertility collapse or the pollinator crisis or overfishing or the growing problem of the freshwater supply. In our industrial growth economy, nearly all our activities—growing food, fishing, building roads, manufacturing products, powering our cars and homes—result in harm to ecosystems and people. After centuries of extraction, consumption, and pollution, we are now reaching the point where we have ecologically overshot the earth's carrying capacity, resulting in what some have called a polycrisis: simultaneous crises that often reinforce each other. To take just one example, the decline of fishing stocks due to overfishing, pollution, and ocean warming leads to hungry people, which leads to social unrest.[8]

Later that Saturday, I listened to a podcast featuring Beaska Niillas, a traditional Sámi activist, kindergarten teacher, and politician. "What breaks my heart right now?" he asked. "It's to see how people with power, nations with power, they literally walk on dead bodies to get what they want. This greed that destroys the land, it destroys nations, it destroys cultures, it destroys values. It's very sad to see what the world has become. I'm not saying that the world has always been a peaceful Eden's garden or something, but I'm saying that people have understood before that you can't burn down the house you are sitting in. And that's what's happening now, but on a global scale."[9] His words speak to my own sadness over what is being destroyed in the name of greed and my own disbelief that we are doing it.

"OPEN MY EYES, THAT I MIGHT SEE . . ."

Each morning, I pray that my eyes might be opened to Christ's presence. I believe that we see Christ not only in resurrection and new life but also in crucifixion, in the places of death.

For years, I have been transfixed by icons from the Eastern Orthodox tradition that depict the harrowing of Hades, or Christ's descent into hell after his resurrection. The Eastern Orthodox Church uses this iconography throughout the Easter season but primarily on Holy Saturday, the day between Good Friday and Easter. On this day, the Eastern Orthodox Church contemplates the mystery of Christ's descent into Hades, the place of darkness and death. We don't often say the Apostles' Creed in my Mennonite tradition, but Christ's descent into hell is found in that creed: "We believe in Jesus Christ . . . who suffered under Pontius Pilate, was crucified, died, and was buried. He descended to the dead. The third day he rose again." Sometime between dying and rising, Jesus descends.

Descent into Hell, icon from the Ferapontov Monastery, public domain.

The icons of the harrowing of Hades show this descent. They show Christ—often riding the cross—descending into the dark belly of the earth, breaking the locked doors of the tomb, and exposing the deepest recesses of creation to Divine Light. Christ is depicted as entering so profoundly into the human condition and into creation itself that he penetrates the deepest realms of sin and death.

It has taken me years to open my eyes so that I can see the sin and death—the crucifixions—resulting from our perpetual growth economy. Of course, my privilege has shielded me from this vision. It would be so easy for me to see only the comfort and security of my life and that of many others in my largely middle-class communities, the steadily growing (until recently) retirement fund, the well-stocked shelves of grocery stores (except during the COVID-19 pandemic). It would be so easy for me to see only the ready access to material goods, my ability to press "buy" and have a garlic press made on the other side of the world land on my porch the next day. It would be so easy for me to accept the myth of unending economic growth and the technological optimism that believes we will surely solve our ecological predicament without having to change our lives.

The dominant worldview has prevented me from seeing the dead bodies that Beaska Niillas describes in the belly of the earth. The dominant worldview wants me to stay above ground, to not see the people and places and animals crushed by our way of life. Or, it may allow me to see the South African town made into a lunar landscape and the Gulf of Mexico fishing waters ruined by oil spills, but only as isolated incidents—and not as the systemic, structural violence embedded in a worldview that views all of this as "business as usual," the price of our economic "progress." But Christ compels me to descend with him into the deepest realms of sin and death. Christ compels me to decolonize my worldview.

CHALLENGING THE DEFAULT MODE OF DOMINANT CULTURE

We have been describing the worldview of the dominant culture as centered in individual self-interest and extractive logic. As part of the work of talking about and more clearly *seeing* this worldview, Sarah and I often use several themes to characterize it: the dominant perspective is *dualistic and hierarchical, reductionistic, abstract,* and *short-term and self-referential.* These adjectives describe the superstructure of dominant culture, its symbolic reality, which provides ideas about what is valuable, ethical, or even what is real or not. As I describe in the preface, there's a direct line between a society's superstructure and its politics and economy (structure), as well as to how it provisions itself (infrastructure). To dismantle colonization, we must make changes at all three levels.

Books could be—and have been—written about these themes. In sketching them out here, I am not trying to present a monolithic Western worldview. Instead, I describe key tendencies in the Western worldview, our cultural default mode, you might say. There always have been, and still are, different worldviews running alongside this dominant one that resist it, debunk it, and try to change it. But as my sociologist husband says, dominant worldviews are like cross-country ski tracks. You can ski anywhere you want, but there's a tendency to keep your skis in the grooves on the trail.

In describing these themes, I am focused only on the shadow side of the dominant worldview. There are more positive tendencies that could be highlighted, but most of us formed by this worldview are quite aware of those. The more we can see the shadow side of this cultural default mode and its dire consequences—even if they were sometimes unintended—the more power we have to push against it and choose something else.

DUALISTIC AND HIERARCHICAL

Western thought is rooted in a dualist strain of Greek philosophy that came to the fore around the fifth and fourth centuries BCE. This dualism posed a split between the body and the spirit—and, of the two, the latter is considered far superior. The spirit was seen as immortal, pure, and as participating in the divine. But the spirit (and the intellect associated with it) was housed as a temporary prisoner in a mortal, changeable, corruptible body prone to unruly passions and disease and death. The good life and indeed salvation itself required escape from flesh into spirit. As Christian ethicist James Nelson puts it, "Now the created world, like the human body, became that from which detachment and escape must be made if one were to find salvation."[10] This dualism came to shape Judaism as well as Christianity, in both its gnostic and more orthodox forms.

Before the Babylonian exile of ancient Israel, Hebrew thought did not share this view of creation, body, and matter as evil or as something to be escaped. To the ancient Hebrews, sexuality was a gift from God—one need only read the Song of Songs! Many scriptures, especially the Psalms, embrace "unruly" passions and emotions. (For sorrow, see Psalm 31:9–10; for discouragement and turmoil, see Psalm 42:5–6; for anger and complaining, see Psalm 88. There are so many others!) Jesus seems more in alignment with this positive view of bodily life. Paul, however, was more ambivalent. As a Jew, Paul affirmed a positive view of creation, but as a person influenced by Greek thought, he was not untouched by dualism. See especially his stated view on marriage in 1 Corinthians 7:7–9, which he sees as a lesser state than those, like him, who are celibate.[11]

After the Babylonian exile, an emerging strand of Hebrew thought took on a more dualistic, apocalyptic worldview. The Christian movement inherited this influence and Greek dualism. Nelson writes, "In early and classic Christianity it was a mixed picture. In some ways the goodness and sacramentality of the earth were affirmed and celebrated. But in competition with this was spiritualistic dualism, represented in forms ranging from the heretical gnostic extreme (matter is evil—the world's creator is not true God but demon) to a highly eschatological faith (redemption comes not in and through this world, but in spite of it and beyond it). Such is the mixture in our heritage."[12]

This dualism is also hierarchical, in that those parts of creation seen as closer to the spirit are superior, whereas those closer to the body are inferior. Ancient Greeks posited a "great chain of being," a hierarchical structure that categorized all matter and life. Medieval Christian theologians further developed this idea, which they saw as decreed by God. God was at the top of the chain, with the angels right below, since neither have material bodies and are pure spirit. Beneath them are humans, who are a mix of spirit and matter, followed by animals, plants, and minerals, which become increasingly "material" or associated with the body as they descend down the chain.

This hierarchy values humans, who are more possessed of spirit, over other creatures and nature itself. But only some humans. As Native theologian and scholar Randy Woodley says, "Along with a worldview of foundational dualism naturally comes the hierarchy of humans over creation and the hierarchy of humans over other human beings via gender, race, class, and

The Great Chain of Being, F. Didcus, 1579, in *Retorica Christiania*, public domain.

such."[13] Women menstruated and gave birth and were identified as more "bodily," and thus inferior. They were supposedly less guided by intellect and more ruled by emotions and bodily passions. Poor and peasant people were often seen as more "animalistic," closer to the earth, and not possessed of the intellect of their social betters. People who were not European Christians were regarded as "savages"—closer to animals than humans—and as not having souls.

Since European Christian elite men were at the top of the ladder and closer to the realm of spirit and intellect, these men "naturally" should have dominion over nature and over those humans identified as inferior. Thus, the earth, certain people, and animals could be made into objects acted upon by the true subjects of history. These superior males were free to control, cage, enslave, manipulate, and dominate the earth, animals, and the bodies of those "lower" than them as they saw fit. This is, of course, the colonizers' rationale. It is the logic behind the African slave trade and the appropriation of land from Indigenous Peoples. It is the logic of white supremacy and many other forms of ongoing oppression, including patriarchy and the abuse of animals and the earth.

Dualism and hierarchy fused into a self-reinforcing, deadly logic. Philosopher and biologist Andreas Weber refers to this hierarchical dualism as the "Western cognitive empire." In this empire, there are two domains: a world made up of dead, non-human things, called nature, and human society, which fights nature in order to obtain security and comfort for humans. This split between those considered objects, which includes all nonhuman beings but also the human other in the so-called colonies, enables the Western cognitive empire to justify their destruction. This worldview is inherently colonialist. Weber writes that colonialism's core motivation lies in this split between human society and nature. It "inevitably leads to a colonial, and hence, violent treatment of extra-societal others." That is, of humans not deemed members of human society, other creatures, and other parts of our planet.[14]

REDUCTIONISTIC

Another characteristic that marks the dominant Western worldview is reductionism. Reductionism breaks complex systems like the body or an ecosystem into smaller constituent parts so that each part can be examined and understood on its own. The scientific method, which has so revolutionized the world, is based on reductionism. In a way, ignoring complexity allowed scientists to devise manageable research topics for rigorous inquiry and experimentation.[15] Breaking complicated systems into smaller, simpler parts yields insights not otherwise available to us. Identifying and studying DNA, for example, enabled the Human Genome Project to map the first genetic blueprint of human beings. This helped identify genes that cause cancers and led to new drugs to treat everything from cystic fibrosis to asthma.[16] Medical care itself offers a form of reductionism. If we have a heart condition, we may be referred not just to a cardiologist but to a subspecialist within the field like a cardiothoracic surgeon, an expert in heart failure and transplant cardiology, or an electrophysiologist. Each of these doctors has specialized knowledge from rigorously studying a smaller, specific part of the heart system.

While reductionism has led to (among other things) medical advances that would seem nothing short of miraculous to people from an earlier era, the Western scientific worldview has rarely integrated this specialized knowledge into a more holistic understanding of the profound interdependence among the separate parts. Physicist and systems thinker Fritjof Capra points out the fallacy of reductionism: "While there is nothing wrong in saying that the structures of all living organisms are composed of smaller parts, and ultimately of molecules, this does not imply that their properties can be explained in terms of molecules alone."[17] Or as Randy Woodley says, "If we try to live out of those reduced categories, we're not living out of a whole reality; we're living out of partial reality."[18] The system of mutual dependence is emblematic of this more holistic system view of Reality.

When we operate without this understanding of the whole, the balance of any system can be thrown off. I suspect many of us have experienced this in our healthcare system—the very specialization that offers expert knowledge tends to view bodies as a collection of parts, each with its own subspeciality to treat problems that arise, rather than an integrated whole. But more problems arise when we don't pay attention to the whole person. I recall when a member of my congregation went to visit his aging father. His father was lethargic and slept for hours a day. At first, my friend was alarmed. He thought his father might be dying. Fortunately, he was a nurse, so he carefully looked at the drugs prescribed for his father. When he did, he discovered that his father was taking many different drugs prescribed by a plethora of specialty doctors. He was clearly over-medicated. My friend talked to the nursing staff, who made changes. Within days, his father was talking and walking again.

On an ecological scale, the twentieth-century use of DDT (dichloro-diphenyl-trichloroethane) illustrates the same problem with reductionism—solving one problem without minding the cascade of effects this "solution" has on the whole system. DDT was among the first synthesized insecticides and was initially viewed as a "wonder chemical" for its ability to control insect populations that cause malaria and typhus and decimate crops. However, some scientists warned that DDT was likely to upset the natural balance of ecological systems by killing beneficial insects and other forms of wildlife that ate DDT-laden insects. This proved true. And since humans are a part of these ecological systems, not magically separate from them, the natural balance of their health was also affected. DDT was banned in the United States in 1972, but the chemical is affecting the *granddaughters* of women exposed to the chemical in the 1960s. The granddaughters of women who had DDT in their blood samples now have a higher risk for obesity and early menstruation, as well as insulin resistance, high blood pressure, and cancer.[19]

Some of the impact of this reductionist worldview has been spiritual, although it is just as material in its effect. Once we started using reason and the scientific method to talk about how the world works, we no longer needed a God to send the sun across the sky each day; that was the earth's rotation. We didn't need to pray to the Creator to send precious rain; we could study meteorological patterns. Science introduced a rational, empirical, reductionistic way of thinking that was a misfit for religious sensibilities. People didn't necessarily become atheists, but the view of God changed quite dramatically. Instead of the Creator animating the world, God now became the clockmaker who designed the world "machine" and then left it alone to function according to mechanical laws. This view removed Creator from creation, which became desacralized, stripped of the animating Spirit of God, de-spirited, and dead.

Born in the late 1500s, René Descartes was one of the main architects of modern philosophy and science. While he declared at least some humans as possessing soul and spirit, he did not believe the same is true of animals or the rest of nature. Animals were organic machines incapable of feeling pain or emotion. He conducted public demonstrations where animals were vivisected. As the creatures displayed visible signs of agony, Descartes would tell the onlookers not to be troubled, because such writhing and howling were simply programmed responses. (Lest we think such attitudes toward animals are confined to an earlier era, we need only look to the horrible conditions in which most animals for our consumption are raised.)

This hierarchical, dualistic, reductionist view almost naturally leads to an *extractive* logic. As Sarah has described, in this view of reality, the earth is a set of raw resources used in service to progress and wealth without much, if any, thought to sustainability or ecological balance. While we have been mining minerals and metals from the earth for millennia, extractivism in the modern era became turbocharged by colonialism, when colonizers exploited resources in the colonies to the advantage of their own economies, and later by drilling for fossil fuels, which powered even more extraction. Many forms of extraction today—fracking, deepwater drilling, tar sands removal, mountaintop removal for coal mining, and industrial agriculture—would be impossible without fossil fuels, especially oil.

Modern extraction comes with huge environmental costs. Name a contemporary ecological crisis—climate change, deforestation, pollution of fresh water, biodiversity loss, soil depletion—and you will find extractive logic at its root. Wherever modern extraction occurs, a "sacrifice zone" of ecological devastation follows in its wake. Nonrenewable resource extraction has increased so much in past decades that scientists warn we may soon run out of these resources, such as the sand needed to produce silica for solar panels.[20] In general, extraction happens without regard for the renewal of even those resources that are renewable. (Note how even the term *resources* engages extractive logic!) Factory farming, for instance, depletes soil fertility until it is essentially a lifeless medium into which farmers pump chemical fertilizers to grow crops. All the fertility of the soil has been wrung out of it.

Extraction has been equally devastating to humans, especially Indigenous Peoples and those from the Global South. Their bodies are polluted by the chemicals used in extraction, their lands are taken for mining concessions, and they lose their traditional lifeways and their spiritual connection to the land.

Human rights violations, unsafe labor conditions, military and paramilitary conflicts, and unequal wealth distribution are all well-documented outcomes of extraction. Environmentalist Hop Hopkins links planetary devastation to the devastation of certain people groups: "You can't have climate change without sacrifice zones, and you can't have sacrifice zones without disposable people, and you can't have disposable people without racism."[21] If our hierarchical, dualistic worldview didn't categorize some people as "less than," we couldn't pollute their bodies, lands, and waters, destroy their homes, or view them as collateral damage in our quest for economic growth. In fact, our economic growth model requires sacrifice zones and sacrificed people, and has ever since the rise of colonization and the African slave trade.

Extractivism is not confined to the mining of minerals or drilling for fossil fuels. The bodies of humans deemed sacrifice-able also become sites of extraction. Labor is extracted from enslaved people and underpaid workers forced to work long hours, often in dangerous conditions. So long as there is a large labor force to be exploited, these humans can be used up and discarded when their usefulness is past, like an abandoned mine.

Some argue that many digital companies operate via extractive logic. "How did Google make its first billion so fast and so unencumbered by all kinds of traditional constraints?" asks sociologist Saskia Sassen. "It got information about all of us for free and then sold it to businesses."[22] In other words, our demographic, economic, and social information was extracted from us and then sold for profit. In the digital economy, time spent on social media is more time spent viewing ads, and our activity provides rich data sets for algorithms. The depletion you feel after you have spent time staring at a screen isn't solely a matter of eye strain. Our very attention is a resource to be mined and extracted.

ABSTRACT

Abstraction is the extreme endpoint of hierarchical dualism. Western culture has become increasingly abstract ever since Plato introduced the idea of perfect forms, which claimed that the physical world is not as true or real as timeless, fixed ideas. Abstraction is the increasing retreat into the world of ideas, or spirit, or other non-corporeal spaces like virtual reality and the Internet. It abandons the inferior body—the body of the earth, our own bodies, and the bodies of other humans. When we live in an abstracted world, we can do horrible things to the bodies of other people or animals or the body of the Earth and not feel what we are doing in our own bodies. When we live in an abstracted world, we can talk seriously about "uploading our consciousness" to the Internet or colonizing Mars. When we live in an abstracted world, we can continue spewing carbon dioxide into the atmosphere or acidifying the oceans or depleting our soils because we somehow don't believe that reality has a biophysical—bodily—foundation.[23]

And why should we? Our economy is based on abstractions. But the *real* economy is the land, water, sun, and soils upon which all life depends. The human economy is "embedded in nature, and economic processes are actually biological, physical and chemical processes and transformations."[24] This seems almost too simple to bother saying. It is a principle of ecological economics, but you can get a degree in economics and never learn it. Modern economic theory has no biophysical foundation. Instead, it attributes all economic productivity to labor and capital, and doesn't count the value of a stable climate, fertile soils, and clean air and water.[25] Not only is the human economy not seen as embedded within the larger, real economy (the biosphere), but when a corporation pollutes this biosphere, the harm is regarded as an externality—something outside of the system, something "out there"—as opposed to something happening to our homes, to our bodies, to the very systems on which our lives depend.

In her 2014 book on the climate crisis, journalist and activist Naomi Klein explores the link between extraction and abstraction, writing, "Extractivism ran rampant under colonialism because relating to the world as a frontier of conquest—rather than a home—fosters this brand of irresponsibility. The colonial mind nurtures the belief that there is always somewhere else to go to and exploit once the current site of extraction has been exhausted."[26] However, as digital economist Douglas Rushkoff says, when a business runs out of extraction sites, it will "go meta."[27]

It is no accident, says Rushkoff, that Mark Zuckerberg rebranded the social media company Facebook as "Meta"—another level of abstraction. In Zuckerberg's "metaverse," we will all work, play, and socialize in Facebook's proprietary virtual world. "Zuckerberg wants the metaverse to ultimately encompass the rest of our reality—connecting bits of real space here to real space there, while totally subsuming what we think of as the real world," says Rushkoff. "It's not that Zuckerberg's simulations will rise to the level of reality, it's that our behaviors and interactions will become so standardized and mechanical that it won't even matter." The more robotic we become, the more at home we will feel in the metaverse.[28]

In time, the line between humans and robots may grow blurry. Historian Yuval Harari predicts that advances in biotechnology, artificial intelligence, and cybernetics will enable a small, elite group of people to "upgrade" their bodies and brains, eventually becoming a new species that Harari has termed *Homo deus*.[29] They will no longer be humans whom God created from the dust of the ground; they will now become "god men." This abstraction is hubris almost beyond imagination.

SHORT-TERM AND SELF-REFERENTIAL

When we are surrounded by people who think like we do, it is hard to imagine that our view is not absolute reality. I (Sarah) may be able to hold in my mind that my experience is just one of many, but it is hard to believe that my experience isn't the *real* reality, with a capital R. It can be so disorienting to glimpse a different view of reality. When a person from the dominant culture who is confident in their worldview spends time in my community, it can feel very disorienting.

I remember when a very smart, ambitious academic moved from California to serve as an executive at the reservation college where I worked for many years. He explained his plans to chart a pathway whereby students could escape from the reservation. His hopes were frustrated again and again as students chose to stay. Why? They were living in a different paradigm, with different norms, values, and interests. Similarly, researchers from the natural sciences came, year after year, and were frustrated when tribal authorities were not willing to share data for student publications. "It is enough that they share their research with us," tribal authorities would say. "We don't need to share our data with the rest of the world." The status and legitimacy offered to individuals by the peer-review process held no allure to a people focused on a priority different from legitimacy in the eyes of the dominant culture. Western science thinks of shared ideas and data as integral to the scientific process. But the process of colonization has not been kind to Indigenous Peoples or their lands, and Indigenous leaders are cautious about sharing data about the natural world with the dominant culture.

Let me share a story of my own about this. Not long after I moved to the Yakama Indian Reservation, a friend and I took our toddler boys to an "Indian taco" sale at the college where I worked. The taco sale was a common fundraiser for student clubs and initiatives. This delicious meal is a large piece of frybread smothered in ground beef, beans, cheese, tomatoes, and all the taco fixings.

As my friend and I entered the small, portable building that then housed the Indigenous Studies program, we were surrounded by college students, Native faculty, community members, children . . . so many people, crushed into a small space. It felt overly warm given the portable fryer crowding the back door, long plastic tables with benches attached set end to end in rows across the room, and people standing, working and chatting in what seemed like every available space. Children were running around in the chaos, laughing and playing loudly. My friend and I surveyed the scene, each holding a toddler son. We made a space for ourselves along one table, and took turns buying tacos and drinks, then carefully arranged a way to share the food with our boys. It was a logistical challenge. The plastic tables with benches attached did not have adequate space between the bench and table to accommodate a mama with a growing son on her lap. We had flimsy paper plates filled with hot food—how to sit there with our children in arms? We stood the boys in a corner momentarily while we tried to arrange ourselves. One of the elder women working the sale watched us with a soft smile on her face and called out to our sons, "Run, babies, run!" The women throughout the room burst out laughing, smiling at us kindly.

From our point of view, we were acting responsibly, working out how to get our food and sit down without causing a ruckus while keeping our children safe from strangers. From the grandmother's point of view, we were acting in a way inconsistent with the nature of toddlers. Toddlers want to explore. So, let them explore. Everyone knows they are vulnerable and need constant monitoring—in this space filled with tribal community, we could free them to toddle and grab, never more than a few feet from the steadying hand of a mother or uncle, grandfather, or cousin.

The grandmother used humor to mildly address the confusion of new mothers. Over time, I learned why our muddle was silly to her. We were in a community space, a space made safe by the tribal mothers and grandmothers, fathers, and elder siblings. We were free to set our children down, let them run, and feed them bites from our cooling plates as they zoomed by. We did not have to think of ourselves as alone in this place— there were plenty of watching adults, our children could toddle safely from table to table, taking bites from all the plates held by parents and grandparents. This space could have been arranged outside, but instead the meal was served in a space that could ensure that no child could wander away from the group. In time I came to understand the meaning of the word *tribe*, but on that day I felt embarrassed and confused.

I had met the limits of my conventional, short-term, reductive thinking, a thinking that places myself at the center.

There was *no* way to eat in that place with a toddler and keep the situation under my strict control. The only way to enjoy my food, my friend, and our children was to release control, to submit to the safety of the collective—to think beyond myself and my own solution. This collectivity carried with it a cost, of course—I too must take responsibility for *every child in the room*, considering each as precious as my own. Any child within arm's reach from me could be the recipient of a bite of my Indian taco or a mild redirection if the behavior became too rambunctious. This corporate responsibility added a measure of complexity I did not feel ready for.

When learning anything new, there is a time of internal challenge when a person wants to reject the new information because it doesn't fit with existing judgments or mental models. We call this culture shock, I suppose. I have witnessed culture shock as folks deemed successful by the dominant culture have tried to relate in a good way with Indigenous ways of thinking and being. It can feel disorienting.

In the dominant culture, we are rewarded for thinking with mental models consistent with the dominant culture. This is often reductive, short-term thinking. Find the fastest pathway between points A and B. We are assigned good grades for doing this and for solving linear puzzles quickly. There is nothing inherently wrong with solving problems sequentially or along the quickest route. But in complex systems, many problems do not unfold sequentially. Many things happen at once across multiple parts of the system, each influencing the outcome of the other. Reductionism resolves the problems posed by complexity by splitting problems into small chunks, addressing them separately. As Sheri described earlier, this process is inherent in the scientific method, which provides us useful tools to measure empirical experience, or what can be measured with our senses. These tools are especially useful when we can control which elements, or variables, are examined in an experimental setting. The usefulness of sequential, reductive examination breaks down when it is prioritized for solving all problems. In the dominant culture, the reference in this type of thinking is the self. How do *I* get from point A to point B? How do I limit the variables to find the most efficient solution *at one specific point in time?*

For several years, I served as a faculty member at the small university on the reservation where I live. In an administrative role, I reported directly to the president, who wanted to add a research arm to what had historically been a liberal arts institution. During a lengthy strategy meeting, I suggested that we work to cast vision for a plan that would span decades, thinking through what programs would serve the community in the long term. We could then plant the seeds of that vision and put systems in place to nurture those seeds. "Why would I do that?" the president inquired. "I won't be here to see it. I'll most likely be here for just four years—and I'm not even interested in a four-year vision. I need to show significant progress to the board in two years!" His vision was outcome-oriented, with an outcome bounded by time and centered around his interests. In this kind of thinking, the goals of the leader are the reference point. For him, the solution was what was most advantageous for him in the short-term. I realize that there were powerful interests at play—his accountability to the university's governing bodies, in addition to his own desire for a positive legacy—and that such thinking often drives decision-makers in our shared culture. Many politicians make decisions based on election cycles. Our news cycle is just twenty-four hours, and this short cycle is an inevitability for many decision-makers. But this sequential, reductive pattern of thinking is not always useful. It can be difficult to imagine a system of thought where the individual is not the reference point.

For Wayana communities I have known, the universal, shared reference is the river. Whether using right and left or cardinal directions when discussing spatial relationships, the point of reference is always the river. If talking about a structure "to the south," a Wayana person would mean to the south of the river, not to the south of herself. In this community, the river, the source of life, is the center and therefore the referent. Imagine how confusing it would be to obtain directions without understanding this vital piece of cosmology.

In my community, it is common to pick up walkers (hitchhikers) looking for a ride. I do this a lot. Many of my friends from the nearby city of Yakima talk about how dangerous this is—how dangerous the reservation is, and how dangerous it is to pick up strangers. But if you believe the entire reservation is a home territory, everyone you pick up is a neighbor, a relative. Giving a neighbor a ride implies that we are already in relationship, even if we don't know each other yet. I assure you it is safe—once you have given the person a ride, you know where they live: where they are coming from or where they are going. An elder on his way to the clinic for a doctor's appointment relies on the neighbor going that way to pick him up. A teenager who missed the bus relies on the neighbor to take him to school (and knows he will get a scolding from whichever auntie picks him up!). This is a view beyond the self as the referent. This community is not a utopia—and there are courtesies to be learned in interacting this way—but its logic is grounded in complexity and not centered on the self.

In conventional short-term thinking where one's self is the referent, what has come before—history—doesn't matter. I need not think beyond the timeframe of the boundaries I set myself for the task. Graduate degrees are awarded for this type of thinking; I define the variables I will study and look at each separately and sequentially. This type of thinking allows mining interests to set targets to extract precious metals based upon access to technology and markets without thinking through the long-term impacts on the aquifer or community health. This kind of thinking built the dams that generate electric power but destroy salmon runs and create sedimentation that is detrimental to the life of the river, to the plants, animals, and to the people in its watershed. The dam gives those with authority what they want *now*, regardless of the health of the whole community and environment. The author of Ecclesiastes calls this chasing after the wind:

> If you witness the poor being oppressed or the violation of what is just and right in some territory, don't be surprised because a high official watches over another, and yet others stand over them. But the land's yield should be for everyone if the field is cultivated. The money lover isn't satisfied with money; neither is the lover of wealth satisfied with income. This too is pointless. When good things flow, so do those who consume them. But what do owners benefit from such goods, except to feast their eyes on them? (Ecclesiastes 5:8–11 CEB)

A fixation with short-term gains—what is in it for me—are pointless, according to the wise king in Ecclesiastes.

We live within a closed system of mutual dependence. Such a view of Reality, which is found in many Indigenous cosmologies, is consistent with ecological reality, with the complex systems that sustain life on this Earth. Worldviews not in alignment with Reality are pointless; they are chasing after the wind, and they will fail. Our individualistic, extractive, dualistic, hierarchical, reductionistic, abstract, self-referential, and short-term worldview has long failed those who have been crushed underneath its weight, and it is now failing all of us.

Second Vision and Poem

I (Sarah) was nineteen when the second vision came.

On the right day, at the right time, I will be there. The ladies are dressed in custom gowns, beautiful in dramatic eye makeup and heels. Everyone important walks up the red carpet—dignitaries, world leaders, generals, captains of industry, artists, actors, and athletes—leading into the crystal banquet room. I am wearing jeans and a grey hoodie, and no one takes notice; I slip right in. The huge building is abuzz with excitement. Everyone looks to see who else is there. There are huge banquet tables, waiters in tuxedos with trays filled with platters and pitchers. Spotlights are trained on a stage at the front. There is an emcee counting down the time, making jokes and telling spirited anecdotes. There are chandeliers, of course, but also giant bells that line either side of the massive crystal hall.

I am standing behind a concrete pillar when I notice cowled figures emerging from the shadows. In unison, they strike the bells. Very slowly, the bells begin to sway. Their sound is deep and resonant, an approaching train still far away. I feel the approach vibrate in my chest, growing louder and louder and louder. The celebrants notice slowly at first—the liquid in crystal glasses registers the rhythm. The volume grows with each beat. The sound is very quickly overwhelming, an earthquake. Celebrants run every direction, screaming. The noise is deafening.

And then, It is there: the One. My knees buckle; an invisible force pulls each of us to the floor, foreheads pressed to the ground. I am terrified. Whatever I thought God was within my small and self-referential world evaporates. My justifications, my religion, all my thoughts are obliterated by the Reality, this Now. I thought I knew God—I was wrong. The One burns through me, fierce, Holy; I am exposed. So is everyone else.

Sarah and I (Sheri) were talking on the phone, and at one point I realized I needed to take down what she was saying because I felt Spirit speaking through her. Later, I made a poem from my notes.

The Way of Life

There is only one truth, and it is the truth we learn by
    participating in Life.
There is only one way, and it is the way of Life.

Those who do not follow in this way will be as grass;
they will wither and blow away;
    they will be scorched in the inferno of their own
      making.
Those who follow in the way of Life will live forever
    because they are one with the forces of the Life,
    which are eternal.

Hell is separation from Life, separation from the One.
Though those living in hell, those acting out of the
      spirit of separation,
    may annihilate life on this earth,
    they can never annihilate Life.
Life endures.

There will always be a home on this planet for those
seeking the way of Life.

Those who practice the way of separation and
domination
are already homeless. Pity these homeless ghosts.
Pity those separated from Life, from the One.
Pity those who seek, in their disorientation,
to destroy the only home they have.
They have been led astray.

We have all been led astray, down the pathways that
lead to death.

Pray for us now. Pray for all of us now.

PART 2

Beyond Green Growth

FOUR

Green Growth Is Unjust

NEARLY THIRTY-FIVE YEARS ago, I (Sheri) moved to Phoenix, Arizona. It was the first time I had lived away from the lush green of Ohio, and initially I felt like I had moved to a moonscape. Over time, the desert wooed me. Here, the bones of the earth were easily seen. The dry air made edges crisp, like a camera lens coming into focus. The plants and creatures I came across were geniuses at living in such a land. (Later, I realized so were the O'odham Jewed, Akimel O'odham, and Hohokam peoples who were indigenous to that place.) Water became a revelation. Unlike the rain-drenched, humid place I was from, the desert showed me what water truly was: life. In what appeared to be a harsh, hot place, I had found a new way to see.

I eventually moved away from Arizona, but in 2022 I traveled back to visit Chi'chil Biłdagoteel (Oak Flat), a site sacred to the San Carlos Apache that is about seventy miles east of Phoenix. I was there with other members of our Coalition to Dismantle the Doctrine of Discovery to witness the beauty of this sacred land and the tragedy of its possible destruction. Two of the world's largest multinational mining companies, Rio Tinto and BHP, and their American subsidiary, Resolution Copper, are poised to decimate the land with a mining technique that would collapse the area into a mile-wide crater a thousand feet deep. It would also heavily deplete and pollute the area's scarce water resources.

Chi'chil Biłdagoteel is on the ancestral lands of the San Carlos Apache and was once part of the San Carlos reservation. Native people don't have rights to their ancestral lands thanks to the Doctrine of Discovery, so much of Chi'chil Biłdagoteel became part of Tonto National Forest in the early twentieth century. In 1955, President Dwight Eisenhower made Chi'chil Biłdagoteel a protected area from mining because of its natural and cultural value. But in 2005, Resolution Copper began lobbying Congress to open the area to copper mining. According to one article, subsidiaries of Resolution Copper spent $1.3 million lobbying Congress in 2014 alone.[1]

In December of that year, Senators John McCain and Jeff Flake of Arizona added a last-minute rider giving Resolution Copper access to this protected land to a massive defense bill that Congress had to pass before it adjourned. McCain justified his actions by saying that copper was needed to maintain the technological supremacy of the US military. Critics pointed out that McCain was the top recipient of Resolution Copper campaign contributions in 2014 and that Flake had also received large campaign contributions from mining companies over his political career.

Eight years later, we traveled to Arizona to meet with Wendsler Nosie, the Apache leader rallying communities across the United States to help them save Chi'chil Biłdagoteel. The

Apache Stronghold, an Apache-led organization, has held mining at bay with prayer, action, and lawsuits for years. However, the land remains at critical risk of being turned over to Resolution Copper. Our coalition, including my church, has joined this struggle. As I stood in Chi'chil Biłdagoteel looking out over a land of exquisite beauty, it seemed almost impossible that it could be a crater one day.

In a presentation to our coalition, I later heard Wendsler's daughter Vanessa Nosie talk about the significance of this land and their struggle. She told us that what's happening at Oak Flat is not just an issue for Apache or Indigenous people. It affects everyone across the globe. "When the environment is destroyed, we have nothing left for our future, for those yet to be born," she said. "What happens at Oak Flat will set the precedent for what will happen throughout the country. There is no way we can live without water. We can't survive if our natural resources continue to be ripped and used for profit." Vanessa asked us to wake up and stop "raping" our natural resources. The Earth is alive, and we depend on its life for our own life. Not only is Resolution Copper destroying a holy site, but the copper mine will use enormous amounts of water in a drought-stricken area that badly needs it for other life-giving uses. The mine is projected to cause numerous health issues in the surrounding human populations, including cancer and asthma. Resolution Copper, said Vanessa, "wants to say this is for the benefit of the people. . . . They are lying to all people."[2]

Vanessa's words are powerful. But it can be tempting to think in response, "How wonderful that the Apache have a way of life so connected to the earth. But that's not how the world works. Why are they calling for us not to mine copper in the name of protecting the earth? To avoid catastrophic climate change, we need to decarbonize our economy. Doing so means we need much more copper and other minerals to build all the necessary electric cars and batteries. One of the biggest successes of the last several years is that solar and wind costs have decreased so much that they are now cheaper than fossil fuels.[3] This is how we will save the earth while continuing to grow our economies."

If that is your reaction, you are not alone. This viewpoint, known as "green growth," is consensus reality. Green growth holds that technology and human ingenuity can allow us to continue growing our economy while simultaneously mitigating ecological crises. It is the underlying philosophy of the Paris Agreement, the work of the UN's Intergovernmental Panel on Climate Change, and many of the largest environmental organizations. It underpins the Inflation Reduction Act, the US climate bill passed in 2022 that many call a game changer. Even Congresspersons Alexandria Ocasio-Cortez and Bernie Sanders, among the most progressive politicians in the United States, put forward plans based on green growth. It is "common sense."[4]

But a closer look at green growth reveals little that makes sense. We know the good that its proponents *say* it will bring. We believe they overlook key understandings of our planet and our history. As people of faith, we are called to seek God's justice and shalom. We live in a time when many of us are becoming more mindful of historical injustices like colonization and white supremacy. As we seek solutions to the climate crisis, we will do well to consider how "common sense" green growth is poised to replicate centuries-old patterns of systemic sin. Green growth is not just, and it is not realistic.

HOW CAPITALISM CAME TO BE

The previous chapters looked at the superstructure of our dominant culture—who and what it values and who and what it doesn't. Now we turn to a key component of structure, the economic system rooted in that worldview. To consider how green growth can replicate historic injustices, we need to tell the story of how capitalism came to be. Actually, we need to retell this story because many of us have only heard one version of it.

While neither of my parents sat me on their lap and told me the story of capitalism, I implicitly received a certain version, and I suspect many of you did as well. Here is an approximate summary:

> Once upon a time, human beings struggled to survive. There was lots of famine and disease, and people spent much of their time just trying to get enough to get by. People didn't live very long, and most people were desperately poor. Then, capitalism came into being. Capitalism, by freeing people to innovate and be creative, allowed much more wealth to be created and allowed lots of people to move out of poverty and into the middle class. This wealth resulted in wonderful achievements you now enjoy like supermarkets full of food, modern medicine, technological innovation, and consumer goods unimaginable to our ancestors. Capitalism ensures our freedom to become who we want and to create the life we want. There are some downsides to capitalism. But, overall, we are blessed to live under the best economic system ever invented. Now, we just have to extend the benefits of capitalism to everyone in the world so they, too, can live like us.

More and more, people are questioning whether this story tells the whole truth about capitalism. Rising inequality, climate change, the recession of 2008–2009, and economic volatility have combined to make people, especially younger folks, skeptical of it.

I want to tell another version of the story of capitalism—one I learned only when I was much older and heard mostly from people who had experienced the underside of capitalism much more than I have as a white, middle-class person. Seeing capitalism's underside more clearly is essential to evaluating the ethics of green growth and how it continues the logic of systems of death. This is necessary to the critical moral work of seeing what is normally hidden from those in the dominant culture. Just as you can see how a rug is made by looking at its underside, I believe we can also understand how our economy is constructed by flipping the rug over and looking at its underside.

I do this with some trepidation. The story of capitalism is complex and one that people have debated for centuries. My aim is not to present a definitive story, as if that were possible, but to add complexity to a too-simple one. In addition, as someone (probably philosopher Fredric Jameson) famously said, "It's easier to imagine the end of the world than it is to imagine the end of capitalism." Our imaginations are so entrenched in capitalism's ski tracks that it is hard to glide out into fresh snow. However, hearing a broader story of capitalism's beginnings helps us break out of those grooves to see our economy as a human creation, not as a natural part of the landscape that will exist forevermore.

Seeing this economic system more clearly will help us determine whether it can meet the needs of people and the planet. We desperately need the voices of people of faith in this discernment. One of the things I love about being an Anabaptist is the emphasis on the "priesthood of all believers." Unlike both the Catholic Church of their time and Protestant Reformers such as Martin Luther, sixteenth-century Anabaptist Reformers believed that the authority to interpret Scripture rested not with learned clergy or bishops but with the gathered community, no matter their education level. A group of "commoners" earnestly seeking together to follow in the way of Jesus has the authority to discern how to live out their faith. In the same way, economics belongs to the people. While we should learn from the work of economists, it is up to us to discern what economic system leads to human and planetary thriving.

For the story I am telling, I am working with the definition that capitalism is a way of organizing societies where social well-being is secured as an unintended side effect of seeking profit and accumulating wealth.[5] This magic is accomplished by the so-called invisible hand of the market. The invisible hand "is a metaphor for how, in a free market economy, self-interested individuals operate through a system of mutual interdependence. This interdependence incentivizes producers to make what is socially necessary, even though they may care only about their own well-being."[6] This sounds nearly like the mutual dependence of Indigenous cosmologies and systems of life, but there is a key difference. In the eyes of capitalism, greed is, well, good. By seeking to accumulate wealth by providing people with goods they want and profiting from it, private owners of capital have their needs met, and so does everyone else.

This definition excludes trade and markets, which predate capitalism. I also do not see smaller, locally owned businesses as problematic in the same way as corporations. For instance, in my hometown, we have a diner called Jim's that employs

local folks and, I assume, makes an annual income for its owners. Jim's is embedded within our community. Photos of Little
League and softball teams it has sponsored over the decades line
its walls. And judging by how I see the same people working
there year after year, Jim's provides good jobs for its employees.
Jim's doesn't seem focused on growth for the sake of growth but
is content to "hold steady" over the years. It's been serving the
same number of people at the same location for decades.

Jim's business is different from corporate capitalism, which
serves global stockholders and is required to produce a quarterly
profit. If corporations don't do this, or if stockholders perceive
them as not making enough of a profit, the workforce is often
"downsized" (meaning people lose their jobs), the business is
restructured (again, people lose jobs), or the corporation moves
to where they can find workers willing to work for less money
or where the cost of doing business is cheaper. Frequently, these
places have more lax labor or environmental regulations or
lower taxes.

Since profits and accumulation drive this kind of capitalism, constant expansion and growth are necessary. In our time,
economists believe our economy should grow 2 to 3 percent
per year, the rate required to ensure positive returns for the
private owners of capital while maintaining a stable economy.
(Of course, many private owners of capital hope for even better
growth rates for their investments.) If capitalism does not grow,
the economy experiences crises—recessions, even depressions.

In the previous chapter, we talked about our tendency to
make things abstract, to untether from the material world of
air and water and soil and bodies. We forget about the biophysical realities of our closed-system economy. I want to point
out something obvious but easy to forget: Constant growth is

not manufactured from thin air. It requires continually increasing extraction and consumption of the earth's resources and increasing levels of pollution or waste resulting from the extraction, production, and consumption of these resources.

To secure the necessary growth, capitalism of this kind requires several interventions according to economic anthropologist Jason Hickel.[7] First, the price of inputs, such as labor, land, minerals, and energy, must be as low as possible. Second, the system needs a constantly increasing supply of these inputs. Third, the system needs markets—ideally, captive markets—that can buy everything being produced.[8] The size and scale of these markets must constantly grow so profits can constantly grow.[9] As Hickel says, capitalism is the first and only intrinsically expansionist economic system in history.[10] To fuel the engine of continued growth, capitalism required four central practices from its very beginning: enclosure, exploitation, imperialism, and colonization, in roughly that order. Though these practices may take different forms today, they remain active within our political economy, including its green growth solutions.

ENCLOSURE: THE DRIVE TO PRIVATIZE

Feudalism is the political economy that structured European society from the ninth century onward. Land was owned by the aristocracy, who rented it out to peasants who farmed the land. Between about 1350 and 1500, European peasants experienced a golden age. The Black Death that had ravaged Europe's population in the mid-1300s meant land was abundant while workers were few. Consequently, peasants could demand more compensation and benefits such as time off and better working conditions. During this period, real wages reached all-time highs. As cracks began appearing within feudalism, peasants stepped into those gaps and began experimenting with cooperative societies rooted in local self-sufficiency. Even the land was healthier and began to heal from deforestation, overgrazing, and soil depletion. However, all of these changes meant that the elites could no longer accumulate wealth as they had before. The aristocracy, the church, and the merchants sought ways to push back against this "people power."

Starting in the 1500s, English manorial lords realized they could make a lot of money by exporting wool and wool fabric as global trade expanded (thanks to improved shipping technologies and the mechanization of cloth weaving). This meant the lords needed large pastures for sheep. So, they fenced in the common land and expelled peasants, through various means, from the commons that had formerly sustained them. This practice of fencing in land that had been once available for communal use is called enclosure. It is a form of privatization, and it took many forms throughout this historical period.

Land—or any resource held for communal use—is called the commons, and the people who use them are (you guessed it) commoners. Much of England's land had been part of the commons for hundreds of years. Even though peasants didn't own the land, it was available for their use to sustain themselves from it. They could farm, fish, graze animals, forage, cut turf for fuel, chop wood for manufacturing household objects, and gather rushes to make flooring and roofs for their cottages. Just about everything they needed came from this common land.

Denying peasants access to the commons proved an effective tool for English elites to wrest control from an empowered peasantry and accumulate more wealth. European elites across the Continent took notice and also began privatizing their commons. If you descend from a "commoner" European family, this may have been your family's story. A few years ago, I read a friend's family history, which mentioned that her great-great-grandparents had immigrated to the United States from the Scottish Highlands in the mid-1800s because the duke had kicked them off their land so he could convert it into sheep pasture. Other now-landless peasants were encouraged to go to overseas colonies as indentured servants.

The practice of enclosure was catastrophic for ordinary people. Turning the commons into private property led to famines in Europe during the 1500s since people lost the ability to practice self-provision. Between the 1500s and the 1700s, for instance, life expectancy dropped in England from forty-three to the low thirties, and real wages declined up to 70 percent over the same period. It took centuries for life expectancies to rise. Ironically, an economy could grow even if people within that economy were worse off. People separated from the commons became consumers who now had to buy food, clothing, and goods that they used to produce themselves. This increased consumption led to economic growth, as measured by the money spent to acquire goods and services.

Enclosures and the poverty they created resulted in massive social strife and even armed conflict between the dispossessed and those they saw as responsible.[11] The Radical Reformation and the rise of the Anabaptist movement were part of the tumult of these times, as commoners sought to claim and retain political, economic, and spiritual power over their lives.

As England and other European countries colonized much of the world, they continued using this strategy of enclosure. English tax policy pressured Indian peasants to stop subsistence farming and turn to raising cash crops for export. They also dismantled communal resources like granaries, irrigation systems, and the woods, pastures, and waters. Just as it had in Europe, enclosure resulted in famines in India. Thirty million Indians died during the last quarter of the nineteenth century.[12]

This same enclosure of the commons is happening in places today where Indigenous people are being forced into the money economy as their commons—their lands, hunting grounds, and waterways—are taken from them or polluted.[13] As these communities are brought into the money economy, that country's gross domestic product increases because people must purchase what was formerly provided by the land. To get this money, many people must move into cities where they become a part of a low-wage, often exploitable, labor force.

This drive to privatize and enclose what was formerly held in common continues in other forms. The patenting of seeds by agribusiness corporation Bayer (formerly Monsanto) encloses humanity's common agricultural heritage. Waterways that provide food and water are part of the commons, but oil spills and other pollution of public resources by corporations that make private profit are another form of enclosure. Our atmosphere, which supports life on this planet, is part of the commons. Some see the demand to make carbon dioxide polluters pay for their emissions as reclaiming the atmospheric commons.[14] In mainstream economic parlance, polluting a shared resource like the atmosphere or a river is a "negative externality." But it a form of enclosure—using what was or should be a public resource for private gain.

EXPLOITATION: THE AFTERMATH OF ENCLOSURE

Exploitation is a direct result of enclosure. People who can no longer support themselves from the commons are much easier to exploit. In the dawn of the Industrial Revolution, English peasants who were kicked off the land flocked to towns and cities, where their low-wage labor was needed in the factories being built at a fast clip. Those who couldn't find work became beggars, a condition punishable by law. Many of us are familiar with the atrocious conditions that workers faced in factories and mines. One evening, the tragedy of this became apparent to me when my sociologist husband told me how factory owners would lock the doors so that the workers couldn't leave. They were working twelve hours days, six days a week, doing mind-numbingly repetitive work in an often noisy, dangerous environment. People had to be forced to work under such exploitative conditions.

The most egregious example of exploitation was chattel slavery. At a time when the world's population was much lower than today, more than thirteen million people from the African continent were captured and sold as enslaved people, a practice that continued for almost four centuries. The wealth of Europe, Canada, and the United States was built by one of the most brutal forms of exploitation ever devised. It took centuries of struggle to end it.

The struggle against worker exploitation and modern slavery continues around the globe. In a 2019 article, journalist Kate Hodal reported that an estimated forty million people live in some form of modern slavery today. Why are there so many enslaved people? The answer is obvious: Slavery is incredibly profitable. As we've discussed, capitalism requires cheap "inputs" such as labor. Labor costs under slavery are cheap to non-existent. In fact, Hodal reports that modern exploiters have lower overheads than earlier slave traders because of advances in technology and transportation. Capitalism also requires a constantly increasing supply of these inputs. Global migration is increasing because of climate change, political instability, and rising inequality due to globalization. This means there is a "large supply of vulnerable, exploitable people [who] can be tapped into for global supply chains in the agriculture, beauty, fashion and sex industries."[15] While many in the Global North view immigrants as an economic liability, the constant supply of exploitable people makes possible our growing consumption of cheap goods and services. Where I live, for instance, the restaurant industry would come to a screeching halt without the low-wage labor of many immigrant workers.

IMPERIALISM AND COLONIZATION: PLUNDERING OTHER PLACES

The economic growth demanded by capitalism cannot endure within an isolated system. A country (or other entity) either overuses and runs out of domestic materials needed for production, or overexploits its domestic population of workers. Hickel says, "If you place too much pressure on your domestic resource base or your domestic working class, sooner or later, you are likely to face a revolution." To avoid this, capitalism has always required someplace external—an "outside"—where it can find cheap labor and natural resources and where it can "externalize social and ecological damages, where rebellions can be contained, and where it does not have to negotiate with local grievances or demands."[16] It has also demanded, as scholar Nafeez Ahmed puts it, "the systemic construction of racial categories designed to legitimize imperial conquest and expansion," which we find in the Doctrine of Discovery and the Virginia Slave Codes.[17]

These "outside" places are the colonies, where racial "outsiders" live. From the fifteenth century on, growth in Western economies has depended on resources (human labor or natural wealth) extracted from colonies on the peripheries.[18] Hickel writes, "Consider the silver plundered from the Andes, the sugar and cotton extracted from land appropriated from Indigenous Americans, the grain, rubber, gold and countless other resources appropriated from Asia and Africa, and the mass enslavement and indenture of African and Indigenous people—all of which exacted a staggering human and ecological toll. On top of this, colonizers destroyed local industries and self-sufficient economies to establish captive markets wherever they went. There was no lag between the rise of capitalism and the imperial project. Imperialism was the *mechanism* of capitalist expansion."[19]

To pick just one example among many: European elites had, for centuries, craved spices for medicinal and culinary reasons. Europe traded with South Asia for these luxury goods. But in the fifteenth and sixteenth centuries, advances in mapmaking and astronomy allowed Europeans to build and sail large boats worldwide. As soon as this technology became available, European powers competed to find the places where the coveted spices originated and seized control of these precious commodities. The Banda Islands of Maluku (now Indonesia), which grew the highly sought-after "trinity" of spices (nutmeg, mace, and cloves) became the prime destination for this domination.[20]

The Dutch formed the Dutch East India Company, the first multinational corporation, to secure these commodities.[21] They initially tried to convince the local population of the Banda Islands to accept various treaties that would have given the Dutch East India Company a monopoly. However, the Indigenous people of these islands didn't have a centralized authority or ruler with whom to form a treaty. (This is historically true and is often still true of Indigenous communities worldwide.) So, the Dutch turned to violence. Their military burnt villages, food stores, and boats. They captured, enslaved, or murdered as many of the Banda peoples as they could. Soon after this massacre, the Dutch East India Company became the largest company in human history, comparatively worth more than present-day ExxonMobil, Apple, and Amazon together. As Jan Pieterszoon Coen, the fourth governor-general of the Dutch East Indies, said in the early seventeenth century: "No trade without war and no war without trade."[22]

Imperialist violence continues today. While this violence is sometimes overt, as in CIA-led coups against governments deemed to be against US economic interests, much of this violence is now baked into our global financial structures.[23] The wealth of the core economies of the Global North still depends on resources from the Global South. In a 2022 study, Hickel and his coauthors point out that the Global South provides about 80 percent of the labor and resources for the world economy. Yet people in the Global South receive only about 5 percent of the annual income generated. In dollars, that equals $242 trillion appropriated from the Global South to the North between 1990 and 2015.[24]

GREEN GROWTH REPEATS THE STORY

Green growth, or green capitalism, is hailed as a novel, inventive solution to the climate crisis. But green growth assumes business as usual—a continuation of our current system based on continuous economic growth—except replacing fossil fuels with renewable energy. We fear that green growth will also mean business as usual and continued enclosure, exploitation, imperialism, and colonization.

Solar panels, batteries, electric cars, and wind turbines require enormous amounts of minerals and metals. Manufacturing electric vehicles require six times more minerals than cars with combustion engines.[25] A 2022 International Energy Agency report said that to get to net zero emissions globally by 2050, we will need to find and extract six times more minerals by 2040 than we do today.[26] Some figures put the total much higher. In addition to increasing extraction exponentially, we need to do this as quickly as possible. What environmental and human rights safeguards will be scrapped in the rush to meet this ambitious timeline? Already, economic development projects rarely obtain the free, prior, and informed consent of Indigenous Peoples, a right required under the UN Declaration on the Rights of Indigenous Peoples. This is a huge concern: over half of the world's energy transition minerals are located on or near land where Indigenous people live. Eighty-five percent of the world's lithium, a key mineral for green growth technologies, is found on or near Indigenous lands.[27]

If history is a guide and industry giants are successful, transition minerals will come from places like Chi'chil Biłdagoteel. They will come from places like the Atacama Desert in northern Chile, the world's oldest desert, a place of exceptional biodiversity, and home to Indigenous communities that have lived there for millennia—and also home to vast amounts of lithium and copper. They will come from Colombia, which hopes to become a primary global supplier of copper.[28] Violence remains tied to capitalism. In 2020, Colombia had the world's highest murder rate of land and environmental defenders, many of whom were Indigenous people.[29]

In all these places and many more, business as usual means that lands and homes will be appropriated from Indigenous and other marginalized communities, people will lose access to their lifeways, food, and water sources, and the people resisting this enclosure and economic imperialism will be the targets of extrajudicial killings. For these reasons, ecological economist William Rees claims that if you factor in all the problems involved in mining, refining, and manufacturing minerals for an average, large electric vehicle, electric vehicles are a *worse* option, both ecologically and ethically, than combustion engine cars.[30]

Already, global elites are racing for the newest versions of nutmeg, mace, and cloves. Billionaires like Jeff Bezos and Bill Gates have invested millions of dollars into KoBold Metals, which is scouring the globe for lithium, copper, nickel, and cobalt.[31] In 2022, the *Washington Post* ran an editorial opposing Chile's new progressive constitution because it would make it more difficult for the United States to source cheap lithium from Chile.[32] Elon Musk, CEO of Tesla and Twitter, stands to make huge profits from the green energy transition. Like the Dutch governor-general of the seventeenth century, Musk explicitly links green energy mineral extraction to imperialism. In a now-deleted tweet about access to Bolivian lithium, he said, "We will coup whoever we want! Deal with it."[33]

Like the proposed copper mine at Chi'chil Biłdagoteel, many mines will ruin land, water, wildlife, and people. A coalition of Native Americans, environmentalists, and ranchers is opposing a project to mine lithium in rural Nevada (which would be the largest in the United States) because it will use billions of gallons of precious groundwater, potentially contaminating some of it for three hundred years and leaving behind vast amounts of waste.[34] Mining requires enormous amounts of water; for instance, a ton of mined lithium requires almost 500,000 gallons of water.[35] Water extracted for mining draws down the water table and limits farmers' ability to irrigate fields. Mining also produces enormous amounts of toxic waste: leaks from mines have poisoned rivers and other waters, sometimes killing off whole freshwater ecosystems. As we have described earlier, current mining practices require sacrifice zones, places that can be devastated by the ecological impacts of the mining, and people and wildlife deemed "sacrifice-able." In short: colonies.

The same communities losing everything because of extraction are also disproportionately affected by climate change and environmental degradation, even though they contribute the least to it. A recent study concluded that the Global North is responsible for most carbon emissions—92 percent!—and that most Western countries exceeded their fair share of their carbon budget decades ago.[36] In addition, high-income countries are responsible for 74 percent of excess resource consumption, which drives most of the planet's biodiversity loss, freshwater depletion, and other environmental pressures.[37] Our excess consumption and pollution in the Global North is triggering ecological overshoot while communities in the Global South and marginalized communities in the North lack the essential resources needed, such as food, housing, and healthcare.

We *do* need to transition to renewable energies and end the use of fossil fuels. But this transition must happen while honoring the self-determination and human rights of Indigenous Peoples and other communities. Many "Green New Deals" proposed by Indigenous and Global South communities meld the goals of an energy transition with ecological and social justice. None of these alternative Green New Deals, however, purport that we can reach these goals and maintain the goal of continual economic growth. Doing so will likely re-create a brutal history, even as we say we want to do justice and right our past wrongs.

THE SPIRIT OF LIFE BECAME FLESH

After he was baptized, Jesus was filled with the Holy Spirit and led into the wilderness. Luke 4:2 says he was tempted for forty days. He lived in a state of prayer and fasting for forty days and nights.

The tempter offered him three things:

1. food, sustenance, and fulfilment of his immediate needs and desires, when he was offered bread from the stones (Luke 4:3);

2. power, privilege, and opulence, when he was offered the authority and splendor of all the kingdoms (Luke 4:6–7); and

3. legitimacy and relevance, when he was taunted to prove who he said he was (Luke 4:9–11).

I (Sarah) think that the church may be in the wilderness now, enduring temptation. We comfort ourselves by saying that we deserve the things that are offered to us.

We want to protect and comfort our bodies by storing up our wealth and attempting to ensure our security. We tell ourselves this is responsible and sensible.

We want power and luxury, and we tell ourselves we should have these things because we are good and responsible—we are the best ones to wield such things so that we can use them for good.

We want legitimacy; we want to be relevant. We believe that what we say and think matters, and we can prove it by befriending the powerful, growing our own power by filling stadiums with the faithful, building important institutions, and collectively owning wealth and property. (The church owns more property than any other private entity on earth.)

I believe that Jesus, being human, wanted these things too. He knew hunger. He had an ego, like we all do. He felt humiliated sometimes and wanted to prove what he could do. But he showed us it is possible to turn away from these temptations.

From my point of view, a central misunderstanding of Jesus' ministry is expressed in our denial that he was like us. We set him apart; we attribute his actions to his perfect nature. We tell ourselves that while he is the perfect example, we can't approximate his vision; only God is perfect and capable of carrying out what Jesus did in his ministry.

But I want to challenge that notion. God became flesh to be with us. Jesus was a man, in the flesh. He felt fear and doubt, exhaustion and disappointment just like we do. But he pursued his mandate every single day of his ministry. He demonstrated that we can do the same. The voice of God made flesh—that Glory on the mountaintop, providing commandments from on high, that tongue of fire leading through the wilderness—now embodied in one of us. How can we dismiss the example of a mortal man? The Spirit of life made flesh: vulnerable, finite. A person who risked all to show us, tangibly, how to live.

After he was tempted, Jesus immediately went back to Nazareth and began his ministry (see Luke 4:14–21). He began by stating his mandate, from the prophet Isaiah, which he called "good news for the poor:" release for prisoners, recovery of sight for the blind, freedom for the oppressed, and the year of our Lord's favor, or the year of Jubilee.

Jesus showed us with his life how to face temptation, how to turn away from what we think we need, what we covet or desire, what we believe we deserve. He walked away from all those things in favor of freedom for the oppressed. He announced, "Today this scripture is fulfilled in your hearing."

It is time for us to claim this same authority with *our* lives. We can choose to endure and exit the wilderness with our integrity intact. We can choose to speak, as he did, with authority. Can you say that with me, out loud? *Today this scripture is fulfilled in our hearing.*

FIVE

Green Growth Is Unrealistic

I (SHERI) OFTEN marvel at how different my life is from that of my grandparents and parents—and how different my son's upbringing is from my own. My paternal grandparents, Ira and Elsie, were born at the turn of the twentieth century. Neither of them ever lived more than seven miles from where they grew up, which was also true for the three generations before them.[1] As children, they walked to school or took a horse-drawn sled. They farmed with horses and cooked their food—most of which they grew or raised themselves—on a wood stove that also heated their homes. They hand-pumped their water from a backyard well. Although they had greater access to a range of store-bought goods and used kerosene lamps, in many respects their lives were not that far removed from those of their ancestors, who were peasant farmers in Switzerland. That changed in the 1920s, when my grandfather proudly purchased a Model A Ford. But despite having an automobile for most of their adult lives, neither of my paternal grandparents ever left the state of Ohio. The idea that they would travel to some destination miles away on vacation was outside their worldview, as was the *idea* of a vacation.

As I noted earlier, my father, Lyman, was born in 1929. He grew up in the small town of Berlin, in a two-bedroom, one-bath home with modern conveniences like an indoor toilet, hot and cold running water, a kerosene cooking stove, and a radio. However, they didn't have a refrigerator or a telephone or electric lights, all of which were expensive luxuries. Even though his family lived in town, they still produced a lot of their own food thanks to the large garden in the backyard and the chicken and pig pens. When my father was ten, his family moved to a small, rundown farm a few miles away. His father used a diesel-powered tractor, but not much had changed between his generation and that of his parents; the house had no electricity or indoor plumbing.[2] My father's job was to chop wood for the large cookstove, which was used for baking, cooking, and providing hot water for the entire home. A pot-bellied stove fueled by wood and coal heated their uninsulated home, although the heat barely made it to the upstairs bedrooms during the winter. My father remembers waking up and finding snow on the interior windowsill.

I was born in 1962 in Berlin in a ranch house that had been built a few years earlier. We still grew most of our vegetables from two large gardens in our backyard and raised a cow in the field beyond them. This was one of the few things I had in common with how my father and grandparents were raised. Unlike them, I couldn't fathom a world without indoor plumbing, electricity, hot and cold water available from multiple faucets, or an insulated home that grew warmer every time I turned up the thermostat. I couldn't imagine a home not filled with machines that made life easier and more entertaining—a refrigerator, electric range, washer and dryer, radio, record player, and television. I spent hours on the phone with my friends, although calling someone long distance was still a luxury. My maternal grandmother owned a small home in the Amish section of Sarasota, Florida, and our family loved to travel there over Christmas break for vacation. I was sixteen when I boarded my first airplane, which took me to a Mennonite high school work camp in Minneapolis. (My mother had not yet traveled by plane.) By the time I finally settled in the San Francisco Bay Area at the age of thirty-eight, I had lived in six different cities in six different states.

My son was born in 2004 in California. Before his first birthday, he logged four flights and had a frequent flyer number with Southwest Airlines. Before graduating high school, he had traveled to ten different countries. With a small device he carries in his pocket, he—along with everyone else in our family—can instantaneously communicate with people across the globe, listen to almost any piece of music ever composed, and access a repository of information that exceeds the Library of Congress, the world's largest. With that same device, he can order Chinese, Japanese, Burmese, Thai, Vietnamese, Mexican, Italian, Middle Eastern, or Peruvian food that will be delivered within minutes, and can purchase almost anything else and have it arrive at his door from halfway around the world within several hours or days at most. I grow a handful of vegetables and herbs in our backyard but nowhere near enough to feed our family. Instead, we rely on the several grocery stores within a few minutes' drive of our home for all our household needs.

HOW I (WE) GOT HERE

Economic historian J. Brad DeLong calls the period from 1870 to 2010—roughly the time span between my grandparents' time and my son's—"the long twentieth century."[3] In a history of the US political economy that became a 2022 bestseller, DeLong argues that technological progress accelerated after 1870, generating an unprecedented productivity explosion that changed almost every aspect of economic life. Humanity's technological competence began doubling every generation, which catapulted families like mine into the growing middle class, especially during the post–World War II Great Acceleration.[4] This exponential change brought with it political instability and conflict, especially for the Global South and oppressed communities in the Global North who were "denied much of the benefit of the world's economic revolutions while suffering the bulk of the harm from the ensuing political and social revolutions."[5]

Fossil fuel energy—coal, oil, and natural gas—powered this explosion. The discovery, extraction, and increasing availability of fossil energy fueled the massive changes DeLong describes between the lives of my grandparents and my son. Up until my grandparent's time, much of the energy needed to produce the food and materials necessary to sustain human life came from the muscle power of people and work animals, wood, and wind—all renewable resources. My grandparents used some coal and kerosene, and coal powered the steam engines and smelters needed for manufacturing the limited number (by today's standards) of household objects. But these fossil fuel inputs pale in comparison to today.

The fossil fuel explosion drastically increased extraction and consumption. A single barrel of crude oil, which costs about seventy dollars as of this writing, equates to almost four and a half years' work by one person.[6] So the 100 million barrels of oil that our global economy consumes annually equals almost 1.2 million years of human labor magically at our disposal *every day*. With this vast increase in "energy workers," we have drilled into the earth's crust to frack natural gas and into the oceans to deepwater drill for oil. We have powered deep-sea fishing expeditions, fueled the tractors and combines needed for industrial farming, and penetrated even deeper into remote areas to mine for minerals.[7] We have powered a global fleet of container ships, trucks, and planes that move everything from tomatoes to can openers around the globe at speeds unimaginable in my parent's generation. This has allowed the average American today to consume *forty-eight times* the goods and services as a person in 1800.[8] This single statistic explains much of the difference between my life and my ancestors.

In his book *How the World Really Works: The Science Behind How We Got Here and Where We're Going*, scientist Vaclav Smil writes that our "increasing dependence on fossil fuels is the most important factor in explaining the advances of modern civilization."[9] Smil grew up in 1950s Czechoslovakia, where most of his family's energy came from the wood he chopped daily. He now lives in a small, energy-efficient house he built himself near Winnipeg. Smil's numerous books are essential reading for understanding the role that energy plays in our economy and, thus, the scope of the energy transition before us. He cites the jaw-dropping statistic that an average, present-day inhabitant of the earth has nearly seven hundred times more useful energy available to them than their ancestors had at the beginning of the nineteenth century. It is as if each adult had sixty adults working for them nonstop, day and night; for those living in more affluent countries, it's more like 200 or even 240 adult workers attending to them. The average middle-class person in the United States of today lives like the nobility of old.[10]

Crude oil is the lifeblood of industrial civilization. This is not only because the gas, diesel, and jet fuel we derive from crude oil fuel our global transportation system—the cars, long-haul trucks, container ships, and airplanes that move people and products around the planet. It's because we also get much more from a barrel of crude oil than diesel, gas, and jet fuel. We also obtain the gooey tar used to make asphalt and pave our roads. (Even electric cars drive on roads derived from fossil fuels.) And we get raw chemical feedstock for plastics, pharmaceuticals, fertilizer, and devices like our computers and cell phones.

We are told that we need to electrify everything to successfully make the green energy transition, but the share of electricity in total final energy consumption globally is still only 20%, a total that includes electricity generated by fossil fuels.[11] That means 80% of our economy still needs to be electrified. Will it really be possible to fly jet engines that run on electricity stored in onboard batteries? Many engineers believe this ability might be decades away, if it's even possible. What about container ships? Finding ways to electrify key industrial processes is even more problematic. In *How the World Really Works*, Smil asserts that the four pillars of industrial civilization—the civilization that has emerged since my grandparents' time—are steel, cement, plastic, and ammonia. All four are manufactured using fossil fuels.

- Steel is in everything: buildings, vehicles, bridges and railways, machines and tools, medical implants and suture needles, and in many of the things we use daily such as household appliances, cutlery, saucepans, computers.

- Since 2007, most of humanity has lived in cities developed out of concrete. Almost every part of the built urban environment relies on concrete, from what is buried in the ground (sewers, subways, tunnels) to what is paved over it (roads, airport runways, shipping piers) to what rises above it (skyscrapers, apartment buildings, bridges). And because cement is not nearly as durable as steel, cement structures must regularly be torn down and replaced. The world now uses more cement in one year than it used during the entire first half of the twentieth century.

- In 1925, global plastic production was 20,000 tons; by 2019, it was 370 million tons. A quick tour of your home will reveal its ubiquity. Consider the healthcare sector: PVC, a plastic polymer, is the primary component of over a quarter of all healthcare products. Think disposable vinyl gloves, gowns, shields, flexible tubes for medical devices and IVs, blood bags, syringes, sterile packaging, trays and basins, bedpans, and bed rails.

- Of the four substances, Smil asserts that ammonia is the most important, calling it "the gas that feeds the world." Synthetic ammonia is used to make nitrogen fertilizers. Without them, Smil believes that nearly four billion of the world's population would not be alive in 2020, as it would be impossible to feed today's population without ammonia-derived fertilizers.[12]

Manufacturing these four materials uses about 17 percent of the world's primary energy supply and causes 25 percent of all carbon dioxide emissions from the combustion of fossil fuels. And, Smil says, "there are currently no commercially available and readily deployable mass-scale alternatives to displace these established processes" on the time scale needed to avert intolerable climate change.[13]

Additionally, our food supply relies on fossil fuels for far more than fertilizers. Plowing, irrigating, harvesting, processing, delivering, and refrigerating food all use fossil fuels, as does the manufacture of everything necessary to grow the food—machinery, fertilizers, agrochemicals, building supplies, and so on. Our food industry is so dependent on fossil fuels that it takes ten calories of energy to produce one calorie of consumed food.[14]

Finally, even the "green" economy will require massive amounts of steel, concrete, and raw earth minerals to build all the solar panels, wind turbines, transmission infrastructure, and batteries needed.[15] Think not only of the fossil fuel inputs necessary for making a wind turbine or battery but the inputs necessary for extracting all the minerals needed for their manufacture. In addition, there simply may not be enough minerals to fuel an energy transition.[16] "Until all energies used to extract and process these materials come from renewable conversions, modern civilization will remain fundamentally dependent on the fossil fuels used to produce these indispensable materials," writes Smil. "No AI, no apps, and no electronic messages will change that."[17] In short, our modern economy will always be bound to colossal quantities of materials and resources.

WHY DECARBONIZING PERPETUAL GROWTH IS DIFFICULT

I know I have just spewed a firehose full of facts! I didn't really believe much of this information when I first came across it. I thought that surely if these things were true, we'd be hearing much more about this. I needed to be convinced that our industrial growth civilization is much more dependent on fossil fuels than I had realized. For the longest time, I wanted to believe people like climate activist Bill McKibben, whom I respect, when he says, "The good news is we don't need to be burning stuff anymore. In the last decade, engineers have brought down the price of renewable energy by about 90 percent. . . . We could stop combustion, stop the spark in your spark plug, stop the fire that's burning in your basement to heat your home, stop the fire that most of us have in our kitchens to cook our food and replace it with the fact that the good Lord hung a ball of burning gas ninety-three million miles away in the sky and we know how to use it."[18]

I have come to believe that McKibben and many others in the climate and green growth movements are, in the words of ecological economist Nate Hagens, "energy blind." Most of us are. We don't fully realize that the world-changing economic growth of the long twentieth century depends on the burning of fossil fuels and that the civilization we have built from this burning cannot be fueled by renewables alone, especially in the short time frame necessary to mitigate disaster.

That time frame is growing shorter as climate scientists increasingly realize that the warming we have already experienced has brought about greater changes than anyone predicted. In 2018, the Intergovernmental Panel on Climate Change (IPCC) concluded that we need to keep temperatures from rising no more than 1.5 degrees Celsius, not the former benchmark of 2.0 degrees. Changes due to increased temperatures at first included things like melting ice caps and endangered habitat for polar bears. They have since accelerated into events that directly affect the everyday lives of multitudes. For instance, in 2022, over 30 million people in Pakistan were displaced by flooding. In the summer of that year, major rivers in Europe dried up and left ships carrying freight stranded. To avert even worse impacts, the IPCC has said we must cut global emissions by half by 2030 and entirely by 2050. However, high-income nations, because they are the biggest climate polluters, need to achieve zero emissions by *2030*.[19]

Decarbonizing our existing economies is challenging enough. Now imagine trying to decarbonize an economy *twice* as big as our present one. Growing the global economy at 2 to 3 percent annually—the rate projected to maintain stability and returns on investment in our perpetual growth economy—will more than double its size in twenty-three to thirty years. Then, that already-doubled economy will double itself again in a similar time span.[20] In other words, when my eighteen-year-old son is of retirement age, our economy will have grown four times larger than today! As Jason Hickel says, this is like trying to fill a bathtub that keeps getting bigger or trying to shovel sand into a hole that keeps expanding.[21] Indeed, scientists have issued a warning to humanity that we cannot decarbonize if we keep growing the economy.[22]

Despite these realities, very few people in the public sphere question the goal of continued economic growth. It's a third rail no politician will touch, and most experts aware of the facts outlined here quickly dismiss the rare suggestion that exponential growth in an extraction economy is unrealistic. Instead, they insist that we can grow so long as we continue to scale up renewable energies as fast as possible while *also* pulling carbon out of the air via carbon capture and developing alternative fuels. These green growth proposals are exceedingly risky gambles.

CARBON CAPTURE

Many experts know it will be impossible to eliminate fossil fuels and grow our economy while keeping climate change under control. That's why IPCC climate models have depended for years on mass-scale carbon capture and storage (CCS) technology to balance the climate numbers. CCS captures carbon dioxide, transports it via pipeline, and then either uses it or buries it in the ground.[23] Proponents argue that carbon emissions can thus be offset by carbon sequestration, referred to as "net zero emissions." In other words, we can continue to overshoot our climate budget and then pull excess emissions from the atmosphere at some future point.

I felt surprised when I realized this. None of the green growth climate goals are about totally reducing carbon emissions. They are about getting to "net zero" or becoming "carbon neutral." And they rely on highly problematic technologies to achieve this balancing act, technologies not yet shown to be effective.

CCS technology is not widely used despite its promotion by politicians, academics, and business leaders for more than two decades. This technology captures emission from smokestacks, separates the carbon dioxide (CO_2) from other components, and then stores or uses the carbon dioxide. However, CCS currently stores barely anything: 0.001 percent of global emissions a year.[24] Nearly three-quarters of captured carbon is injected back into oil fields to—get this—extract more oil and gas.[25]

Direct air capture (DAC), another carbon capture technology, uses big fans to vacuum in lots of air and filter it through chemicals that remove carbon. Unlike carbon capture and storage, DAC can handle "legacy emissions," the nearly one trillion tons of carbon dioxide we've put into the atmosphere since 1750. But, again, there's the problem of scale. Supposedly, the largest DAC facilities will eventually capture one million tons of CO_2 each year. That means we'd need to build thirty-seven thousand plants just to capture the thirty-seven billion tons of CO_2 we currently emit each year.[26] This doesn't account for any legacy emissions. In addition, DAC is energy- and material-intensive. And in order for direct air capture to be green, it must use renewable energy, not fossil fuels.

Building out these carbon capture technologies to scale would be one of the biggest building projects ever attempted. And that would be in addition to the incredible infrastructure feat of transitioning to renewable energy. As Smil says, it took us over one hundred years to develop our oil industry infrastructure, and capturing even 10 percent of our annual CO_2 output would require the same infrastructure that now supports the entire global oil industry. "Something like this can't be done in five, or 10, or 15 years," he says. "Simply on the matter of scale, carbon sequestration is just simply dead in the water."[27]

A 2022 report on government climate pledges from around the world found that they relied on land-based carbon removal approaches, like reforestation, that would require 1.2 billion hectares of land, an amount *equal* to the world's current cropland. Needless to say, this is not realistic. Interestingly, the report recommends that Indigenous Peoples and local communities be given secure land rights and self-determination to manage their lands and forests because these communities are much better than government or private landowners at conserving existing primary forests.[28] These primary forests, which hold much of the earth's biodiversity, store far more carbon than harvested and replanted forests or monocrop tree plantations, like the palm oil plantations that have replaced rainforests in Indonesia and other countries.

It's amazing the flights of fancy we are willing to take to maintain the status quo of unending economic growth. The land, resources, and money needed for carbon capture seem to be based on a fictional world, not the one we actually have. This unrealistic thinking pervades many of the proposed solutions for avoiding catastrophic climate change while maintaining the same levels of consumption. Choosing a societal goal other than growth might seem unrealistic, but is it actually more unrealistic than the alternatives?

ALTERNATIVE FUELS

Like carbon capture, biofuels are often touted as part of the solution to the climate crisis. Biofuels, which are manufactured from organic material, emit only about half as much CO_2 as fossil fuels when burned, and the plants grown for biofuels absorb CO_2 as they grow. However, when we factor in how biofuels are grown, made, and transported, they may emit more CO_2 than fossil fuels—according to one report, an average of 1.8 times as much.[29]

Growing biofuels also requires vast amounts of land. Already, humans have converted half of the earth's habitable land into agricultural land. If we continue growing our population and eating the way we do, we will need to clear more land equal to one and a quarter Indias by 2050 to meet world food needs.[30] Now add to this equation the enormous quantities of land needed to grow biofuels. That's a lot of land, possibly more than we have. Many experts say that the amounts of land needed to generate adequate biofuels are unrealistic. In the United Kingdom, for example, even if all arable land were used to make bioethanol, it would only produce 45 percent of the demand currently met by petroleum in that country.[31]

Other alternative fuels like hydrogen and fusion require more energy to produce than we get from their creation and are not scalable in the aggressive time frame needed. This scaling issue holds true for nuclear power. While many people are rethinking the need for nuclear power and believe it has a role in our energy transition, nuclear power is no easy or quick fix. As mentioned earlier, of global energy consumed, only 20 percent comes from electricity, and only 10 percent of that electricity is generated by nuclear power plants.[32] Therefore, nuclear currently makes up a quite small proportion of our overall energy use. Building enough nuclear plants to change that will take a lot of time and money—nuclear plants are expensive to build and often take several years or longer to construct. Furthermore, nuclear power is politically unfeasible in many areas because so many people oppose it. In other areas, nations don't have the capacity to build nuclear power plants. (As of 2023, only thirty-one countries have nuclear power plants.[33])

While some experts (like Smil) believe that we have overreacted to the perceived environmental and health risks of nuclear power because of catastrophic events like Chernobyl and Fukushima, real risks remain, especially considering our future trajectory. In a climate-changed world that experiences more hurricanes and wildfires, could we safely maintain the several hundred existing nuclear plants (and their waste), much less many more? Can we guarantee their maintenance two hundred years from now? What if a breakdown in social complexity makes it impossible to maintain them, or what if nuclear plants or waste sites become targets of warfare?[34]

Let's imagine that we somehow manage to become carbon neutral. Let's wave our magic wand and say that the world electrifies everything it can in the next three decades, that fuels made from hydrogen and fusion are available tomorrow, and that we will start sucking billions of tons of carbon from the air the day after that. Problem solved! But all these solutions only solve the problem of carbon emissions. They don't address the other planetary thresholds we have crossed or the ones we are in danger of surpassing. In fact, as we'll explore in the next chapter, some of the proposed climate solutions may increase the risk of crossing other planetary boundaries. As Jason Hickel writes, "Even if we had a 100 percent-clean-energy system, what would we do with it? Exactly what we are doing with fossil fuels: raze more forests, trawl more fish, mine more mountains, build more roads, expand industrial farming, and send more waste to landfills—all of which have ecological consequences our planet can no longer sustain."[35] The destruction of the earth would continue, even if we stop emitting carbon dioxide.

THE HUNGRY CYCLE MUST CEASE

There is a story poem titled "call that story back" that I (Sarah) heard many times during childhood. It comes from Leslie Marmon Silko's novel *Ceremony*, which explores the cosmic forces of life and death through the cosmology of her Pueblo (Tewa) people. Her people are the Laguna; in the lines of our shared ancestors, her people and mine are relatives. As the characters in the story grapple with the aftermath of war and violence, stories are a road through which the characters make meaning from the trauma they endure.

Silko's story poem "call that story back" had a profound impact on me. It describes a witch gathering, where the spiritual forces of darkness gather to impress each other with the evil they can imagine and bring to life. Near the end of the strange gathering where witches brag about the violence they could bring about, the last witch, whose origin and gender is unknown, offers a story that weaves reality in its telling. The witch calls into being the worst thing any of the gathered foes of creation could think of: colonization. They describe a people from across the sea as beings that "grow away from the earth," from the sun and other beings, because they only see objects; they see the earth as "a dead thing." They live in fear, and destroy the things they fear, making killing machines that destroy life in a blink. The death machines bring drought, hunger, and genocide. The living world is taken over from sea to sea, and the colonists destroy even each other in a competition for the resources they find in veins of rocks deep within the earth.

The other witches and sorcerers are horrified by this vision, and cry, "Call that story back." But it is too late. In its imagining, the story is already set in motion.[36]

Imagining. There is an irony here worth exploring. The powerful hands on the levers of the systems of death in our world do not fear imagining any technical or biological weapon, any technology, however unethical, whatever the cost. But the ordinary humans who live here in this place, who are shaped by the benefits and the costs of this continual hungry race toward destruction, are too timid to imagine different systems, systems that comply with the Reality of mutual dependence. If we are to survive as a human race, we *must* collectively imagine systems that comply with life. Who will have the courage to imagine? Will people of faith finally rise and resist the systems of darkness with one voice? Time will tell.

Silko's story poem describes colonization from Silko's cosmology, through the lens of her (my) people. This experience is not one of progress or achievement; it does not boast of great technological strides, or democracy, or the triumph of human ingenuity. It is just an experience of death, wrought by evil. The Pueblo people revolted against the Spanish in armed conflict in 1680. They had already been occupied for eight decades.[37]

One hundred eighty years later, the Suquamish people of the Pacific Northwest met with colonial forces.[38] In an 1854 speech addressed to the US government, Chief Seattle recounts the events of colonization through the cosmology of his coastal Suquamish people:

> To us the ashes of our ancestors are sacred and their resting place is hallowed ground. You wander far from the graves of your ancestors and seemingly without regret. Your religion was written upon tablets of stone by the iron finger of your God so that you could not forget. The Red Man could never comprehend or remember it. Our religion is the traditions of our ancestors—the dreams of our old men, given them in solemn hours of the night by the Great Spirit; and the visions of our sachems, and is written in the hearts of our people.
>
> Your dead cease to love you and the land of their nativity as soon as they pass the portals of the tomb and wander away beyond the stars. They are soon forgotten and never return. Our dead never forget this beautiful world that gave them being. They still love its verdant valleys, its murmuring rivers, its magnificent mountains, sequestered vales and verdant lined lakes and bays, and even yearn in tender fond affection over the lonely hearted living, and often return from the happy hunting ground to visit, guide, console, and comfort them . . .
>
> Every part of this soil is sacred in the estimation of my people. Every hillside, every valley, every plain and grove,

has been hallowed by some sad or happy event in days long vanished. Even the rocks, which seem to be dumb and dead as they swelter in the sun along the silent shore, thrill with memories of stirring events connected with the lives of my people, and the very dust upon which you now stand responds more lovingly to their footsteps than yours, because it is rich with the blood of our ancestors, and our bare feet are conscious of the sympathetic touch. Our departed braves, fond mothers, glad, happy hearted maidens, and even the little children who lived here and rejoiced here for a brief season, will love these somber solitudes and at eventide they greet shadowy returning spirits. And when the last Red Man shall have perished, and the memory of my tribe shall have become a myth among the White Men, these shores will swarm with the invisible dead of my tribe, and when your children's children think themselves alone in the field, the store, the shop, upon the highway, or in the silence of the pathless woods, they will not be alone. In all the earth there is no place dedicated to solitude. At night when the streets of your cities and villages are silent and you think them deserted, they will throng with the returning hosts that once filled them and still love this beautiful land. The White Man will never be alone.[39]

The force of evil that Silko imagined through the experience of our people, both living and dead, has now conquered this land from ocean to ocean. But we and our northern relatives are not alone as victims in its wake. Now every human on earth, every one of us, faces destruction from the evil of extractive logic, the assumption that the earth is a dead thing, a commodity to be exploited. The hungry cycle we set in motion is spinning faster and faster toward our demise. It is not some distant enemy force that will destroy us or even a virulent virus—our commitment to feeding our own consumption will destroy us.

In moments of despair, when I shout into the dark for another year but still cannot seem to wake the people of God, who are seemingly enthralled by a horrible dream, I remember Psalm 37:7–17 (NIV).

> Be still before the LORD
>> and wait patiently for him;
> do not fret when people succeed in their ways,
>> when they carry out their wicked schemes.
> Refrain from anger and turn from wrath;
>> do not fret—it leads only to evil.
> For those who are evil will be destroyed,
>> but those who hope in the LORD will inherit the land.
> A little while, and the wicked will be no more;
>> though you look for them, they will not be found.
> But the meek will inherit the land
>> and enjoy peace and prosperity.
> The wicked plot against the righteous
>> and gnash their teeth at them;
> but the LORD laughs at the wicked,
>> for he knows their day is coming.
> The wicked draw the sword
>> and bend the bow
> to bring down the poor and needy,
>> to slay those whose ways are upright.
> But their swords will pierce their own hearts,
>> and their bows will be broken.

Better the little that the righteous have
    than the wealth of many wicked;
for the power of the wicked will be broken,
    but the LORD upholds the righteous.

Are we not, as the children of God, the meek? Or are we the wicked, content with the plots of the mighty against the meek? It is time to take a stand. Will we stand with death or with life? Do we see ourselves in Silko's story poem or in Chief Seattle's words? We have a choice. The Creator, the Spirit of Life, stands with the meek. Will we stand with that Spirit and live?

SIX

Green Growth Is Limited

IN 1972, WHEN I (Sheri) was ten years old, a group of MIT scientists released a book called *The Limits to Growth*. New computer technologies allowed the scientists to explore the dynamic patterns of living systems. These tools made possible the fields of complexity science and systems dynamics, allowing Western science to more easily overcome the reductionist approach that had dominated for so long.[1] Now, scientists could begin to grasp, at least partially, the integrated whole that is our dynamic, living earth system.

Their conclusion? If population, consumption, and pollution continued to grow as predicted, global society would reach the limits to economic growth due to depleting natural resources and the finite capacity of earth to absorb pollution from industry and agriculture. This overshoot would result in decreased industrial output and declines in food production, services, and other consumption. The end to growth could take the form of a collapse, an "uncontrolled decline in both population and human welfare." Or it could take the form of a "smooth adaptation of the human footprint to the carrying capacity of the globe."[2] The authors urged us to immediately begin to return to an ecological balance on a finite planet and recommended various policies to achieve that goal, including stabilizing the world population, introducing radical efficiencies in how we use resources, shifting our societal goals from consumerism and consumption to providing high-quality education and health care for all and promoting cultural activities, identifying and adopting less polluting ways of producing goods and food, and promoting sustainable agriculture.

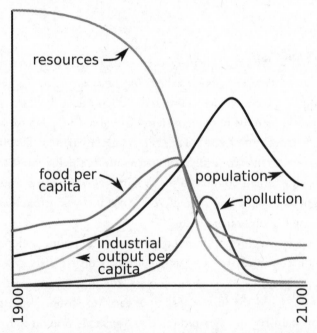

"Standard" world model run as shown in *The Limits to Growth*, figure 35, page 124, graph reconstruction by Reuben Honigwachs (@YaguraStation), CC BY-SA 4.0.

The Limits to Growth shocked the world and helped make the public aware of the concept of global overshoot. Mainstream media and economists quickly denounced the book and its conclusions. The authors were branded as "Malthusians," named after the eighteenth-century British scholar and economist who predicted that population growth would eventually outpace food production, resulting in catastrophic deaths from famine and war. Malthus's theory became widely discredited when it didn't occur. Notably, critics of both Malthus and *The Limits to Growth* argued that technology and human ingenuity would always find a way to get beyond these limits. Still, the book sold millions of copies, was translated into thirty-seven languages, and is the bestselling environmental book of all times.

The book marked its fiftieth anniversary in 2022. Many folks dusted it off and revisited its conclusions. They found its predictions about where we would be fifty years later to be right on track. In fact, scholars have been validating the book's conclusions since around 2008. The most recent analysis by sustainability researcher Gaya Harrington in 2020 compared current data on population, fertility rates, and resource use, among others, and found that the business-as-usual scenario from *The Limits to Growth* was correct: If there aren't major changes in consumption, economic growth stands to peak and rapidly decline—possibly leading to collapse—by around 2040.[3]

But how could this be? Even today's worst climate change scenarios don't predict such imminent collapse! Remember, the original book was written before the impacts of catastrophic climate change were known. The authors had based their startling conclusions on a bigger picture than carbon dioxide emissions alone. They were instead modeling a more holistic, systemic scenario of the impact of human activity on our planetary system.

ACKNOWLEDGING PLANETARY BOUNDARIES

More than thirty-five years after the publication of *The Limits to Growth*, another group of scholars provided an even sharper, more comprehensive picture of the dilemma we are facing through the framework of planetary boundaries. In the mid-2000s, an international, interdisciplinary team of scientists gathered in Stockholm to define the "safe operating space" for humanity. Since the start of the Holocene era twelve thousand years ago, human civilizations have operated within a delicately balanced earth system that maintains the atmosphere, oceans, and ecosystems. In 2009, the Stockholm group detailed nine planetary boundaries that govern the stability and resilience of the earth system: climate change, biodiversity integrity, ocean acidification, depletion of the ozone layer, atmospheric aerosol pollution, biogeochemical flows of nitrogen and phosphorus, freshwater use, land-system change, and environmental pollutants, or what the report calls "novel entities."[4] If we surpass these boundaries, we risk instigating large-scale, abrupt, or irreversible environmental change.

The 2009 report, as well as updates in 2015 and 2022, found that we have already overshot the safe operating space for six of these nine boundaries: climate change (due to CO_2 emissions), biodiversity integrity, biogeochemical flows of nitrogen and phosphorus, freshwater use, land-system change, and environmental pollutants. Exceeding climate change and biodiversity limits is especially worrisome since scientists consider each of them "core" planetary boundaries that, on their own, could destabilize the entire earth system. Johan Rockström, who led the Stockholm gathering, has said, "There's enough science today to say that [human-induced climate change] on its own can knock the planet away from the Holocene state. Similarly, if

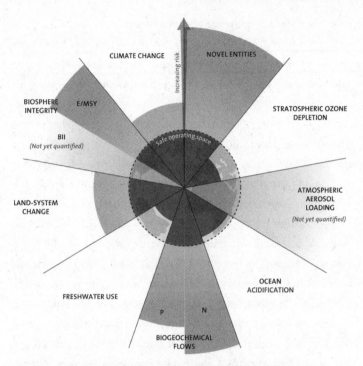

Planetary boundaries pollutants update 2022. Azote for Stockholm Resilience Centre, based on analysis in Persson et al., 2022, and Steffen et al., 2015, https://www.stockholmresilience.org/research/planetary -boundaries.html, CC BY 4.0.

we just continue our mass extinction, losing more and more species, from phytoplankton to top predators, you will come to a point when the whole planet [system] collapses."[5]

Formerly stable systems—like oceans, ice sheets, climate, and ecosystems—can cross a tipping point that changes them quickly and irreversibly into a new, self-reinforcing state. This new state may be one that can't support humanity, Rockström says.[6] And scientists are unsure where the tipping points for each of these nine boundaries lies. As one article on planetary limits reports, "What we don't know is how long we can keep pushing these key planetary boundaries before combined pressures lead to irreversible change and harm. Think of humanity, blindfolded, simultaneously walking toward nine cliff edges, and you gain some sense of the seriousness and urgency of our situation."[7]

Many of us are already familiar with climate tipping points and that we are perilously close to them. We know that ice sheets are melting at an accelerating rate alarming to scientists and could potentially raise global seas to catastrophic levels. We know that Arctic Sea ice is retreating so much that there may be no summer ice by 2035, a condition called the "blue ocean event" that could bring its own extreme changes to the earth system. Many of us have lived through the droughts, wildfires, heat waves, huge storms, and cyclones that suggest we are reaching a climate tipping point. In fact, catastrophic human-caused climate change has already occurred. We now know that coal burning in European countries during the Industrial Revolution led to the shutdown of the Sahel Monsoon in sub-Saharan Africa during the 1960s, which caused massive deaths due to starvation and political instability.[8]

But we may be less aware of the biodiversity crisis and its tipping points. Two sobering statistics: A 2019 Intergovernmental Science-Policy Platform on Biodiversity and Ecosystem Services (IPBES) assessment found that 25 percent of plants and animals worldwide are threatened with extinction.[9] A 2020 study found that the population of mammals, birds, amphibians, reptiles, and fish declined by nearly 70 percent on average between 1970 and 2016.[10] As with climate change, scientists don't know how much biodiversity loss ecosystems can tolerate before it triggers irreversible change. Extinction threatens 40 percent of insect species, which provide pollination, pest control, nutrient cycling, decomposition, and food for other species. Ecologists question whether humans could even exist without the "ecosystem services" of these insects.

Frighteningly, some of the climate solutions that reduce carbon emissions may speed up the biodiversity crisis. Wind and solar require ten times more land per unit of power than coal or natural gas power plants. A scientist investigating the impact of the renewable energy "gold rush" on the environment of the American West says that "utility-scale solar is just as bad as urbanization and development" on habitat destruction, a key contributor to our biodiversity crisis. And the increase in global mining, largely targeted at China and the Global South, will be catastrophic to ecosystems in those areas, leading to massive biodiversity loss.[11]

Finally, because of the complexity of the earth system, researchers are also unsure how exceeding one planetary limit might lead to other tipping points. For example, converting forests to farmland is the leading cause of deforestation worldwide. Chopping down rainforests reduces water released to the air from plant leaves, which reduces rainfall, which produces droughts that can lead to abrupt shifts where rainforest becomes degraded savanna, a change that releases vast amounts of stored carbon, which exacerbates climate change, which causes more droughts . . . . The cycle continues.[12]

DEBUNKING DECOUPLING

In our look at whether we can continue growing the economy while not exceeding planetary boundaries, we need to consider one last green growth argument: decoupling. Decoupling refers to the idea that economic growth can be separated from environmental impacts like biodiversity loss, carbon dioxide emissions, overuse of finite resources, and excess pollutants. The argument for green growth relies on the assumption that we can permanently, globally, and quickly decouple growth from environmental pressures that would cause us to exceed (or keep exceeding!) planetary boundaries.[13] This "decoupling" argument had better be correct because, again, we are gambling our future on a livable planet on this possibility.

Let's look first at the argument that we can continue to grow our GDP and decouple from energy usage. Reporter David Wallace Wells, who sounded a huge alarm about climate change with his book *The Uninhabitable Earth: Life After Warming*, recently revised his dire predictions based on how drastically and rapidly the cost of renewable technologies has declined. He reports that since 2010, the cost of solar power and lithium-battery technology has fallen by more than 85 percent and the cost of wind power by more than 55 percent.[14]

However, even with the incredibly rapid deployment of cheap renewable energy thus far, fossil fuel use has not declined. Consumption is leveling off, but total usage has not decreased. Because economic growth increases the energy needed to fuel the economy, rising renewable energy use has fueled growth, not reduced fossil fuel use. Global carbon dioxide emissions increased in 2022 despite a record growth in renewables of 10 percent in the same year.[15] Globally, we are producing eight billion more megawatt hours of clean energy each year than we were in 2000, but economic growth caused energy demand to increase by forty-eight billion megawatts in the same period. As economic anthropologist Jason Hickel says, "Growth keeps outstripping our best efforts to decarbonize."[16]

The fact is, since at least 1800, humans have never reduced existing forms of energy use as new energy sources become available.[17] In 1800, we primarily burned biomass such as wood or crop waste. As the Industrial Revolution cycled up, we added coal into the mix—a fuel my grandparents were familiar with. Around 1950 and on the cusp of the Great Acceleration, oil consumption began to rise. A couple of decades later, natural gas came online, making a small dent in coal consumption. Cleaner energy sources like nuclear, hydropower, wind, solar, and biofuels followed. But none of these cleaner fuels have replaced fossil fuels. Overall use has only grown. Some experts say that our energy transition to renewables is more of an energy *addition*.[18]

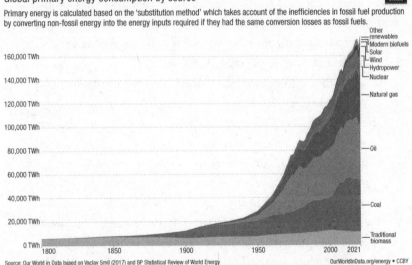

Global primary energy consumption by source

Primary energy is calculated based on the 'substitution method' which takes account of the inefficiencies in fossil fuel production by converting non-fossil energy into the energy inputs required if they had the same conversion losses as fossil fuels.

Source: Our World in Data based on Vaclav Smil (2017) and BP Statistical Review of World Energy

OurWorldInData.org/energy • CCBY

Global energy substitution chart. The slight dip toward the end of the chart is 2020, the year that COVID shut down the global economy. From Our World in Data, based on Vaclav Smil, appendix A in *Energy Transitions: Global and National Perspectives*, 2nd ed. (Santa Barbara: Prager, 2017), and BP Statistical Review of World Energy, https://ourworldindata.org/energy-production-consumption, CC BY 4.0.

Exponential energy use isn't the only foil to decoupling growth from its impact on the earth's life support systems. We also need to decouple our economy's broader material footprint, a process known as dematerialization, which refers to using less material *and* energy to make stuff. Mainstream experts assert that dematerialization is possible and has been happening for decades. A recent example of this argument is the book *More from Less: The Surprising Story of How We Learned to Prosper Using Fewer Resources—and What Happens Next*, which claims that advanced, wealthy economies have been producing more with little to no increase in resources for years. Author Andrew McAfee, an MIT scientist, assures us that capitalism and technological progress are allowing us "to tread more lightly on the earth instead of stripping it bare."[19] Perhaps not surprisingly, many mainstream economists, CEOs, Silicon Valley celebrities, and writers have heralded McAfee's book.

But this argument contains a critical accounting error, an oversight in logic that ecological economists have known about for a long time. *More from Less* focuses on domestic material consumption, or the resources a nation extracts and consumes. This domestic data doesn't factor in resources used to extract, produce, and transport *imported* goods. Since the United States and other wealthy countries have been shifting their manufacturing sectors to other countries for nearly half a century, looking at only domestic data gives a skewed picture of whether decoupling or dematerialization is happening. "What looks like 'green growth,'" says Hickel, "is really just an artifact of globalization."[20] Total resource use in the United States and other major industrial economies hasn't fallen at all; it has increased nearly in line with rising GDP. Since 2000, resource use has risen faster than global GDP.

Far from dematerializing, the world economy is *re*materializing. Ecologists estimate that the planet can handle about 50 billion metric tons of resource use annually. But we blew past that boundary in the late 1990s and are now overshooting it by more than 90 percent.[21] We already know that the energy transition we must make will require vastly larger amounts of minerals, as well as other materials. For instance, an onshore wind plant uses nine times more mineral resources than an equivalent gas-fired power plant. Just one wind turbine needs five hundred kilograms of nickel, which requires one hundred tons of coal to be refined. A gigawatt of solar power requires eighty metric tons of silver, since solar panels use silver in their manufacture.[22] A group of scientists concluded in 2016 that GDP "cannot be decoupled from growth in material and energy use. It is therefore misleading to develop growth-oriented policy around the expectation that decoupling is possible."[23]

If technological improvements enable efficiency, why haven't we managed to decouple? Part of the problem is that we've already used up the cheap, easy-to-get-to fossil fuel energy; it takes a lot of energy and resources to get to what's left, such as fossil fuels extracted via fracking or tar sands. Economists talk about the energy return on investment, or EROI, of a given energy source. Back in the days of the oil boom, when you could drill a shallow hole in a field in Texas and crude oil would often fountain up, the EROI could be almost 100: nearly one hundred times the energy invested. The EROI to extract tar sands fuel, which is very energy and resource intensive, is around 5. It's estimated that the EROI from fracking is around 1.5.[24] EROI values for wind (including the need for energy storage) are below 4, while the same calculation for solar varies between 1.6 to 9.[25]

Furthermore, economic behavior proves remarkably resistant to decoupling. In the nineteenth century, the British economist William Stanley Jevons discovered that increased efficiency in coal-burning technology did not decrease coal consumption. Use *increased*. Because it was cheaper to power steam engines with coal, the prices of products went down, which meant people had more money to buy more stuff, which increased the demand for coal to fuel increased manufacturing. This is known as Jevons's paradox. Growth-based companies use savings from efficiency improvements to expand production and stimulate consumption, which causes total resource use to rise. For instance, if a soda company finds ways to use less metal in its cans, it will invest any savings into expanding the business by, say, producing advertising to get people to buy more soda.[26] Another fact: Since 1995, we've become 33 percent more efficient in generating energy, but because of growth we've used 50 percent more energy during the same time frame.[27]

Perhaps someday, sometime, we will find some way to dematerialize. But we've shown no indication to do so thus far. And it's unclear whether we could manage to dematerialize before we start reaching unknown planetary tipping points—all while still growing our economy. Experts are increasingly skeptical. "Climate change is not a standalone issue," said a member of a consortium of scientists who issued a public warning about climate and overshoot in 2022. "It is part of a larger systemic problem of ecological overshoot where human demand is exceeding the regenerative capacity of the biosphere. To avoid more untold human suffering, we need to protect nature, eliminate most fossil fuel emissions and support socially just climate adaptations with a focus on low-income areas that are most vulnerable."[28]

ADMITTING ECOLOGICAL OVERSHOOT

I've always been struck by Jesus' repeated invitations to new ways of seeing and hearing in the Gospels. "Come and see," he says to those he invites to be his disciples in John 1:39. He restores physical sight to those who have lost it and metaphorically opens people's eyes so they can see this realm of God that he has come to announce and enact, this realm already in their midst. He tells parables about this realm and says, "If you have ears to hear, then hear" (Mark 4:23). I often wonder: What does it mean to have eyes that see? What does it mean to have ears that hear?

The rise of capitalism, the colonization it engendered, and especially the turbocharged growth of fossil fuel usage have propelled our civilization on a juggernaut toward ecological overshoot.[29] As we've described, overshoot occurs when humans (or any species) use renewable resources in their environment faster than they can be replaced or dump waste into it faster than the ecosystem can assimilate it. William Rees, an ecological economist with deep knowledge of ecological overshoot, says that we are already overshooting earth's carrying capacity by anywhere from 50 percent to 70 percent. He gives the stunning statistic that if we continue to consume energy and resources at our current rate, we will consume more in the next thirty-five to forty years than we have since the beginning of the Industrial Revolution![30] To put it another way, if the whole world consumed at the rate of France and Germany—which have far lower rates of consumption than the United States—we would still need two or three Earths to sustain that consumption.[31]

In other words, we are taking resources from the future and spending them now, like binge shoppers drawing down the savings upon which they plan to live in coming years.

Indigenous people have told us for years that the colonizers' way of life is unsustainable. But we have not had ears to hear. The more affluent among us keep extracting and consuming such that there are now too many of us demanding too much from our ecosystems. We have overreached the biophysical carrying capacity of the earth. We are overfishing, overextracting, overpolluting, and depleting topsoil and fresh water. It has taken me years to see this—years of study as I tried to alter my vision to see the world as it truly is, years of believing that some smart person or technology would somehow alter these accumulating facts. But I have concluded that, remarkably and oddly, we are living during a unique time in human history when this centuries-in-the-making ecological overshoot is becoming a fact.

I have described the shifts between the lives of my grandparents and parents and my life and my son's: the overshoot is clear. My grandparents never left the state of Ohio; my son visited ten countries before the age of eighteen. My grandparents lived what we now call hyperlocal lives: they produced most of their own food, sewed much of their clothing, and supplied a good portion of their energy needs through work animals, wood from their land, and physical labor. While my family tries to buy locally as much as possible, many of our household needs (and wants) are met via a supply chain that stretches across the globe. And despite our efforts to live more simply than those around us, the consumer goods that flow into and out of our home would astonish my ancestors.

Scholars of the Great Acceleration bear out my observations with statistics. Since 1945, three-quarters of the human-caused emissions of CO_2 have taken place. The human population has tripled. Motor vehicles have increased from 40 million to 850 million. Plastic production has grown from about 1 million tons to more than 300 million (as of 2015). As the authors of an environmental history of the Great Acceleration write, "The entire life experience of almost everyone now living has taken place within the eccentric historical moment of the Great Acceleration, during what is certainly the most anomalous and unrepresentative period in the 200,000-year-long history of relations between our species and the biosphere."[32]

Ecological overshoot is a common, albeit devastating, biological phenomenon. Most organisms, from yeast to insects to mammals, will grow their consumption and population when the environment allows it—in biology jargon, when the environment has a surplus of carrying capacity, or the "average maximum number of individuals of a given species that can live in a habitat without wrecking that habitat."[33] Consider wine-making: As yeast cells gobble up the sugar in grape juice, they multiply exuberantly. Eventually, they eat all the sugar, their environment is "polluted" by the conversion of sugar into alcohol, which is toxic to the yeast, and their population crashes. The same happens to squirrels in a forest with initially abundant food sources.

Humans often fancy ourselves different from other organisms. We are surely not subject to the same biological phenomena as yeast or squirrels! Yet like all others, we live within an interdependent ecological web. We cannot magically rise above it, and neither can we control nature as if we are not subject to its laws and limits. Unlike yeast or squirrels, who do not drill or frack, we used cheap fossil fuels to gobble up our environment much faster than we would have otherwise. Like other biological beings, we must still live within the carrying capacity of that environment.

However, while nonhuman animals do not have the ability to control ecological overshoot and ecological collapse, we can anticipate and understand these dynamics; we can respond proactively. We have the capacity to establish what one theologian calls "graced limits," to restrict what we take from the earth so we can sustain life for generations.[34] Many Indigenous cultures throughout the centuries have done this. My own fellow Anabaptists, the Amish, have placed religious and culturally imposed limits on their production and consumption. But these cultures are the exceptions rather than the rule. "Modern techno-industrial culture," says Rees, "is systematically—even enthusiastically—consuming the biophysical basis of its own existence."[35]

Unfortunately, most people who sincerely want to save the earth propose solutions that only address discrete symptoms like excess carbon pollution, not the wider systemic problem. Climate change has been siloed as an issue separate from deforestation, soil degradation, microplastics in rainwater, depleted fresh water, collapsing fisheries, the giant gyres of trash in our ocean, desertification, extinctions, and more. I believe this is because of reductionist tendencies in Western thinking. But once we have eyes to see, we can see how climate change is another symptom of ecological overshoot, which results from both overconsumption of finite resources (fresh water, topsoil, rainforests, fossil fuels, and rare earth minerals) as well as over-pollution of the environment past what it can sustain (carbon dioxide).

Economist and Quaker peace activist Kenneth Boulding supposedly said, "The only people who think infinite growth is possible on a finite planet are either madmen or economists." Like Boulding, we believe green growth is a concept that will fail. It is unjust and unrealistic. Instead, those of us in the wealthier Global North need to stop our patterns of over-consumption and devise a new societal goal other than endless economic growth so that those in the Global South unable to meet their basic needs can consume more—and so all of us can remain within safe planetary boundaries. We need to divest from systems of death emotionally, intellectually, imaginatively, theologically, and economically. We need to begin to imagine and build new economic and cultural structures that are in alignment with the kindom of God.

BEING PEOPLE OF THE GOD OF SOIL AND SEED

I (Sarah) met theologian Wati Longchar in 2012 in New York at an expert consultation at the invitation of the World Council of Churches. Quick-minded, bright-eyed, and cheerful, Wati is deeply kind. He is also thoughtful and curious—he kept me on my toes during the consultation where we both served as participants, querying the ideas of each co-participant with quick insight. He treated me with respect and careful courtesy, and over the next two years, we became friends. Wati's cosmology has deeply influenced how I think about the world.

Wati is a liberative voice among Indigenous theologians in Asia. In one conversation, he told me, "Sarah, without the land, God ceases to work. God is a co-parent with the earth." In Nagaland, he told me, there are twenty-three festivals related to the soil. "There are multiple *names of God* related to the soil," he said. He carefully wrote in my notebook "*Li-jaba*" and under this he wrote "soil-real"; "*Li-zaba*" and under this "soil-enter."

"Do you see?" he asked me, smiling brightly.

"Not yet," I admitted.

"*Li-zaba* means the one who enters the soil with the seed. The one who enters the soil is *God*."

This idea blows my mind. The Creator, present during the process of germination. The Spirit of God present in the germination of *every seed*. I love this. It reveals the faithfulness of the Creator as well as the ongoing *process* of creation. God enters the soil with the seed, the miracle of life is born with each seed that sprouts, and we are nourished by the food that miraculously grows. We literally eat the Spirit of God—and no food is possible without the Spirit's descent into the soil. Each bite of food we eat is consecrated by the Spirit that embodies it. We eat the host at each meal. While many of us in Christian traditions give thanks for our food before we eat, how many of us reflect on the miracle of life within each bite we consume? Yet what Wati describes is reverence for the Creator on the scale of each morsel of food—life given and received.

Here are a people living in balance with the Creator and the earth, acknowledging the web of mutual dependence that binds us together. Here is a process of living in balance. Yet all Indigenous Peoples daring to live in a culture not rooted in a market economy are under attack.

In the anthology *Doing Indigenous Theology in Asia*, Wati writes, "In the globalized free market, the only people who count are those who have goods to sell and money to buy. This in turn drives many to the margins of economic life. The Indigenous community who depends on land and forest resources has little chance to survive in this system. In short, globalization works for the benefit of the rich, while the poor and the Indigenous become commodities, used for cheap labor."[36] People who live in harmony within the limits of the earth are under attack. Yet Indigenous cosmology gives us an inkling of how to live in Reality. Wati writes: "The land is not only sacred but also co-creator with the Creator. The Genesis account also speaks of the earth as the co-creator of God. 'Let the *earth* bring forth living creatures according to their kinds' (Gen 1:24). It is the land that owns people and gives them an identity. It is also a temple in and through which people become one not only with the Sacred power, but also with their ancestors, the spirits, and other living creatures. Political, economic, and social justice can be attained only in relation to land."[37] This succinctly expresses mutual dependence.

The earth is not *only* sacred (a passive role) but also co-creator with the Creator (an active one). As co-creator, it lays down its life for us, reenacting the redemption story on a cosmic scale. Even now, we crucify the earth.

As we crucify the earth, we crucify particular peoples of the earth. In *The Principles of Mercy*, Spanish liberation theologian John Sobrino writes, "We well know that in our world there are not just wounded individuals but crucified peoples, and that we should enflesh mercy accordingly. To react with mercy, then, means to do everything we possibly can to bring them down from the cross. This means working for justice—which is the name love acquires when it comes to entire majorities of people unjustly oppressed—and employing in behalf of justice all our intellectual, religious, scientific, and technological energies."[38] Indigenous Peoples suffering under colonization are crucified peoples. And, with them, the earth suffers on the cross. To provide mercy to the earth, we must take the earth down from the cross.

How can we as a church embody mercy? "The complete human being," Sobrino writes, "is the one who interiorizes, absorbs in her innards, the suffering of another . . . in such a way that the interiorized suffering becomes a part of her, is transformed into an internal principle, the first and the last, of her activity. Mercy, as a reaction, becomes the fundamental action of the total human being. . . . We hold that the principle of Mercy is the basic principle of the activity of God and Jesus, and therefore ought to be that of the activity of the church."[39]

The activity of the church, according to this logic, is to employ all our intellectual, religious, scientific, and technological energies toward mercy and justice. We must imagine together systems that are consistent with the principles of creation, systems of life, and work together to embody them, using all our imagination, skills, and creativity.

The Naga cosmology tells us the Earth is alive, constantly unfolding in the process of creation. It feeds us in germinating seeds, it nurtures us, it owns us. We are in a relationship of mutual dependence.

"Sarah," Wati my friend and teacher said to me, his eyes twinkling, "humans are made of soil and breath. *What are we but soil and breath.*" These words unlatched a door in my mind. We receive God's breath, and so live. Not only in times of old, not only at our creation, but in an ongoing process of life happening right now—God's breath provided to us now, with this very breath, and the next, to the last one we take. This understanding has been with me in my mind and heart for more than a decade. The Creator provides us each bite of food and enables *every breath*.

The Earth is our mother, literally. We are made from her and of her. We belong to her. As Wati says, *it is the land that owns people*.

The Earth lays down its life for us. In a paradigm of perpetual growth, it is crucified—and we must take it down from the cross.

Third Vision and Poem

It is early morning.

Outside, the black sky is littered with dirty clouds that obscure what little light is possible at this hour. A grey-green smear at the horizon is the only hint that day will come.

I have not slept this night. I am traveling alone up a gravel road, without a coat or a bag—without bearings. I don't know where I am. I have left the only home I know, stumbled into the dark, stupid with rage. I could be anywhere. I am nowhere.

I have been walking without direction for hours. It is late winter. The black fields around me lay dead. A shallow wind blows debris in my path intermittently; an abandoned nest or a twig jerks around my feet, then blows on.

The scene of my departure plays over and over. I watch it again: anger, accusations, violence. My body is numb from cold, my rage long gone. Dread lies like a stone inside me.

I am alone. It is dark and so cold. I can't go back. I am cast out. Paralyzed by cold.

Terrified of stray dogs. I am alone. I am alone. Where will I go? I know no one. The rage that moved me is forgotten.

No one pursues me. I thought they would chase me, try to drag me back there. But they have no power on this endless plain, this big flat world. I am gone and that is all. Is this freedom? I am so cold. The green-gold strip at the horizon is widening but gives little hope.

And then, a presence. Someone there on the road. The distant heat of another's breath. Crunch of another's step. I am afraid but don't look back. We walk this way a while. A dim, grey light leads us toward morning.

"Leave the road," a distant voice calls. I turn back, squint into the dark to catch a glimpse—nothing. But where will I go?

"Follow the wind." A plastic bag blows at my feet. So flimsy a thing. I stoop to pick it up. It looks bright white in the dark, but it's dirty, so I put it down. It's blown here and there then slips off the road, heading north. I will go north, for now.

A dirty bag? So flimsy a thing? The freezing dawn illuminates the sky. I stumble, numb, through my first morning, following a plastic bag. I've followed it since. A shining, battered apparition floating a few paces before my feet.

This poem references the experience of being in my husband's small boat on the Pacific Ocean when there are large swells, as well as Wisdom, who appears in the Hebrew Scriptures as a feminine face of the Divine. Many New Testament and later Christian authors saw Jesus as the personification of Wisdom.

The Way to Wisdom

Wisdom cries out in the street;
*   in the squares she raises her voice.*
At the busiest corner she cries out;
*   at the entrance of the city gates she speaks.*
*   —Proverbs 1:20–21*

I can't find the way to Wisdom.
I'm in the trough of the wave.
I can only see the swell,
and it is big.
I can only see the smallness
of our boat.

But I am not alone in the boat,
and, somehow, I am not afraid
that the swell will overtake us.
That's not how waves work
this far from shore.
They don't crest and break
on top of you.

They hold you up,
from underneath.

Your only job is to stay in the boat,
as it rises and falls,
sways and startles.
Your only job is to hold on,
to make sure others are doing the same,
and to hold onto those who can't.

Wisdom will make Her way known.
She will call to you.
Hold on.

PART 3

Imagining a Decolonized Future

SEVEN

Describing Decolonization

MY LIFE IS a product of colonization.

I (Sarah) grew up in a regular cycle of eviction and homelessness in a city located on the traditional homeland of my people. I experienced hunger and neglect. My parents were raised in Catholic institutions themselves and passed on an inheritance of desperation and dysfunction to their children. Wards of the state, my parents had no community, culture, or family wealth to pass on to me. While I am the descendant of an ancient people who developed complex math, physics, astronomy, agriculture, hydrology, and a rich and complex cosmology, I grew up in the underclass in the United States, unclaimed by my tribe and separated from my people.

My life demonstrates the concrete outcome of colonization.

In earlier chapters, we have traced the story of capitalism and the default habits of thinking that led to colonization in the Americas and the Global South. Colonialism is the policy or practice of acquiring political control over another country, occupying it with settlers, and exploiting it economically.

Colonization is the action or process of settling among and establishing control over the Indigenous people in an area. There is great overlap between these practices, and we use these terms interchangeably throughout the book.

Colonialism takes various forms in specific contexts, but reflects common themes. Mohawk scholar Taiaiake Alfred describes colonialism in the Canadian context as "an irresistible outcome of a multigenerational and multifaceted process of forced dispossession and attempted acculturation—a disconnection from land, culture, and community—that has resulted in political chaos and social discord within First Nations communities and the collective dependency of First Nations upon the state."[1] Colonization takes land and other resources from Indigenous and other vulnerable populations over generations and forces them to assimilate into the colonizing culture.

European colonialism was inspired by Western thought and sanctioned by the Doctrine of Discovery. As research scientist Rishi Sugla summarizes, colonialism "facilitated a system of resource extraction that not only includes practices such as fossil fuel manufacturing, but also clear cutting of forests, industrial agriculture, and water-intensive mining." Sugla describes how these practices "fed industrialization and a culture of consumption that neatly tracked the rise of greenhouse gas concentrations in the atmosphere." Resource extraction, he says, "hinges on the displacement of Indigenous Peoples—a reality that is intentionally hidden from most of the world, in an attempt to justify business as usual."

In the above words we can see the intersection of the movement for climate justice and the movement for Indigenous liberation: displacement of Indigenous Peoples is a precursor of extraction, which causes ecological overshoot and climate change. "Extractivism justified by the urgent need for an energy revolution is . . . analogous to the system that fed the furnace of industrialization in the first place: colonialism," writes Sugla. "Colonialism, the centuries-long effort to dominate other peoples and exert political and economic control over their territories, is the very foundation of the modern-day climate crisis."[2]

Colonization is frequently accompanied by genocide. Genocide toward Indigenous Peoples is not just part of our deep past; it remains an ongoing global process. Sociologist Vahakn Dadrian, in his typology of genocide, talks about "utilitarian genocide" as a focus on obtaining material and economic wealth, often for the benefit of another population deemed superior.[3] This is happening today. Extractive industry pollutes the lands and bodies of Indigenous Peoples in the Guyana Shield, which is a subject I have written about extensively. I have joined with Indigenous Christians around the globe who are facing the same catastrophic impacts, who cry out for the death to stop. Christians in Mexico, Guatemala, Peru, the Philippines, Indonesia, India, Australia, New Zealand, Greenland, Sweden—I know the names of people in these places who are struggling right now, today, for their lands and lives. We cry out to the church to stand with us, not symbolically but physically, in our struggle for survival. We cry out for decolonization.

Recently, a clever and astute colleague asked me, "When you say you want decolonization, do you expect for all the European descendants to leave North America and go back to Europe?" I realize that this statement was meant to be glib; of course we do not expect the descendants of those who colonized North America to return to Europe. But I appreciate the question because I think this is what many Christians fear.

Technically, decolonization means that the colonizing powers and their beneficiaries relinquish control of a subjugated people, and then identify, challenge, and restructure or replace assumptions, ideas, values, systems, and practices that reflect a colonizer's dominating influence.[4] "The decolonizing project seeks to reimagine and rearticulate power, change, and knowledge through a multiplicity of epistemologies, ontologies and axiologies."[5] In other words, decolonization uses our knowledge (epistemologies), our understanding of life (ontologies), and our value systems (axiologies) to dismantle harmful, colonial power structures and establish noncolonial, life-giving systems. This "demands the valuing of Indigenous sovereignty in its material, psychological, epistemological, and spiritual forms," write scholars Aman Sium, Chandni Desai, and Eric Ritskes. "We cannot decolonize without recognizing the primacy of land and Indigenous sovereignty over that land."[6]

If colonization is a complex of ideas and actions that form the context of the injustice where we find ourselves, decolonization is a complex of ideas and actions that seek repair. I will attempt here to identify a framework for active decolonization.

DECOLONIZATION MUST BE GROUNDED IN INDIGENOUS PEOPLES' KNOWLEDGE

From the start, decolonization must be grounded in Indigenous cosmology and sovereignty. We emphasize Indigenous lifeways and cosmologies because they choose life; they stand in stark contrast to extractive logic, the foundation of colonization. Indigenous cosmologies acknowledge the Reality of mutual dependence within a finite earth. They align with and represent systems of life.

In his deeply moving work *Principles of Tsawalk: An Indigenous Approach to Global Crisis*, Nuu-chah-nulth scholar Umeek talks about how his people remember this Reality. His book explores *haḥuułism*, which refers to the interconnection of all life in the native language of his people. *Haḥuułism* is centered around the well-being of family and community, which includes all life. *Tsawalk*, which means "one" in the Nuu-chah-nulth language, is central to this worldview. Umeek describes a ceremony where his people acknowledge Reality: "A central ceremony of *haḥuułism* involves periodically, publicly, and reverently acknowledging that humans are characterized by short-term memory. Humans have a tendency to forget; they are easily distracted. Humans have a tendency to prefer the 'quick fix.' . . . The ancient Nuu-chah-nulth guarded against falling into such times with a periodic remembrance ceremony called a *ƛuukʷaana*, which means 'we remember reality.'"[7]

I would like to hold Umeek's vision as a model for how we as a Church can move forward: Decolonization means actively remembering Reality grounded in Indigenous Peoples' knowledge.

This view is not exclusive to the Nuu-chah-nulth. In his work on Indigenous pathways to decolonization, Cherokee scholar Jeff Corntassel writes about his people's understanding of Reality: "As a refutation to a resource extraction-based economy, Indigenous peoples practice and honor their sustainable relationships. A Cherokee word that describes a sustainable relationship is digadatsele'i or 'we belong together.' Belonging to each other in the broadest sense means that we are accountable and responsible to each other and the natural world."[8] But colonization threatens Indigenous Peoples' understanding of what is real.

Corntassel draws on the ideas of both Umeek and Indian scholar and activist Vandana Shiva, who posits that the free market economy—capitalism—eclipses two other economies: nature's economy (the ecological system) and the sustenance economy (where people work to maintain their lives).[9] Though the dominant economy can't exist without nature's economy or the sustenance economy, it has exploited them "to the point of depletion." As Corntassel writes, "Colonization and the false premise that there are no legitimate alternatives to the market system serve to weaken the confidence of Indigenous people and challenge one's ability to imagine anything other than economic development as a viable pathway to resurgence. Under the guise of a 'green economy' or 'sustainable development,' corporations and other colonial entities are 'in violation of natural hahuulic law.'"[10]

Umeek echoes this sentiment: "For corporations, the creation of wealth has become a purpose in and of itself rather than a fulfillment of hahuulic law's requirement for well-being of family and community, which includes all life forms on planet earth."[11]

I'll repeat what I said above: Decolonization *must* be grounded in Indigenous cosmology and sovereignty because Indigenous ways of knowing stand in stark contrast to systems of death, to extractive logic. For Christians, this is the choice set before us by the Creator in Deuteronomy 30: choosing life over death, blessings over curses, and true prosperity over destruction.

DECOLONIZATION MUST BE TANGIBLE, NOT METAPHORICAL

Decolonization rooted in Indigenous knowledge must be concrete and relevant in the physical world. Decolonization is not a metaphor or a series of symbolic actions. Portuguese scholar Pablo Luke Idahosa warns, "There is a danger in seeing decolonization as strictly the liberation of the mind." African anti-colonial leader Amilcar Cabral explains, "People are not fighting for ideas, for the things in anyone's head. They are fighting for material benefits, to live better and in peace, to see their lives go forward, to guarantee the future for their children."[12] The scholars mentioned earlier—Sium, Desai, and Ritskes—emphasize that decolonization is defined as the urgent struggle to restore traditional territories now separated by state borders: "We cannot decolonize without recognizing the primacy of land and Indigenous sovereignty over that land."[13] While beneficiaries of colonization may seek to intellectualize decolonization and make it abstract, Indigenous and vulnerable peoples cry out for real, material justice: land return and sovereignty. Decolonization demands concrete action beyond the performative.

Land return means returning back land that was wrongfully taken to Indigenous Peoples. In the United States, this includes land held by federal and state governments, like national and state forests, as well as land owned by corporations and churches and even land that is privately held.[14] Sovereignty means acknowledging the right of Indigenous tribes to govern their own affairs on their own lands. Standing with Indigenous tribes in pursuit of sovereignty means supporting Indigenous movements for self-determination. For example, the Indian Child Welfare Act (ICWA) of 1978 grants federally recognized tribes' "exclusive jurisdiction" in determining child welfare placements for their enrolled members, rather than Christian organizations or State child welfare agencies. At the time of this writing, ICWA is being challenged at the US Supreme Court.

Affirming Indigenous sovereignty in this example includes supporting tribes' bid to retain this crucial jurisdiction.[15]

Many years ago, my husband Dan and I accompanied a Matawai community documenting the presence of cyanide in their traditional homeland. The gold mine that had invaded their territories released cyanide seasonally into the river that served as their community's sole source of fresh water. In the Suriname rainforest where this Matawai community lives, there are two rainy seasons each year, which reliably flooded the mine's cyanide retention pool. The mine simply released the contaminated effluent into the river. When confronted about this egregious pollution, mine executives denied it. The community decided to learn how to collect evidence of cyanide release. Dan and I provided cyanide test kits and simple training for community members to test the water regularly.

I asked more than one Christian professional peacemaker to help us mediate direct negotiations between the community and the mine. Most were not willing. Only one young monk agreed to accompany us to Suriname, but only so he could observe proceedings and write for his blog. "I am willing to go with you, but only to bear witness," he said. While I appreciated his sentiment, direct involvement was what I craved and requested.

Christians confronted with injustice often focus on bearing witness, which can be a legitimate position of solidarity—but can also justify remaining at a remove. Creating liturgy and educational materials are effective tactics for mobilizing the church, yet the next necessary step is to directly engage in concrete support for Indigenous Peoples' sovereignty. When Christians get directly involved as colleagues and friends to Indigenous and vulnerable peoples, they can see the injustice of the extractive logic and colonization that threatens all of us via climate change and ecological degradation. Direct involvement helps Christians see past the privilege that creates the illusion of safety. By transitioning from the role of sympathetic bystander to a relative who fully shares the fate of those threatened by extraction, Christians can cross the line.[16] Direct involvement helps us to transform from observers into co-resisters. We can resist from a position that acknowledges that all our survival is at stake.

To confront the climate crisis, we must transition from protest, which is mainly symbolic, to dismantling, which attempts to change reality. We must do more than to simply ask an institution in power to stop what it is doing; dismantling requires imagining different structures that are designed to do different things. Our current, extractive economy is doing what it was designed to do. If we use an extractive economy to fight climate change, we will simply change what we extract: minerals rather than fossil fuels. The purpose will remain the same: to extract. If we want our economy to do something else—for instance, to ensure the well-being of families and communities, which include all life forms on planet Earth, as Umeek proposes—then we need to build an economy designed to do that.

DECOLONIZATION IS UNSETTLING

Decolonization challenges colonial systems of authority. It therefore *must* be unsettling. As someone who works in the Anabaptist context—a faith tradition that seeks to live the peace of Christ—a big challenge in my work is helping people distinguish between direct activities that seek justice and smoothing over difficult interactions or avoiding conflict and discomfort altogether. When we affirm the status quo by reinforcing comfortable practices, it may feel like peace, but peace cannot be achieved without seeking justice. Structural violence, or violence baked into society's rules and systems, feels comfortable for those who benefit from it. Structural violence is often invisible to them because they often have little interaction with those who are victimized by it. When we challenge structural violence, however, these actions are commonly interpreted as "causing trouble."

I remember a conversation with a church leader who told me, "Sarah, for a pacifist, you sure create a lot of discord." When I challenge structural violence, like church financial investments in companies that poison the bodies, communities, and lands of Indigenous Peoples, it feels uncomfortable. It leads to interactions that are uncomfortable for me and for the representatives of implicated financial organizations. Conflict can result, which feels uncomfortable, especially when the people with whom I am in conversation are friends and neighbors. It is unsettling! But it is necessary to ask for change when the status quo is creating violence in the families and communities of the vulnerable. For us to enjoy peace in our home church communities, we must *all* be able to enjoy peace, including Indigenous Peoples, who are *also* my people. I cannot be at peace if my people are suffering while church institutions benefit.

I seek to follow Jesus' radical mandate to peacemaking. He proclaimed his gospel of good news for the poor as expressed in Luke 4, where we find Jesus concluding his time of fasting and temptation in the wilderness and returning to Nazareth. He goes to the synagogue and reads a prophetic passage from the book of Isaiah:

The Spirit of the Lord is upon me,

because the Lord has anointed me.
He has sent me to preach good news to the poor,
    to proclaim release to the prisoners
    and recovery of sight to the blind,
    to liberate the oppressed,
    and to proclaim the year of the Lord's favor.
                                    (Luke 4:18–19 CEB)

Jesus says, "Today, this scripture has been fulfilled just as
you heard it." (Luke 4:21 CEB) With these words, he claims
these prophetic words as his mandate. He will proclaim release
to prisoners and recovery of sight to the blind. He will liber-
ate the oppressed and proclaim the year of the Lord's favor,
or Jubilee. When Jesus claimed this passage from Isaiah and
when he spoke these words with authority, people were upset.
His words were unsettling. His mandate necessarily upset the
status quo because it challenged the systems and institutions of
Empire and extractive logic.

Decolonization is unsettling, for everyone. It is uncomfortable to realize that one inhabits a position of supremacy and
privilege in a society designed to advantage some and disadvan-
tage others. It is uncomfortable to imagine a reorganization in
land tenure, which is implied in Jesus' reference to the "year of
the Lord's favor," or the year of Jubilee.

Jubilee is a year to release people from their debts, release
all slaves, and return property to its original caretakers. As described in Leviticus 25, God provides Moses with a plan for
managing land, mandating that every seven years the land must
be allowed to rest, without cultivation. At the end of fifty years
is a year of Jubilee, or forgiveness. Jubilee provides a reset for
the whole society. While Jubilee means liberation for captives

and slaves and land return for its original inhabitants, it means loss for those who have amassed land. A year of rest for land also means a loss of profit for those who benefit from cultivation. Jubilee is unsettling in the same way decolonization is unsettling.

DECOLONIZATION IS FOR EVERYONE

Just as decolonization unsettles everyone, it also must be the work of everyone. In their essay "Decolonization Is Not a Metaphor," educators Eve Tuck and K. Wayne Yang write, "Settler colonialism and its decolonization implicates and unsettles everyone."[17] Central to decolonization is returning land to Indigenous Peoples, including acknowledging Indigenous sovereignty over that land. Land return is crucial in our current society, which actively removes Indigenous Peoples from their lands.

In the inaugural issue of *Decolonization: Indigeneity, Education, and Society*, education scholars Aman Sium, Chandni Desai, and Eric Ritskes assert that "there is no room for settlers to claim innocence in the ongoing colonial violence and dispossession of Indigenous land. *We each have the agency to participate in this violence (or resist it).*"[18]

Since its formation, the United States has made the removal of Indigenous Peoples from their lands an ongoing policy. These policy eras include extermination; removing Native people from their lands in the east to west of the Mississippi River; forcing sovereign peoples onto reservations; further reducing reservation lands via allotment; and terminating federal tribal status.[19] Our national narrative places the removal of Native people from their land safely in the past. But colonial violence and dispossession are ongoing. This includes child removal, which has been the most effective policy for draining Indigenous Peoples from their lands—and subsequently annexing and controlling Indigenous lands. The logic here is that the fewer Indigenous people there are, the less resistance there will be.

By forcibly moving Indigenous children to boarding schools and White Christian adoptive and foster homes, state child welfare agencies have effectively removed Indigenous citizens from their families, people, cultures, languages, and lands. This is happening now. At the time of this writing and as mentioned above, the US Supreme Court is considering the constitutionality of the Indian Child Welfare Act. The ICWA is a federal law passed in 1978 to protect Native American families after an alarming number of Native children were removed from their homes by public and private agencies. The law promotes the children's interests by keeping them connected to their extended family, community, and culture. When Native children are placed in foster care, the law ensures that tribal authorities can determine the best placement for their children.

The ICWA has faced more legal challenges than the Affordable Care Act. If the Supreme Court finds the ICWA unconstitutional, as the plaintiffs claim, Native American tribes will no longer have the right to determine placements for foster children in their tribes. This will not only be a blow to the sovereignty of Native American tribes but will also remove protections for Native American foster children that ensure Native children are housed with kin among their own people. Ordinary people belonging to the dominant culture must resist the colonial drive to remove Indigenous children from their families and homelands. Ordinary people can resist by saying no—by confronting authorities and demanding that tribal sovereignty is honored.

Ordinary people belonging to the dominant culture must also resist the casual co-optation of Indigenous lands when resources like water, copper, and lithium are found within Indigenous borders and then claimed in the name of economic development and national security. They must resist the continuous contamination of Indigenous lands in service to the dominant communities that surround them, such as pipelines that cross Indigenous watersheds (the Dakota Access Pipeline at Standing Rock), toxic waste trucked across Indigenous lands (the derailment spill on the Swinomish reservation at Padilla Bay in March 2023), and waste dumped in Indigenous territories (nuclear waste stored at Yucca Mountain on Western Shoshone Nation lands).[20] They must resist the seizure of Indigenous resources. Extraction takes many forms:

- *Dams on Indigenous waters that produce hydropower.* One example is the dam at Celilo Falls on Yakama lands that creates electric power for the state of Washington.[21]

- *Water extraction from Indigenous lands where water is piped to high-population areas.* On the Diné reservation in Arizona, water rights are held by municipalities which pipe away water and deny water to the people on their own lands.[22]

- *Economic development projects within Indigenous territories.* In the Yucatan Peninsula of Mexico, the Mayan people decry the pollution and violence that the Mayan Train will bring to their lands and people.[23]

These three examples are among thousands across the world. Ordinary people can resist by saying no—by joining with Indigenous Peoples to confront authorities and demand justice by ceasing extraction on Indigenous lands.

Embracing decolonization provides a pathway to survival for everyone. We must acknowledge the reality of our world: we live in a closed system of mutual dependence. This acknowledgment, and the actions that accompany it, necessarily lead to decolonization. The project of colonization has led us to ecological overshoot with devastating consequences like climate change. To divest from systems of death with their logic of extraction, we all must actively embrace decolonization and shape a future *without* colonialism as our central paradigm.

DECOLONIZATION RESISTS COLONIAL INSTITUTIONS

In the eyes of the United Nations and its member states, Indigenous sovereignty is a threat to nationhood and national borders. Jeff Corntassel notes, "While Indigenous peoples do not tend to seek secession from the state, the restoration of their land-based and water-based cultural relationships practices is often portrayed as a threat to the territorial integrity of the country(ies) in which they reside and thus, a threat to state sovereignty."[24] I witnessed this firsthand when the Wayana people wished to map the Wayana language territory in the transborder region that spans the borders of Suriname, French Guyana, and Brazil. The national governments do not acknowledge the Wayana map of their own territory. Because the Wayana Language Territory map was not created by the colonial powers according to established national borders, the state authorities do not acknowledge the reality of the Wayana traditional homeland or the existence of their people within it.

This perceived threat is expressed even in the United Nations Declaration on the Right of Indigenous Peoples, which contains this disclaimer in Article 46: "Nothing in this declaration may be interpreted as implying any State, people, group or person any right to engage in any activity or perform any act contrary to the charter of the United Nations or construed as authorizing or encouraging any action which would dismember or impair, totally or in part, the territorial or political unity of sovereign and independent States."[25] In other words, even the Declaration on the Rights of Indigenous Peoples must protect the interests of colonial states.

If colonial institutions view Indigenous sovereignty as a threat, it is understandable that the "solutions" offered by these colonial institutions are unlikely to benefit Indigenous Peoples. Many of the mechanisms do not provide the solutions that people from the dominant culture think they do.

Human rights mechanisms provide a powerful example. In the United States, rights are seen through the lens of the individual, and the state is presumed to sit in benevolent authority. Supposedly impartial institutions, like courts, serve as arbiters between the government and individuals and ensure that the rules we agree to in our society, or laws, are justly applied. This presumes a level of impartial justice not experienced by the vulnerable.

Both national and international human rights mechanisms offer state recognition of Indigenous Peoples. But Indigenous independence declares that rights are *unalienable*—they do not require recognition. We, as people, are not asking for rights which no person or nation can give to us. We are born with dignity and sovereignty, whatever the dominant culture believes. We do not need the recognition of colonial institutions. Yet theoretical recognition by colonial institutions is offered to Indigenous Peoples as a legitimate remedy—as if recognition would provide actual redress. It is not in the best interest of colonial institutions to offer *concrete* redress to Indigenous Peoples. It is not in the best interest of institutions designed to enforce colonialism to undermine the authority of colonial nations by enforcing land return or Indigenous sovereignty. Therefore, petitioning colonial institutions for recognition, access, and redress is often fruitless.

As an alternative, I—with the support of many others—have advocated for direct negotiation between Indigenous communities and extractive industry. As we change our focus from identifying actions we can take at an individual level to identifying systemic interventions, we must include the most vulnerable (and often the most impacted) in decision-making. This inclusion is necessary to bring about true decolonization. We asked the Christian financial services company Everence to help us by requesting negotiations between Newmont mine in Suriname and Indigenous communities impacted by the mine. Since Everence—and by extension, its stockholders—holds stock in Newmont mine, it has the positional power to at least arrange a meeting with the leaders of the Newmont mine. We are currently in negotiations with Everence regarding this request.

Such negotiation would honor the sovereignty and self-determination of those most impacted by extraction. Direct negotiation has the power to address impact and redress without the endless delays created by layer after layer of bureaucracy that are designed to deny claims for redress. International bodies like the United Nations have neither the authority nor the will to provide redress. The United Nations does not have the authority to mandate redress, because it cannot impose any directive that threatens the sovereignty of a *member nation*. It does not have the will to mandate redress, because it is designed to serve member nations.

While attending a UN Permanent Forum on Indigenous Issues in New York in 2014, I was privileged to hear the testimony of a woman from Bolivia. We were both attending this global caucus, where communities from around the globe negotiate what message should be shared with the UN Economic and Social Council. (The Permanent Forum is an advisory body to this council.) The Bolivian woman explained that her family would go without food during her time in New York—their sacrifice so she could come to appeal to the United Nations.

Regardless of people hearing her moving testimony about land-grabbing and the murder of children in her community by settlers overtaking her traditional lands, the Permanent Forum does not provide any mechanism for intervention or redress. Regardless of the sacrifice of her family to make her trip possible, the most any of us could hope for that day was that a sentence or phrase would be included in a report to the Economic and Social Council.

The UN was created to serve nation states, not constituents within them. The unit served by the UN is, therefore, the nation state. The International Court of Justice, one of the constituent organs of the UN, has approved the legal and legitimate occupation and acquisition of sovereignty by another nation under the Doctrine of Discovery, which the International Court of Justice has approved as a legal method for acquiring territory.[26]

The Organization of the American States (OAS) is the multilateral decision-making body of the Western Hemisphere. The purposes of the OAS follow the logic of the Doctrine of Discovery: exploitation and extraction of natural resources for economic gain as a collectively acknowledged "good."[27] According to the OAS charter, the General Assembly is "composed of the delegations accredited by the governments of the member states. All member states have the right to representation in the General Assembly. Each state has the right to one vote. The delegations of the member states are composed of the representatives, advisers, and other members accredited by the governments."[28]

Like the United Nations, the OAS serves its constituent nation states. The OAS regulates trade in the Western Hemisphere *and* composes and convenes the Inter-American Commission on Human Rights. The same member states regulate both. When constituents like Indigenous Peoples appeal to the Inter-American Court, they must navigate an institution where the member states who hear their claim are the same member states who have perpetrated human rights abuses.

When we as Indigenous Peoples are viewed as "them"—as objects of either charity, aid, or sympathy—and when we are viewed as *separate* from the beneficiaries of privilege, the solutions offered to us reinforce the inequality created by colonial structures. We are not separate from members of the dominant culture. We are one—your people and mine. The injustice meted out to us will ultimately be felt by all. Climate change and its consequences do not single out Indigenous Peoples; they impact all life on earth. We—all of us—require institutions that reflect Reality: a closed system of mutual dependence. Colonial institutions will not save any of us. We must imagine together alternative institutions that acknowledge Reality and serve all of us.

DECOLONIZATION REQUIRES SYSTEMIC ACTIONS

Let's summarize our definition of the values and activity of decolonization:

- Decolonization is a framework for resistance to colonial reality centered in Indigenous Peoples' struggle for traditional lands and self-determination.

- We acknowledge our embeddedness in a society formed by a colonial reality; thus, we need to "pick a side." Decolonization asks that we side with Indigenous people by supporting their struggles for sovereignty and land.

- Decolonization is not a metaphor but has a bearing on the physical world here and now and includes *actions* for everyone.

- We affirm Reality from an Indigenous perspective (that is, we live in a closed system of mutual dependence).

- We are committed to dismantling colonized institutions at every level and imagining new alternatives.

Enacting these commitments requires that we untangle the difference between individual action and systemic or structural action.

Individual actions are what most of us typically pay attention to. Where we work, where we live, whether and who we marry, our family size, the products we buy, even what we eat are all individual-level actions. These individual actions are nested in a larger society. Our society is formally and informally governed by a series of agreements that most of us buy into. We agree to pay our taxes, to obey traffic laws, to send our children to school, and acknowledge the formal decision-makers we elect to public office.

When we participate in these agreements together, we participate in what seventeenth-century philosopher Thomas Hobbes called the social contract. For many of us, the social contact feels effortless, because we have grown up with it and benefitted from it. We pay taxes so that we have safe, maintained roads, first responders during times of crisis, public safety provided by authorities who understand our needs, courts that settle disputes, and libraries and public schools to educate our kids, who are the next generation in a free society. In short, we have been socialized to participate in the social contract. It feels natural to us; it feels like reality. It seems to us that this agreement "just makes sense."

However, some categories of people are excluded from the social contract. Society is made up of institutions that comply with a set of rules and norms—laws. And these laws define our experience. They exercise the power to empower some categories of people and limit the choices of others.

Historically, enslaved people were excluded from the social contract since their very humanity was denied in the US Constitution. Laws protected enslavers, ensuring that even those who aided enslaved people would be punished. People of color living under segregation were likewise excluded from the social contract and subject to sanctioned violence like lynching, unjust incarceration and forced labor on chain gangs, housing redlining, exclusion from labor unions, and denial of the right to vote.

The Black Lives Matter movement has underscored how African Americans are still systematically excluded in American society. For example, racial profiling and discrimination by law enforcement, prosecutors, juries, and schools target African Americans, who simultaneously face disproportionate sentencing and incarceration. One in three Black men will experience incarceration in his lifetime and, in most states, will be subsequently stripped of his right to vote.[29] The individual actions of all African Americans are thus limited. Likewise, undocumented immigrants are excluded from the social contract because they do not have legal standing to participate in the legitimate economic system; therefore, their individual-level actions are limited.[30] Native Americans in the United States are still designated as the dependents of the federal government, and the Bureau of Indian Affairs is mandated to manage their affairs.[31] Decolonization requires systemic actions and interventions because it seeks to change the rules of the social contract.

Some of you may want to stop me there, saying, "But I thought the purpose of inclusion is to ensure everyone has access to public institutions, or the social contract." Inclusion does not really provide access to justice in American society. Native American people make up between 1 to 2 percent of Americans today.[32] Genocide, termination, and child removal are responsible for our small numbers. We simply do not have a large enough population to influence laws in a meaningful way. Our status in the US Constitution also ensures that Indigenous tribes are presumed to have the same sovereignty as states, yet we are not represented in Congress.

To put it another way, some members of our society hold a greater share of power than others. For example, those who hold or control the largest share of wealth have a much larger impact on our society than most of us. Think for a moment about our elected officials. What does it take to run an effective campaign for a national public office? It requires personal connections, sponsorship for races where costs often run into the millions, and a considerable commitment of time. While not all of those elected to national office are wealthy, most of them are.[33] If our national elected officials create legislation that reflects their own fiscal interests, the policies they create do not reflect the financial reality of at least half of the population in the United States. The rules of our society, our laws, and policies, are created by people who share more interests with each other than they do with much of the public.[34] To rectify this, there are no individual actions for us to take. *Collectively*, we need to change laws and policies, as well as the very institutions that make and enforce them.

Similarly, we need systemic change to bring our structures into alignment with Reality—the carrying capacity of our earth and our mutual dependence. That also means changing laws and policies, and the very institutions that make and enforce them. Colonization will not be alleviated if every European descendent takes individual-level actions. Similarly, climate change cannot be alleviated if every individual in North America drives an electric vehicle.

Climate change is a result of ecological overreach. We are putting more carbon in the air via fossil fuels than our atmosphere can safely hold without causing changes in our climate. Because our economy is designed to grow *perpetually*, every economic system is set to consume more fossil fuels than the year before. This is a systemic issue. While individual-level actions, like installing solar panels on an individual home, may have a slight impact, household electricity use comprises only a modest share of total carbon emissions.[35] Even if every single household installs solar panels, the impact will be small.

Don't get me wrong: operating with integrity in our own homes is important. It is not wrong to erect solar panels! But individual actions will only get us so far. Sixty-five percent of carbon emissions come from transportation, and these emissions are reflective of our transportation *system*.

The transportation sector uses the lion's share of petroleum, one of the largest inputs of carbon emissions. This includes transporting products across the country by truck and airplane.

Our economic *system* depends on a paradigm of perpetual growth: for the economy to work effectively, more products must be consumed every year. To meaningfully impact macro issues like climate change, the economic *system* must change to rationally comply with the boundaries of the earth's life support systems. Every person must participate in systemic change because every person participates in the economic system, but individual-level actions are not the locus of change. If a family invests in the installation of solar panels on their home, this will not affect the transportation of products, such as the food the family buys at the grocery store or the clothing and home products they purchase at the local big-box store. Systemic issues require systemic interventions—and this means a change in laws and policies. It also means changing the institutions that make laws and policies.

In our current economic system, we are rewarded for taking more than we need—in fact, our economy depends on it. According to the World Trade Organization (WTO), global trade has consistently grown between 1 and 6 percent per year over the past decade.[36] We are rewarded for domination—for subjugating weaker populations. Extractive activities are in the Global South, on Native lands in North America, and in low-income, usually BIPOC (Black, Indigenous, and People of Color) communities, in that order.

Those who advocate for defense of the earth, or curbing consumption, are denigrated as irrelevant or even as obstructionist. For instance, the WTO regulates global trade and promotes economic development practices that include pressuring farmers to use certain pesticides and fertilizers and grow produce that is not only hard on the environment but also too expensive for the farmers themselves to consume.[37]

Even institutions meant to be neutral are enlisted in prioritizing and enforcing commerce. The World Health Organization's International Health Regulations, which are meant to ensure health standards across the world, state that health can be prioritized *only* if it does not interfere with trade or transportation.[38]

The core assumptions of perpetual growth victimize vulnerable peoples and hurt everyone. *Decolonization includes challenging these core assumptions.*

Colonization is grounded in extractive logic; it makes extraction concrete. The laws and policies of colonization named European monarchs and their beneficiaries the correct and just owners of all lands in "discovered" territories. Authority of those lands has been transferred to nation states, who determine the "highest and best use" of land consistent with their financial and military interests. This arrangement is the opposite of mutual dependence.

Decolonization reverses extractive logic. It seeks right relations, consistent with the Reality of mutual dependence.

Those who benefit from colonization get to decide whether they believe in the "reality" of mutual dependence in a closed system. They get to decide whether they want to participate in dismantling systems of oppression. Many of us may ask ourselves, "What does this have to do with me?" Those victimized by colonization do not share in this privilege.

Engaging in decolonization requires collectively working for institutional change and for change in laws and policies. In the United States, for example, what if control of every fracking permit and every oil and gas permit had to be approved by the Native American tribe that would be most affected by the proposed project? What if ordinary people petitioned the Department of the Interior, asking that they require Indigenous approval of all land use permits? How might this affect drilling and fracking? How might this kind of change in perspective and leadership affect carbon emissions?

This would require collective action: getting on the phone with your legislators, and also getting on the phone with friends, coworkers, neighbors, and family members, and encouraging *them* to get on the phone to their legislators. It would mean setting up meetings, writing editorials, and using all the leverage at our disposal to push this agenda forward. This is not work that many Christians feel comfortable doing. Many will decline to act and say, "It's too political." Politics is the process of making decisions collectively. The opposite of political action is individual action. Individual action will not get us where we need to go.

This is the work to which we are called. Actively seeking justice requires all of us, working together.

DECOLONIZATION REQUIRES SACRIFICE

In the months after my father's death, the communion of saints felt very real to me now that both of my parents had joined them. I (Sheri) found myself drawn to connecting with my ancestors who had lived and died in my homeland of Ohio, whose bones lay in the same ground that now held my mom and dad. I began a quest to identify the gravesites of ancestors buried in that place so I could visit, thank, and honor them.

My family on both sides have lived in that part of Ohio for almost two hundred years, so there are a lot of ancestors to visit. It is an incredible privilege that my family has lived in one place for centuries and a privilege that I even know where my ancestors are buried. The Lenape people forced to leave before my ancestors arrived don't have that privilege, nor do those whose ancestors were enslaved or the many who came to the United States as political or economic refugees.

Still, it wasn't easy to research these gravesites, given that my earliest ancestors are buried in Amish farm cemeteries in fields, in woods, and atop ridgelines that are scattered across the countryside. Fortunately, I discovered that an Amish man named Leroy Beechy had published a directory of these farm cemeteries in 1975. I soon found myself traipsing through fields with my Pennsylvania Dutch–speaking brother, Phil, at my side.[39] So far, we have only been able to visit a few of the gravesites, but we plan to continue doing so every time I return.

However, there is one grave I am unable to visit: that of Jonathan Hostetler, my maternal grandfather's great-great-grandfather. No one knows where he is buried. It's possible he was laid to rest on the farm where he lived, one mile west of the town where I was raised. *Lived* is the key word here. Jonathan didn't own the farm, because he "believed land should be free for all to use as needed."[40] Unlike every other ancestor, Jonathan was buried alone. (His wife, who died a few years later, is buried in the family farm cemetery belonging to her brother-in-law.) Two stones and a sassafras tree once marked his grave, but they have since been removed. Only two sentences in Leroy Beechy's cemetery directory now mark his existence.

I think about Jonathan Hostetler when I read this passage in Matthew 10:34–39:

> Do not think that I have come to bring peace to the earth;
> I have not come to bring peace, but a sword.
>> For I have come to set a man against his father,
>> and a daughter against her mother,

and a daughter-in-law against her mother-in-law;

and one's foes will be members of one's own household. Whoever loves father or mother more than me is not worthy of me; and whoever loves son or daughter more than me is not worthy of me; and whoever does not take up the cross and follow me is not worthy of me. Those who find their life will lose it, and those who lose their life for my sake will find it.

Among the hard sayings of Jesus, none may be harder than "Do not think that I have come to bring peace to the earth; I have not come to bring peace, but a sword." My way will bring conflict, says Jesus. It cannot help but do so. Drawing deeply on Jewish prophetic tradition, Jesus announces a kindom that challenges the structures and arrangements of the Roman Empire. The result is conflict. Just as storms and violent weather form where two weather systems collide, so too will conflict develop when two ways of ordering the world encounter each other.[41]

Jesus specifically names that conflict will arise in families. In his time, the male-headed family was the location of identity and security. The head of this household, the *paterfamilias*, determined most things, including what religion household members would observe. To deviate from the *paterfamilias* could bring serious personal, domestic, societal, and economic consequences. It could expose you to the same vulnerabilities as orphans and widows, who were without the protection and status that came from belonging to a household. You could be cast off, alone, exposed. This is why the Torah and the prophets command the community to care for orphans and widows, and why treatment of the most vulnerable was a hallmark of a society's righteousness.

I think about my ancestor Jonathan's belief that land should not be owned and his tenacity in hewing to that belief over many years. I wonder whether Jonathan's vision of a world without private property was so radical that it brought conflict to his family. Is this why he was buried alone and none have tended his grave? Was this his cost for "taking up the cross"?

This hard saying from Matthew tells me that announcing and enacting the new order, the good news, will bring conflict and division. It will be *unsettling*. It will be disorienting, as old ways of seeing and structuring the world are called into question. It will be uncomfortable. It will hit us where we live—in our sense of identity and security.

I cannot visit the grave of my great-great-great-great-great-grandfather Jonathan. But alone among my ancestors, I am thanking and honoring him with these words. He inspires me with his radical vison of the commons, a world where land is not owned by one but free to use as needed by all. He inspires me to believe bold things despite the conflict such beliefs may bring. He inspires me to lose one form of identity and security so that I might find another.

I don't know much about Jonathan, so all I have is my imagination. I imagine him buried under the sassafras tree, his body returning to the land he honored with his life, his spirit free. On his headstone are the words "Those who lose their life for my sake will find it."

EIGHT

Decolonizing Economic Systems

WHEN I (SARAH) began working in the Guyana Shield in 2004, I thought that if I found an alternative source of uncontaminated water for Indigenous Peoples living in a gold mining impact zone, it would provide the solution to pollution in the river system. My husband Dan and I worked to provide rainfall water catchment tanks and even to convince a mining company to dig wells for impacted communities. Simple! Problem solved, right?

Well, no. Because the Indigenous communities living with the death, disease, and disability caused by resource extraction (gold mining in this case) do not have land rights or self-determination. Even if alternate sources of water were enough to provide potable drinking water, which is questionable given how the river aquifer and deeper aquifer are connected, this solution does not address the contaminated food web, or land grabbing by a host of participants in the gold rush, or the militarization of their lands to protect mineral resources that has effectively made self-determination impossible, or transportation problems caused by the river dredging practiced in alluvial gold mining, or the malaria caused by pools of stagnant water that are the byproduct of river dredging . . . the impacts of mining are widespread because of *complexity*.

Understanding complexity is important because "systems consist of numerous interacting and interwoven elements, parts, or agents defined by the structure of the system, the types of interactions between system elements, and the dynamics and patterns of the system that emerge from these interactions."[1] Read: Everything is related. *We are joined to each other in a closed system of mutual dependence.*

The Indigenous communities I describe are embedded in a system: the global economic system. The purpose of this system is to extract raw resources at the lowest cost possible and to export these resources to consumers so that corporate individuals can earn a profit. A host of elements must cooperate in the system to make this happen: International trade agreements must be made; environmental laws must be managed; national consent must be gained. But at the end of the day, the economic system is meant to generate profit for corporate individuals. Providing water catchment tanks or digging wells does nothing to alter this system. Therefore, while one symptom of the problem may be momentarily addressed, nothing in the system has changed.

Over the past two decades, in advocating for Indigenous communities in the Guyana Shield, Dan and I have tried to challenge economic institutions, negotiate with corporations, change national laws and policies, impact international human right laws. None of this has worked. Our friends' situation has only deteriorated. The system is still chugging away, doing what it was designed to do.

CHANGING THE SYSTEM

A *system* maintains its existence and functions as a whole through the interaction of its parts.[2] In other words, a system is a collection of elements or components that are organized for a common purpose.[3] This is the opposite of the reductionistic mindset that characterizes the default mode of Western thought. Here, we are looking at a systemic whole made up of multiple parts, and especially their interactions with each other.

Because systems are complex, simple and even complex actions like providing water tanks or changing a national law have insignificant impact on a system. So how do we change a system? Systems theory proposes two primary mechanisms: first-order change and second-order change.

First-order change in a system impacts a *process* within the system but does not change the nature of the system itself. In a factory that produces cars, automation that exchanges robots for human labor does not change the output (cars) or purpose of the system (profit).

Even social change that is considered radical does not necessarily change a system's output or purpose. Let's consider the movement in the twentieth century to ordain women in most mainline Protestant churches. First, we must consider: What is the purpose of ordination? Does ordaining women change that purpose? I propose that ordination sets select individuals apart to carry out ceremonies, provide pastoral care, and act as leaders in the church. From a systems level, the ordination of women simply includes additional persons in the function of ordination.

The purpose of ordination and the system established to pursue this purpose remain the same. In fact, changing processes within a system, or "tinkering" with a system, often reinforces its purpose and strengthens the system. In this case, even something we perceive as large societal change, like allowing women's ordination, reinforces the system created to establish legitimate church leadership. More people are included into the practice of ordination, increasing society's cultural and even emotional investment in the practice.

Another example of first-order change is the green economy. In the proposed green economy, the types of resources extracted will change, as will the pollution created in energy generation, but the system itself will still serve the same purpose: to produce more and more energy to fuel an economy of perpetual growth, which in turn produces profit for individuals.

Second-order change is change to the system itself. This changes not just processes (tinkering), but also the purpose and structure of the system. A factory that stops producing cars and is repurposed to house unhoused community members has experienced second-order change. Its output has changed (from producing a consumer product to providing shelter) and its purpose has changed (from producing profit to providing a public good).

Let's take the example of ordination more broadly. Some denominations, like the Quakers, do not ordain clergy, but depend on lay leadership. The reasoning is that anyone has access to God—no special dispensation or qualification makes one person more able than another to lead, or to access the divine. If mainline churches chose to stop the practice of ordination altogether, this would equate to second-order change. If the purpose of ordination is to identify legitimate leadership in the church, the end to ordination demonstrates a divestment from valuing legitimacy in leadership. Second-order change will have occurred because the purpose and output of religious affirmation has changed. Ordination as a practice, and its sanctity, would neither be affirmed nor enforced. This would change the nature of how we view leadership or hierarchy in the church. The very meaning of leadership would change; anyone might have access, or just as easily, no one. Church institutions themselves would necessarily change, and I presume that permanent positions, or even a career in the clergy, would become obsolete.

First-order change tinkers with the process. Second-order change transforms a system's purpose and structure. If we wish to significantly change our society to challenge ecological oversight and climate change, we must accomplish second-order change in our economic system.

TURNING TO INDIGENOUS PERSPECTIVES

When we talk about sustainability, we often do so from the vantage point of individuals rather than systems, although individuals have little impact on whole systems. In his book *Sand Talk*, Aboriginal scholar Tyson Yunkaporta explores the pattern of creation from the perspective of his people, and how to live within those patterns (as opposed to trying to force creation into our human systems). He expresses frustration about academic contexts that discuss "sustainability from an Indigenous perspective":

> I have been to many conferences and talks about Indigenous Knowledge and sustainability. . . . Most carry the same simplistic message: First Peoples have been here for x thousand years, they know how to live in balance with this place, and

we should learn from them to find solutions to sustainable issues today. . . . They offer some isolated examples of sustainable practices before colonization, and that's it. The audience is left wondering, "yes but how? What insight does this offer today, for the problems we are experiencing now?"[4]

Yunkaporta is describing a lack of systems analysis. He observes that the Indigenous contexts described at conferences were sustainable because those contexts were designed to be sustainable. Exploration of Indigenous systems and what they were designed to do could gesture toward second-order change. Rather than simply describe "sustainable" practices, we could query Indigenous systems—what are the intended outputs or purposes of Indigenous systems that result in sustainable practices?

I have also attended conferences on sustainability and heard presentations about successful individual "sustainability projects." Discussion then revolves around how to "upscale" a successful project that is small and context-specific. There is no attempt to explore the local system that supports such a project. More to the point, there is no discussion about how to design a system where sustainability is the purpose, where individuals don't have to try to embody sustainable practices against the grain, because the system itself requires it.

"We rarely see global sustainability issues addressed using Indigenous perspectives and thought processes," writes Yunkaporta. "We do not see econometrics models being designed using Indigenous pattern thinking. . . . Any discussion of Indigenous knowledge systems is always a polite acknowledgement of connection to the land rather than true engagement. It is always about the *what*, and never about the *how*."[5] I have found this to be true. Indigenous thought is often provided as a garnish, an accessory to the narrative offered by the dominant culture. When I am asked to speak in church contexts, I am most often asked to provide a short homily or reflection rather than facilitate a dialogue or exchange of ideas. When I am asked to be present on boards, committees, or commissions, it is frequently to fulfill a diversity requirement, not to share my worldview. In these contexts, it is rare to engage in problem-solving using the unique perspectives of Indigenous Peoples.

Yunkaporta offers us a valuable perspective for second-order change to our economic system. We can engage Indigenous scholars and thinkers by investigating how Indigenous systems work. Indigenous Peoples built complex economies that functioned for millennia. Indigenous cosmology can guide us in learning about the purpose, assumptions, and outputs of these economies.

UNDERSTANDING CAPITALISM'S DESIGN

Any time we want to advocate for change in a system, we must first understand what it was put in place to accomplish. We must ask: What exactly is this system created to *do*, and *who* exactly was it created to serve?

An economy is a system of interrelated production and consumption activities that determine the allocation of resources within a group. Our economy is rooted in capitalism, where trade and industry are controlled by private owners for profit. Earlier in this book, we retold the story of capitalism, narrating the shadow side of an economic system that has likely been central to all our lives. Many of us would also likely agree that capitalism has resulted in many astonishing things: the development of amazing technology, lifesaving medicines and treatments, exploration of the stars, distribution of food at a magnitude of complexity never imagined, and so on. For now, let's set aside our preconditioned thoughts about capitalism and merely consider its purpose.

In Adam Smith's influential, eighteenth-century work *The Wealth of Nations*, Smith explains that private ownership of capital is the best way to ensure the wealth and security of nations. By allowing individuals to freely pursue their own self-interest in a free market, without government regulation, nations will prosper. The common purpose of our economy is profit. For the sake of this thought experiment, let's agree that profit is neither bad nor good; it is simply the objective of our economic system and what capitalism is designed to generate.

In my first year as a graduate student in sociology, my instructor described the basic units of capitalism as a system. Capitalism, she explained, contains households and firms. Firms provide employment and products to households while households provide workers and consumers to firms. Other elements come into play, of course, but they are all subsidiary to the basic elements of firms and households, with the objective of producing profit. Governments, for example, provide governance and representation for households and rules and regulations for firms.

My instructor then asked us, "What is missing in this system?" Whatever social unit we thought of—whether nonprofit organizations (firms), churches (firms), clubs or associations (firms), schools (firms)—she could easily fit it into the simple dichotomy of households and firms. Raised and educated in American society, I was stumped. Was there anything that did not fit into this elegant model? She raised her eyebrows at our silence. "What about air?" she asked. "What about water?"

Since then, I have discovered many things that cannot be easily accounted for in the system of capitalism: community health, well-being, nature, life.

From a systems perspective, capitalism is an elegant and clever system—elegant in that it serves a simple purpose (profit) and clever in that it requires complexity (that is, a lot of actors, who in turn form many overlapping relationships). Successful systems benefit from complexity because the relationships between actors have as much value as the actors themselves. Many actors creating and applying different strategies ensures the survival of the system. Complexity is important because it breeds creativity. Ineffective actors in the system fail or fall away, and successful strategies are rewarded, creating a rich environment for innovation. Innovation is necessary for any system to thrive because external conditions are constantly in flux. For example, in a natural ecosystem, a diversity of species ensures that if external conditions change at least some of the species will survive. If all species share the same survival strategy, a change in external conditions will wipe them all out. In a capitalist system, new technologies are developed, while others become obsolete. Complexity makes market conditions difficult to predict—they are constantly in flux.

Capitalism does well what it was built to do: create profit for self-interested individuals. Capitalism is rooted in the core assumption of individualism. Each household represents individuals and their interests. Corporations, nonprofits, and organizations are likewise legally defined as individuals and enjoy the rights of individuals. Individuals are the unit of our society. We look through the lens, the perspective, of the individual. Civil and human rights: viewed through the lens of the individual. Property taxes and retirement funds: viewed through the lens of the individual. Those things that do not fit into an individual identity often go unaccounted in our system, like animals, streams, air, and community health.

The US Constitution values private property at its core, and the American Dream holds property ownership as the fundamental form of wealth accumulation. All of this seems to make sense, especially for those of us who have grown up in American society.

What outcome does our current system serve? To find out, let's begin by asking who it was created to serve. The US Constitutions says the United States was established by "we the people," but we know that the laws at the time of the country's formation were written to benefit male property owners of European descent. So "the people" meant a narrow demographic of people sharing geographical proximity at the time. System beneficiaries have since broadened, although they still don't include every human living in close geographical proximity, and certainly not all life.

To reiterate: Capitalism is an economic system designed to generate, transport, and sell products to consumers. It is designed to keep the cost of labor and other inputs as low as is feasible, to keep the cost of products as low as possible. An ever-growing population of consumers buy more stuff so firms can reap more profits. The accumulation of wealth for firms and some households, especially the descendants of those who created the current political system, is the intended and desired outcome. Simple. *Capitalism is not designed to protect life, to uphold equity, to ensure that life continues, to cooperate with the support systems of the earth, or even to ensure the well-being of humans.* It has a simple purpose—to generate profit. That is why its success is measured in economic growth. This is not a bad outcome or end. However, I want to suggest that we must be clear about what our capitalist system is designed to *do*.

CONSIDERING ISSUES OF SCALE

The pursuit of self-interest in a free market described by Adam Smith generates some dissonance when viewed from differing levels of scale. A scale is a metric that describes the spatial and temporal dimensions of an object, pattern or process. While capitalism may have one assessment of benefit and risk from the perspective of an individual, when viewed from the perspective of a society or an ecosystem a different range of benefits and risks emerge that are not obvious from the individual perspective. Let's imagine that a marketing research firm (a corporate individual) can either hire labor for twelve dollars an hour in the firm's headquarters of a large American city or pay two dollars an hour in a developing nation with many English speakers. From the individual perspective, choosing the call center with cheaper labor will clearly generate the most profit for the individual (the firm).

If we look at this same example at the scale of the community, exporting jobs to another country has a different impact. The potential jobs taken from the city where the firm is headquartered means that wages will not be available in the local economy. Potential workers' taxes will not be paid to support the local schools, first responders, or infrastructure, wages will not be spent at local stores, and homes will not be built in the local economy.

Viewed at the scale of the society, sending jobs offshore from the US to foreign labor markets has a detrimental impact on the working class. The trend of moving production to areas where labor is cheap has drastically increased income inequality in the United States, where skyrocketing profits are enjoyed by the upper class while the working class lose ground economically. Some social scientists credit the loss of working-class jobs with the rise in authoritarian movements among displaced White workers in North America and across the developed world.

From an ecological level, placing a call center in a developing country will require oversight of a remote workforce, including development of transnational infrastructure in a region likely to have weaker environmental protections. It would also include transnational travel via airplane. The carbon deposited in the atmosphere by this arrangement will have a negative impact on everyone in the closed system we share, including the individual (firm) for whom cheaper wages are viewed as a benefit at the individual level.

When we look at the individual level alone, we miss the impact at different levels across scale. Capitalism is not bad for neglecting to do this, because it was designed to do a specific thing: generate profit for individuals. But the unintended consequences and harmful impacts of generating wealth for individuals are obvious when viewed at different scales. Particularly, when we examine shared resources or any goods not owned by any individual or even regulated by any government (like air), capitalism creates a dissonance we call the tragedy of the commons.

Earlier in this book, we discussed how enclosure of commonly held property led to famine and sweeping changes in European society, including the rise of capitalism. Since then, conventional economic wisdom has discredited the very idea of commonly held property, arguing that individuals with access to a public resource will act in their own interest and, in so doing, deplete the resource—thus, the tragedy of the commons.[6] British scholar William Forster Lloyd conceptualized this theory while observing pastures in 1830s England. He noticed that cattle in common grazing areas looked stunted and the commons looked bare, whereas private property looked better cared for. Multiple farmers in the community each had some privately enclosed land and also a shared commons. Each farmer had to calculate herd size based upon land access. While adding additional animals might confer an advantage to the farmer, it could be detrimental to the shared grazing land. So from the scale of the individual, adding animals to one's herd had an obvious profit benefit. But at the scale of the community, adding too many animals could lead to overgrazing, or depleting, a shared resource.

This tragedy of shared resources has been used as an argument for privatization. In 2009, Elinor Ostrom won a Nobel Prize in economics (the first woman to do so) for debunking the idea that publicly owned resources would always be mismanaged. She documented many communities around the world that cooperate successfully to govern waterways, grazing land, forests, and fishing rights. Most communities within the feudal system similarly worked out community guidelines for equitably sharing the commons without depleting those resources for future generations.

But within a capitalistic system based on private property and seeking short-term profits for a few, the tragedy of the commons *does* occur. Capitalism is designed to benefit individuals seeking self-interest, not communities or even the public good. Many tragedies of the commons are the result—including excessive carbon emissions that have led to climate change. Under US law, corporate directors have a fiduciary duty to make decisions in the best interests of the company, which is often interpreted as maximizing shareholder return.[7] The single-minded focus of "shareholder primacy," says economist Lenore Palladino, "often comes at the expense of investments in workers, innovation, and long-term growth . . . [and leads to a] high-profit, low wage economy."[8] This brings us to our current climate conundrum. Many, many individuals seeking individual profit are destroying the commons on which everything depends: our earth's ability to support life.

RECOGNIZING EMERGENCE AND EXTERNALIZED COSTS

Systems exhibit *emergent properties*. Emergence is what happens when elements in a system exhibit properties beyond the ability of any individual element.[9] Emergence refers to the existence or formation of collective behaviors—what parts of a system do together that they would not do alone.[10]

An emergent property of capitalism is externalization, where individuals in the system, often corporations, convey business costs to the public. As described in previous chapters, externalized costs are those generated by companies but carried by society.[11] For example, a factory may pollute water by dumping waste in the river without paying for it. Fifty miles downstream, the local government must clean the water for drinking. Those costs are caused by the factory, but the factory does not pay them; the local government does. Externalizing costs means companies show higher profits, but society pays for them.

Another example of externalized costs are transportation costs. While corporations like Amazon have a fleet of trucks and planes to transport their products to consumers, they are not responsible for building and maintaining roads, freeways, bridges, and other infrastructure upon which the transport of goods depend. Governments (and by extension taxpayers) fund these things necessary to do business. When industry deposits toxic waste in vulnerable communities by extracting heavy metals, minerals, or oil, they need not build the cost of this pollution into the cost of doing business. The communities who live in the area bear the cost in their bodies. This is why industries seek resource-rich environments with the least environmental regulations.

A UN research study found that the activities of the three thousand largest companies caused $2.2 trillion in environmental damage in 2008 alone.[12] The cost of this impact is born by the public. Were these companies to pay the true cost of this impact, it would amount to one-third of their earned profits. A 2013 study demonstrated that the global top one hundred environmental externalities cost the economy worldwide $4.7 trillion per year in greenhouse gas emissions and loss of natural resources.[13]

Externalized costs are good for individuals seeking profit but bad for society. This tragedy of the commons includes ecological overshoot and climate change: individuals (including firms) profit from overextraction, and all of earth's life-support systems bear the price.

IMAGINING A NEW ECONOMY

Capitalism was designed to generate profit and wealth for individuals. To this end, globalization has made it possible to extract raw resources and labor from across the globe to minimize costs of labor and inputs and maximize profits. The byproduct is environmental catastrophe, including climate change.

We need an economic system that maintains balance with the life-support systems of earth to create community well-being. We need an economy that generates well-being, not profit. We need an economy designed for communities rather than individuals, or households and firms.

Such an economy must be rooted in certain assumptions:

- It is ruled by the first law of thermodynamics, namely that *energy can neither be created nor destroyed, only altered in form*. While our current economy says it creates new products by way of innovation, it is only converting natural resources into consumables plus waste. An economy that generates well-being would acknowledge that we live in a closed system, one where nothing can be added (no new air, water, or soil) or deleted (there is nowhere else for toxic waste we generate to go).

- The actual existence of a concrete, measurable food web, where we are dependent upon the life-support systems of earth, and we must live within a natural budget intrinsic to those systems (that is, in balance with the systems of life). While our life-support system can integrate and process some pollution, we cannot alter our need for healthy water, air, and soil systems or that we are currently polluting the earth past the point where it can process our waste.

- The Reality of mutual dependence, where substantial damage to any portion of the system results in cascading damage to other elements in the system and, eventually, the entire system.

Let's call these assumptions Indigenous assumptions since they are based on systems that Indigenous Peoples created and inhabited prior to colonization. What might our imagined economy look like?

Very often, I am told it is incorrect to point out what is wrong with our current economic system without offering a concrete alternative. This is quite linear thinking. It assumes that a discrete, fully formed "solution" need only be discovered, and that one must imagine, design, and offer an alternate whole cloth. In my experience, this is looking for a solution from the wrong direction—the end—rather than identifying a process for designing something that does not yet exist.

We must invest our efforts into something that does not yet exist, and build it piece by piece. One does not wait to become a new parent until she can envision her adult child, the person he or she will be when full-grown. A new parent begins with a baby and engages in a process rooted in relationship: building a family. Her child changes many times as he grows. Creation is a process, after all, not a product. We must set the assumptions and output we desire, then engage many, many imaginations, relationships, and tools to build a system to meet our needs.

We begin with intention, we articulate our assumptions, we set conditions, define the desired unit and output, and then build a system that complies with these.

I suggest here that we turn to Indigenous cosmology for help imagining what a system might look like that meets our needs while remaining in balance within ecological limits. It is nearly impossible to imagine a system like this while living within a paradigm using the assumptions of our current system. It follows, then, that we need the help of those who live with a different set of assumptions.

If we do this—if we carefully construct the elements of a system we need, solutions will emerge. That is, in imagining and creating a new system, it will have within it emergent properties!

- A system is dynamic, complex, interconnected, interrelated, and non-linear.

- A system's behavior is determined not only by the parts of a system but by the interlocking relationships of those parts.

- Relationships are dynamic and fluid, and they cannot be easily summarized or defined or predicted. All of this makes systems *complex*.

- Emergent properties grow from complex systems. Sometimes these properties are negative—like the externalized costs mentioned earlier—and sometimes, they are positive.

I do not mean to be evasive by not offering a "ten-point plan" to produce a new system, but rather I mean to express humility. It is foolish for me to believe that one woman, myself, has the imagination or the breadth of tools required to create such a complex system. Can't we follow the guidance of Tyson Yunkaporta and design an economic system based upon Indigenous patterns of thinking? Many of us don't know what that would mean, but there is a way to find out: we can ask Tyson Yunkaporta, along with other Indigenous systems thinkers, to guide us.

It is not for me alone to define what it will be. Many imaginations must generate it, try it, reflect on it, and try again and again, until we succeed. Our survival depends on it.

JOINING THE GREAT TURNING

I (Sheri) have spent the past several years coming to grips with the true scope of our predicament. Initially, of course, this was overwhelming. If fixing our mess is not as simple as switching to renewables and driving electric cars, if our progress is not as easily measured as the parts per million of carbon dioxide emissions each year, then God have mercy on us.

But I soon began to see this predicament as an opening to a bigger transition I knew was necessary. Humans have created an economic system based on profit and wealth accumulation for individuals, and we can experiment with creating a new system with new goals. I don't care what we call it—capitalism, socialism, whatever-ism. I care about having an economic system that supports life on this planet.

If I sound hopeful, it's because I am. As Sungmanitu Bluebird, an Oglala Lakota writer and activist, writes, many of his elders have said: "There will come a time when white men will have to choose between destruction and salvation." Bluebird thinks that time is upon us, and I believe this is true. Many people do. Eco-philosopher and activist Joanna Macy calls this transition from an industrial-growth society to a life-sustaining civilization "the Great Turning." I believe this Turning is what Jesus of Nazareth called us to when he set foot in human form on this beautiful planet to announce and enact the kindom of God.

I am also hopeful because I believe this transition is already happening. All around the world, people are realizing that we can't go on this way, that the system is broken. They are also realizing that we can meet human needs without destroying the world. As Macy says, "We have the technical knowledge, the communication tools, and material resources to grow enough food, ensure clean air and water, and meet rational energy needs."[14] We can and must create an economic system based on the Indigenous assumptions that Sarah has described. We can and must shift our economic goals from growth and wealth accumulation to well-being and planetary health.

There are movements all around the planet working on this shift. I mention the ones that I know about; there are many more! I encourage you to do your own research. You may come away similarly hopeful that change is possible and is already happening.

- For decades, economists have been studying and imagining economic systems based in ecological reality and a more just allocation of resources. These schools of thought include ecological economics, Herman Daly's steady-state economics, post-growth economics, Kate Raworth's doughnut economics, and the degrowth movement, which is well known in Europe and part of Latin America.

- In 2010, more than thirty-five thousand people attended the World People's Conference on Climate Change and the Rights of Mother Earth held outside of Cochabamba, Bolivia. The conference deliberations resulted in "The People's Agreement of Cochabamba." Based in Indigenous wisdom, it serves as a blueprint for a way forward.

- Buen Vivir is a political and economic philosophy based on Indigenous, feminist, and environmental thought that is influential in Latin America.

- Rights of Nature is a legal theory that views ecosystems and species as having rights similar to fundamental human rights. As of 2022, twenty-four countries, at least seven tribal nations in the United States and Canada, and over sixty US cities and counties had instituted nature's rights laws.

- Anti-globalization and pro-localization movements like Local Futures and Transition Towns encourage people to relocalize their economies, resulting in greatly reduced use of energy and resources. These movements include local currencies and local food initiatives like farmers' markets, community gardens, and community-supported agriculture.

- Permaculture is a system that designs sustainable human communities, although it is best known for its agricultural practices. Permaculture is rooted in two core concepts: "an understanding and acceptance of the diversity of whole systems, as opposed to the soil-degrading effects of industrial monoculture," and the "relational, slow-yet-dynamic practice of observing the land, and its many complex ecosystems."[15]

- Ever more promisingly, agroecology combines agronomy and ecology and also addresses injustice and inequity in food systems, as well as advocating for Indigenous knowledge and land rights. The movement is associated with the world's largest organization of small farmers, La Via Campesina.[16]

- Many initiatives further the sharing and repairing economy by, for instance, establishing local lending libraries for tools and other goods as well as "repair cafes" and "maker spaces."

- More than electric vehicles, we need good public transportation, and many people in Canada and the United States are advocating for this. In addition, numerous "fifteen-minute city" initiatives attempt to provide all necessary urban functions—education, health care, parks, commerce, entertainment, and so on—within a fifteen-minute walking distance.

- "Commoning" philosophies and initiatives provide guidelines and practices for restoring and rejuvenating the commons, or publicly owned and governed resources. See especially the work of Dave Bollier and Nobel-prize-winning economist Elinor Ostrom.

I love the Greek word we translate as repentance in the New Testament—*metanoia*. It means "to change one's mind or purpose." It isn't just about being sorry for your sins. It means to turn—to change one's priorities and direction. This sort of repentance is at the heart of Jesus' message. In the gospels of Mark and Matthew, Jesus begins his ministry by proclaiming the good news of God: "The time is fulfilled, and the kingdom of God has come near; repent and believe in the good news" (Mark 1:15). *Metanoia* was not about individual salvation (a concept unknown in Judaism at that time) but about turning toward God's vision for the world and away from the status quo of the oppressive and ever-expanding Roman Empire. Instead of believing in the good news (*euangelion*) of the supposed peace and security offered by the Pax Romana, Jesus asked people to believe in the *euangelion* of the kindom of God, which alone offers true peace and security.

I have often been struck by the process that second-century Christians went through when they were baptized into the alternative community called the church. Candidates were "deschooled" in the ways of Empire and "reschooled" in the ways of the kindom of God. They had to let go of professions that were inconsistent with the values of Jesus' *euangelion* (like being a gladiator). If they became soldiers during this process, they were rejected from the church; if they were already soldiers, they had to pledge not to kill anyone. They had to demonstrate a "turned" life by sharing food and material possessions and behaving in ethical and just ways.

The baptismal ritual was also politically subversive. Candidates ritually turned away from the direction of Rome and toward the direction of Jerusalem to demonstrate their changed allegiance. They would then make a public oath of faithfulness to God's kindom—an oath called a *sacramentum*. The *sacramentum* was originally the oath of loyalty soldiers would make to the Roman Emperor. Early Christians "appropriated" this term to describe the oath of loyalty they made to Jesus and his kindom upon baptism. Marcellus, a Roman centurion, was executed in 298 CE for violating his *sacramentum* to the emperor by being baptized.

I wonder: What it would mean for the church to lead the way in a collective *metanoia* now—a turning from an extractive economy to one based in the Reality of God's dream for creation? What if the church repented of its complicity in colonization by doing what Sarah suggests? What if we humbly followed the guidance of Indigenous pattern thinking in imagining a new economic system and then announced and enacted this *euangelion*—good news—to the world?

NINE

Decolonizing Cultural Systems

AMONG THE PEOPLE where I (Sarah) live, it is believed that in ancient times all the different people could talk to each other—the bear and chipmunk people, the elk and bird people, and the human people. Within this context, the salmon people gave salmon as a gift to humans so that they might never go hungry. The Haida people of the Pacific Northwest tell the story of the salmon boy to illustrate the symbiotic relationship between the Haida and salmon:

> All the people knew that after salmon were taken from the water and eaten, anything left over, including the smallest bones, must be returned to the water because the bodies of the salmon are sacred—their remains must be returned to the salmon people. But one disrespectful boy refused, and threw salmon bones on the ground after he ate without a care. He even threw cooked food on the ground if he felt like it.

One day during the season of the salmon run, he swam into the river instead of showing the spawning salmon respect by staying away, as was the custom of his people. While he was swimming, he was caught in a whirlpool and drowned. The salmon people swam all around him, and took him to their home in the ocean. They were kind to him and taught him respect and kindness. They showed him their mysteries, and he became a shaman. In time, he swam up the river to the village of his people wearing the salmon skin the salmon people had given him. His mother recognized him and brought him on shore where he was able to show himself as a person and teach the people. When he died a short time later, his people put his body in the river so that he could return to the salmon people.

This story is one of many about the salmon people in the Pacific Northwest. These stories illustrate the relationship between Native peoples and the community of life that surrounds them. Humans are not separate, but part of a community of life; prey are not subordinate, but revered. Stockpiling food makes little sense in this cosmology. Seeking profit for one individual makes no sense when he is connected to those around him. Disregard for externalized costs is unthinkable in a system where even waste is treated with reverence. The salmon people in this story are not vengeful, but generous. This cautionary tale ends with wisdom and honor for a disrespectful boy who grows to be a wise man. Competition for scarce resources does not make sense in an ecosystem of interdependence. This story provides a window into a cosmology that explains a system of mutual dependence. Importantly, the values expressed in this cosmology run counter to the dominant culture.

Several years ago, when my son was small, our family was in relationship with a principal in our community who claimed to drink five Big Gulps each day. A Big Gulp is a thirty-two-ounce soda. I don't know whether this statement was hyperbole or an accurate assessment of how much soda he drank, but it is true that I never saw him without a large soda in tow.

This big, friendly, smiling man was beloved by children and parents alike. This principal—let's call him Nathan—welcomed the children who lined up for school every morning and greeted each person by name. He was ever-present and available. He was good at his job and a valued community member. But he struggled with health problems, and those of us who surrounded him watched sadly as his health declined, watched as his hospitalizations became more frequent, and watched as he began to depend on a wheelchair for mobility. But we watched from a remove, detached.

Five Big Gulps equals 160 ounces of soda each day, or one and a quarter gallons. According to the University of California at San Francisco, consuming a single twelve-ounce soda per day for a year equals consuming fifty-five thousand calories, which is the equivalent of fifteen pounds per year.[1] Not surprisingly, this principal faced multiple health challenges. He used a wheelchair to aid his mobility since walking was challenging. He suffered from heart disease and diabetes. Like one in three American adults, he dealt with many of the health risks that accompany obesity. Unfortunately, the obesity prominent in American culture can be directly linked to our current food system.

Our food system, and how it came to be, provides a good model for exploring the dominant culture in the United States. The way we provision ourselves embodies a logic of perpetual growth. To effect systems change, to challenge unjust laws and policies, we must also challenge the elements of our culture that normalize individualism and consumerism, meaning the norms that reinforce perpetual growth. In other words, to effect changes at all three structural levels of society, we need to attend to changes in our superstructure, our symbolic reality. What are we taught to value and to pay attention to by our culture? What decisions and choices flow "naturally" from this largely unconscious training?

"GET BIG OR GET OUT"

In 1955, the only soda size on offer at McDonald's was seven ounces. Today, a small soda sold by the same chain is nearly twice the size at twelve ounces, while a large is thirty. This change reflects more than the strategy of one fast food chain; it reflects a national policy to maximize production of commodities, industrialize food production, and reduce the cost of food.

At the end of World War II in 1944, US households spent 36 percent of household income on food.[2] By contrast, in 2021 we spent just 10.3 percent of household income on food. Only 5.2 percent of that was spent on food at home, while 5.1 percent was spent on eating out.[3] According to the American Enterprise Institute, Americans per capita have the most affordable food on the planet; residents in European countries spend twice as much on food as a share of their total consumer expenditures, and countries like India (36 percent) and Kenya (45 percent) spend much more. In the United States, the true cost of food production is partially masked by federal food subsidies. The federal government subsidizes corn, wheat, and soy, which in turn provide feed to produce cheap eggs, dairy, and meat.[4]

The transition to cheap food began in the 1970s, when federal policies under the Nixon Administration increased food production and drove down food prices. Secretary of State Earl Butz even coined the slogan "Get big or get out."[5] This is when the government began providing the subsidies mentioned above.[6] An overabundance of food drives down prices, masks the true cost of food production, and pushes small farmers out of the market, since they do not benefit from subsidies reserved for large-scale farms. These policies made way for the growing fast-food industry and the manufacture of cheap processed foods. They also increased exports of subsidized commodities, which meant farmers in other countries could not compete with the flood of cheap subsidized food coming from the United States. Factory farms, in turn, came to depend on cheap fuel and fertilizer, overuse of water, and extraction of food from depleted soils. Our overproduction of food follows the logic of extraction.

This food transition came about not by accident but by design. While our consumption practices appear to be driven by individual "choice," our choices are embedded in a system that drives outcomes. (Ironically, this system is not rooted in capitalist principles, because subsidies make some foods cheap and readily available artificially. True capitalism would rely on the market to regulate the true cost of food.) When just a fraction of household income is needed to buy food, a large percentage of disposable income—in the case of US households, more than 25 percent of household income—is then freed up for consumer spending on products like smartphones and computers, cars, and vacations. In short, cheap food feeds the growth monster.

I have no difficulty with government subsidies for small-scale or family farms. But our food system was created to form export markets, support corporate vertical integration (where one huge corporate conglomerate owns the fuel, feed, and protein production, controlling costs at every level), and create the hungriest consumers in the world: American consumers.

While an artificially subsidized food system hurts all of us, the vulnerable, as always, are disproportionately affected. In 2021, the Rockefeller Foundation published a study explaining the hidden, externalized costs built into the food industry. The results, using data from the year 2019, found that while we spend $1.1 trillion on food each year, we incur over $2 trillion in externalized costs due to diminished human health and a degraded environment. "That [$1.1 trillion] price tag includes the cost of producing, processing, retailing, and wholesaling the food we buy and eat. It does not include the cost of healthcare for the millions who fall ill with diet-related diseases. Nor does $1.1 trillion include the present and future costs of the food system's contributions to water and air pollution, reduced biodiversity, or greenhouse gas emissions, which cause climate change."[7]

A dramatic example of these hidden health costs is the impact of diet and health on hospitalizations during the COVID-19 pandemic. In the United States, most adult hospitalizations were attributed to one of four pre-existing, diet-related conditions: obesity, hypertension, diabetes, and heart failure, in that order.[8] These conditions disproportionately affect racial or ethnic groups. For instance, diabetes diagnoses among Latino Americans are 1.7 times higher than white Americans; diabetes diagnoses among Black Americans are 1.5 times higher than white Americans.[9] As a respiratory illness, COVID-19 infections were also exacerbated by other health and environmental conditions, which also have a disproportionate impact. Black Americans, for example, are exposed to air pollution at a rate

25 percent higher than the national average, and Latinos are exposed to air pollution at a rate 41 percent higher.[10] Indigenous Americans are nineteen times more likely to have reduced water or sanitation access than white Americans. In all, COVID-19-related hospitalizations and deaths were disproportionately higher within minoritized communities. COVID-19's impact was not equal—the vulnerable bore more of the cost.[11]

Our society's dependence on cheap food results in oppression. Scholar, environmental activist, and food sovereignty advocate Vandana Shiva has described the industrial global food system as "an anti-food system spreading hunger and disease." It is not a food system, she says, but "an inefficient profit generating commodity system with high ecological and social costs externalised to society and nature."[12]

What is the impact of our national policy on Nathan, the principal in my community? According to a study by Oxford University that analyzed a million people around the globe, moderate to severe obesity reduces life expectancy by three to ten years, respectively.[13] According to the same study, one in three deaths from heart attack or stroke are attributed to obesity. The excessive consumption of sweeteners like corn syrup in Big Gulps is life-threatening. It will kill you; that's a fact.

I see the Big Gulp as a metaphor for ecological overshoot. Just as we are overconsuming fossil fuels and other resources, many of us, like Nathan, are overconsuming Big Gulps. Our overconsumption results in climate change and environmental degradation just like drinking too many Big Gulps lead to excess weight, strain on the heart, and diabetes.

If Nathan is given insulin to manage his diabetes, this treats only one symptom of overconsumption. It won't address the strain on his musculoskeletal structure, which necessitates a wheelchair. The obvious solution is to stop drinking so much soda. Similarly, reducing carbon emissions may impact one symptom of ecological overshoot—climate change—but will do nothing to protect precious aquifers and fragile food webs. The solution to the quandary of ecological overshoot is to stop the process of perpetual growth—to live within our means on our planet.

Even if Nathan uses insulin and drinks only one Big Gulp per day, that consumption would equal forty pounds of weight gain in a year. He can't change the rules of basic biology and chemistry; overconsumption of sugar equals added weight. No medicine or technical solution will change the reality that over-consumption of sugar will result in adverse health outcomes. Similarly, we can't change the rules of ecological overshoot— the chemistry, biology, and physics of the earth. Ecological overshoot will damage the life-support systems of Earth and make it impossible for people to live on this planet, regardless of whether we fuel our consumption with fossil fuels or with minerals and rare earth used to build renewables. All the wealth and privilege in the world will not change this fact. It doesn't matter how smart we are. These are the rules of reality. It is an abstraction to believe that we somehow exist outside of the rules of reality. We are not outside these rules—we are mutually dependent within a closed system!

Ecological overshoot will kill us. That is a fact.

BELIEVING THE MYTH OF PERPETUAL GROWTH

As I (Sheri) have learned to see in new ways, it began to seem so obvious that perpetual growth is not survivable. If so, why does the current strategy continue to have such staying power? I believe we remain in thrall to a central cultural myth. We believe that for us to be happy and for our society to function in a healthy way, growth is the only way forward, specifically growth as measured by gross domestic product. Economists, journalists, and politicians closely watch GDP numbers, and as soon as GDP growth dips, alarm bells ring: Warning! Everyone breathes more easily once the numbers start going up again.

I was surprised to learn that this emphasis on economic growth as measured by GDP is only several decades old. In fact, gross domestic product has been used as an economic measure only since 1934. The originator of the concept, Simon Kuznets, warned against using it as an indicator of the welfare of a country rather than simply a measure of the monetary value of goods and services purchased within a given time span. Senator Bobby Kennedy famously said of GDP: "It measures everything in short, except that which makes life worthwhile."[14] One would think we would have developed other metrics.

But starting in the 1970s, neoliberal economic thought and policies become dominant. Neoliberalism is the idea that (1) the unregulated free market will result in robust economic growth, defined by rising GDP, and (2) economic growth can solve social ills and provide for social goods. Do you want to end poverty? Don't enact policies that redistribute wealth by taxing those who are better off financially and spending that money on social welfare programs. Grow your economy, and that wealth will trickle down to the least well-off members of society. Do you want your people to live longer, more healthy lives? As counterintuitive as it may sound, don't provide good public healthcare. Grow your economy: a rising economic tide will indirectly lead to improved health as people's standards of living rise. These are the claims of neoliberalism, which is also known as trickle-down economics.

Under the spell of neoliberalism, Global North economies like the United States and the United Kingdom began cutting government spending (except for the military), eliminating environmental and labor protections that supposedly stymied economic growth, and easing barriers to global trade. These same economic policies were essentially forced upon the Global South. To qualify for loans, the World Bank and International Monetary Fund mandated that developing countries cut public spending and make their countries more attractive to economic development by eliminating trade barriers, cutting business taxes, and easing environmental and labor protections. These so-called reforms were officially referred to as "structural adjustment programs."

But these growth-based policies did little for human well-being. Trickle-down economics has been largely discredited.[15] Income inequality is on the rise across the globe. The United States now has the highest income inequality among wealthy countries. Neoliberal policies helped decimate the US manufacturing sector, leading to the loss of working-class jobs that paid good wages, included benefits, and provided job security. The anger and frustration over these economic changes helped fuel political polarization along lines of class and education.

As disastrous as these policies have been for people in the Global North, they have been even more devastating for those in the Global South. Structural adjustment programs gave the Global North renewed access to cheap labor and resources in the Global South, access which had diminished during the postcolonial era as formerly colonized countries began reclaiming sovereignty over their own economies and resources. Throughout the 1980s, the Global South exported more commodities to the

Global North while their total revenues declined. As economic anthropologist Jason Hickel puts it, "By depressing the costs of Southern labour and commodities, the North [appropriated] a significant quantity effectively *for free*."[16] This is why these policies are referred to as neocolonial economic policies. Direct rule may have ended, but the Global North was enclosing, expropriating, and extracting wealth from former colonies via global capitalism.

While rising GDP doesn't magically lead to better social outcomes, investment in public welfare does improve social health. In the early part of the twentieth century, life expectancies began to rise in countries in the Global North. Some economists point to steadily rising GDP as the reason for this, but research bears out that much of this increase in life expectancy was due to public sanitation measures. Water sanitation measures alone accounted for 75 percent of the decline in infant mortality in the United States between 1900 and 1936 and half the total decline in mortality rates. Universal access to healthcare and education also lead to higher life expectancies.[17] The Social Security and Medicare programs established in the 1930s are among the most successful, effective, and popular programs in the United States. We enjoy these social goods because people before us advocated for them, often against severe opposition.

Their victories greatly benefitted my family. My grandma Anna had to leave school in eighth grade so she could take care of her ailing mother while her father worked. Had my mother or I ever faced such need, we would have had access to public assistance. The Rural Electrification Act of 1936 brought electricity to isolated rural areas of the United States, including where I grew up. Social Security allowed my grandparents to retire without falling into poverty or relying exclusively on their children to take care of them.

But without growth, how could a society get the money it needs to fund these great things like healthcare and education and sanitation? Some developing countries *do* need economic growth to fund these necessities. But developed countries do not need more economic growth to ensure the welfare of their citizens. In fact, the economies of most developed countries could "shrink" and still—with a just distribution of resources—ensure high social outcomes. GDP doesn't need to be that high to meet social needs, since providing public health care and education is more cost-effective than private avenues for these social goods.[18] One need only think of the United States' expensive and inefficient private healthcare system. Americans pay more for healthcare than any other country yet experience far worse health outcomes.

Countries with a far lower GDP per capita than the United States provide good lives for their citizens. Portugal provides good healthcare and free childcare and enjoys higher life expectancies, among other social goods, even though people there make 65 percent less income per capita than in the United States. Costa Rica also has a higher life expectancy than the United States even though they have 80 percent less income per capita. As Hickel notes, Costa Rica achieved many of its gains in life expectancy during a time when its GDP didn't grow at all. Estonia has one of the world's best education systems and boasts health outcomes far better than those of people in the United States, and it is a country with 66 percent less income per capita.[19]

We can meet human needs on far less GDP than we think. In fact, past a certain threshold of economic growth, human progress goes down as GDP goes up. If we compare US GDP growth to a metric called the genuine progress indicator (GPI), which includes the social and environmental impacts of economic growth, we see that GDP and GPI grew together through the 1970s. But after that, GDP continued growing and GPI went down. Interestingly, studies show that happiness rates in the United States peaked around the 1950s, when GDP was far less than today and when our society had far less wealth inequality—and when the Great Acceleration began to rev up. I am not the first person to wonder if there is a correlation between the rapid increase in consumption, widening inequality, and declining happiness.

I think most people of faith already know this. We know that past a certain level, money does not buy happiness. What makes us happy is living lives of purpose with others in community. What makes us happy is knowing that there is justice—right relationship—in the land, that all residents have enough and that our planetary home is not threatened. We long for a restored garden where we walk humbly with our Creator. But if pushing for continued growth is actively working against our happiness, then why do we keep it up? Why do we overconsume?

OVERCONSUMING FOR UNMET NEEDS

I (Sarah) do not know why Nathan, the beloved principal in my community, consumed Big Gulps to the point of severely deteriorated health. Nor do I fully know why I and many other community members only watched from a distance as his health worsened. But I know that soda is broadly accessible, inexpensive, and advertised in ways that normalize or even glamorize its consumption. Our society does not talk about food in healthy ways. And I suspect that a certain element of overconsumption is part of this story. Many people use food as a source of emotional comfort.

The Mayo Clinic describes emotional eating as "a way to suppress or soothe negative emotions, such as stress, anger, fear, boredom, sadness, and loneliness. Major life events or, more commonly, the hassles of daily life can trigger negative emotions that lead to emotional eating." They note that food can serve as a distraction. "If you're worried about an upcoming event or stewing over a conflict, for instance, you may focus on eating comfort food instead of dealing with the painful situation."[20] A depressed or anxious person may cut down on sugar consumption, but this will not change the need for emotional comfort.

Why didn't those in the community, myself included, intervene with Nathan? It is a disturbing occurrence in our dominant culture when a man turns to sugar rather than human relationship for comfort. Our cultural propensity to blame every action on personal choice dismisses the needs that overeating brings to the surface. "Most of the time, emotional eating has nothing to do with a lack of self-control," says dietician Kasey Kilpatrick. "Since food rules are all about encouraging self-control, it's not surprising that they don't always solve emotional eating in the long run."[21] If overeating is not a matter of will, then perhaps it is a response to an unmet need.

In the same way, excess consumer spending also expresses a need for comfort, reassurance, status, and belonging. The credit score reporting agency Experian characterizes emotional spending as "impulsive spending that's fueled by big emotions, such as stress, anxiety, or sadness." They cite research which suggests that "consumers who are stressed may spend more on products they consider necessities. The theory is that it provides a sense of control when other areas of their life feel uncontrollable."[22]

It's not wrong for people to meet these needs. Nor is it rational to deny underlying needs. But when we attempt to meet these needs via consumption, our spending does not nourish us—it provides empty calories, thus degrading our overall well-being. Overspending exacerbates our vulnerability, contributing to household debt and climate change. We turn to consuming, whether eating or spending, to fill ourselves—to tend to our need for comfort and safety. We *could* collectively choose instead to turn to one another, to community, and systems of connection—to systems of life.

Our dominant culture is making us sick. The racial superiority, hierarchy, and hegemony embedded in our individualist, capitalist culture result in obesity, depression, anxiety, and unhappiness. Perhaps it is time to consider changing our culture.

IMAGINING THE KINDOM OF GOD

One definition of culture describes it as "the way of life for an entire society" that includes beliefs and institutions passed down from generation to generation.[23] What is our way of life? Based on my research, our culture seems designed to provide products for our consumption. Our culture is engineered to support the logic of extraction by providing the products of extraction to a willing society of super-consumers.

We know that consumption does not meet our needs. So what do we want our culture to provide?

The *More-with-Less Cookbook*, by home economist and Mennonite Doris Janzen Longacre, was first published in 1976. It remains one of the bestselling books of all time for Herald Press, our publisher. As such, many Anabaptists have decades-old, spattered, dog-eared copies on kitchen counters and in pantries. When I received my first copy as a young woman,

I didn't read the theology and philosophy contained in its early chapters, but I've been reading it lately.

Something about the crisis we now find ourselves in caused me to recall the Haitian proverb printed on the flyleaf of the book: "A full stomach says: a ripe guava has worms. An empty stomach says: let me see." When I read this many years ago, it stuck with me, because I knew that when your life is on the line, you are willing to be persistent, to negotiate, to not give up. Because I grew up hungry—literally without enough to eat—I related to this proverb. I have returned to it many times over the years. Inaction is a common and even rational response to despair, but not when life is on the line. When life itself is at stake, we can kick into another gear. And that is what is required of each of us, and of all of us collectively, at this time of climate crisis and ecological overshoot.

While I have relied on *More-with-Less* in my kitchen over the years, I recently tuned in to Longacre's call to Christians to live our values in the most practical way I can think of: choosing how and what we eat. Longacre lays out a vision of reducing consumption in North America so that we can share vital resources with those facing food shortages in the developing world. She challenges the core assumptions of privilege and entitlement in North American culture. She writes, "As Christians dealing with human hurts, we have to remind ourselves again and again that we are not called to be successful, but to be faithful."[24]

Longacre writes that while nine-tenths of the world is starving, in North America we are overweight. I am sure this was true when she was writing in the 1970s at the beginning of the transition to large-scale agriculture, when 13 percent of adults and 7 percent of children were obese. It is even more true today: roughly 65 percent adults and 30 percent of children are overweight or obese in the United States. Longacre says that we must reduce the amount of sugar and animal protein in our daily diets; if we do this, we can free up these calories for others. Her cookbook serves as a practical guide for how North Americans can seek right relationship with nine-tenths of the world through simple eating. For her, seeking right relationship is not a metaphor, but grounded in concrete action. Her work was and is still radical!

Taking responsibility for our consumption is not a matter of "charity;" reducing consumption is not a sacrifice. Living in balance and in right relationship is generative. It makes our lives better. When we choose to live in balance, we are more connected to each other across the world, and with our inter-connected ecosystem. I am not suggesting here that our individual actions are the locus of social change, although reducing our personal consumptions benefits us personally. Rather, working collectively and standing together for structural change will build a collective movement.

How might we extend Longacre's vision of more with less to our culture and be guided by her vision to seek right relationship?

I propose that our culture could meet our real needs by supporting right relationship: connection to each other, the earth, and all of creation—true shalom. Ecological economist Kate Raworth describes this as meeting the needs of all within the means of the planet.[25]

We did not get to where we are by accident or by the conscious and rational choice of millions of individuals. Our institutions are designed to reinforce the priority of consumption. We are socialized to view ourselves as consumers, where the outcome of any interaction is transactional. We are encouraged to meet even our needs for emotional connection and comfort by consuming. But we are not stuck here. We can acknowledge reality as it is and turn away from the norms, practices, and behaviors that are making us sick, away from systems of death.

Jesus' ministry showed us how to do that—how to break the bonds of the rules and the pressure to go along with societal norms that are selfish and unjust. In speaking with the Samaritan woman at the well, Jesus dismisses purity norms by calling someone who had been rejected by society to receive living water (John 4). Jesus instructs the rich ruler that discipleship and divestment of wealth provide the pathway to eternal life (Mark 10). He announces his anointing to bring good news to the poor, heralding in the year of Jubilee when the oppressed are freed and the captives released (Luke 4). Jesus rejects conventional wisdom about who is important by valuing substance over appearance, justice over conformity. We can commit to following him in seeking right relationship.

To turn away from systems of death, *decolonization is necessary*. Colonization created the systems that have led to our situation. Decolonization is a process to dismantle these systems. But we don't know what we don't know. For those of us stuck in a paradigm of perpetual growth based upon extractive logic, it is hard to imagine what else is possible. We must turn to people outside this system to seek healthful systems of life. We must know what an alternate system looks like in order to figure out how to build one.

I return to the Nuu-chah-nulth people of the Canadian Pacific Northwest, who practice *Tsawalk*, or "one," which acknowledges that all living things form an integrated whole that must continually work for harmony through constant negotiation and mutual respect. "This is the time of decay, when people begin to take the easy way through life, when the ego assumes superiority and the human identity becomes lost in the contradictions of polarity, when nations and empires begin to fall, when people lose their way and forget their teachings," Elder Umeek explains. He points to the remembrance ceremony of *X̌uukʷaana*, which "addresses the problem of collective memory." He explains, "Many nations that dismiss Indigenous participation in their histories do not have a collective memory. If it is true that humans have a tendency to forget, then a new education and socio-political system might be developed in concert so as to collectively address this problem."[26]

As the church, we could join with our Indigenous siblings to cast vision and create an education and sociopolitical system designed to remember Reality. Systems theory tells us that embedded systems are nearly impossible to reform. Rather than spending generations pushing for systems change of the dominant culture that might result in superficial change, we can join with Indigenous siblings to create a counterculture in the church—a culture where right relationship is the output.

DREAMING OF A REIMAGINED CHURCH

Public health literature provides some helpful ideas for imagining how the church might pursue this cultural vision. Scholars at the University of Warwick Law School articulate a vision of three publics in the international health arena. In a 2013 paper, the scholars explore the relationship between the general public, or what they call the "primordial public"; the legitimate hierarchical bureaucracy that they call the "civil public"; and those with some positional power that are neither part of the general public nor the ruling structure/bureaucracy. They call this group the "third public," which they describe as "un-co-opted elites."[27] My read is that "un-co-opted" means those in this group are not indebted to the legitimate bureaucracy and yet have more power or access to power than the general public, who are subject to the authority of those in power. Because this third public is not indebted to the legitimate authorities yet has more power than the general public, they can agitate for transparency and accountability.

I believe that the church could serve as this third public in creating a vision for a system designed to create shalom or right relationship.

Let me be precise about what I mean by "church." Many church institutions *are* compromised by financial investment in resource extraction. I know this because I have spent more than a decade lobbying church bodies to stand with the oppressed actively and vocally, to little effect. Some argue that church bodies are indebted to the legitimate hierarchical bureaucracy in that they are willing to give up autonomy and prophetic voice in favor a of tax-free organizational status and profit. Many activists find it difficult to move church institutions to challenge other legitimate institutions.

We know that the church in its current manifestation in rich countries is troubled. In the United States, Canada, and Europe, the church is shrinking year by year. While 70 percent of Americans claimed church membership in 1976, by 2018 less than 50 percent were church affiliated.[28] During COVID-19, one in three practicing US Christians dropped out of attending church completely.[29] I wonder if, in its effort to retain its legitimacy with authorities, the institutional church has lost its way. I question whether the institutional church is relevant in a world with such savage inequality, where the powerful use up the life-support systems of earth upon which we all depend to feed the appetites of the mighty.

The church I am dreaming of and talking about is the people of God joining together to follow the Spirit of Life in co-imag-ining a world built upon shalom. Theologian Noel Moules de-scribes shalom as "one wholistic vision of the dynamic harmony and interrelationship of all things—everything and forever—one wholistic wholeness."[30] This system is not something I can imagine alone, and it is yet to be discovered.

Is it time for another reformation? I long for a church that will stand up to the systems of death on this earth and say, "Enough! We stand with the systems of life; we repent of our complicity with the systems of death, and we repudiate the sys-tems of extraction that are victimizing the vulnerable and de-stroying the possibility of life on this earth." That is the church I will stand with. That is the church I dream of and pray for, the church that is within us and around us, that animates us in response to the Great Animator. And to tilt my hand just a bit—it is the church many of us are *organizing*.

We could choose to create a system together that attempts to meets the needs of all within planetary limits and model this for others. Where life is, there is the Spirit. Where the Spirit is, there is life. We can follow the Spirit of Life in living into the kindom of God.

We cannot do this alone, because we do not know how—we are socialized to consume in a society of perpetual growth. While many of us do the best we can to live simply and sus-tainably as individuals, we are perplexed by how we might do this collectively, systemically. This is where collaboration, ac-knowledgment of mutual dependence, and humility come into play. We can seek out those who know how to do this and join with them to learn how. We can engage in conciliation with Indigenous siblings that leads us to a place of mutual acknowledgment and respect, to each other and to the earth.

Many skeptical voices will say this vision is silly: utopian and unrealistic. To this I respond: How else should I use my life energy at this time? Calamity is upon us. Should we not try everything, even acting as audaciously as believing in the gospel of Christ? My job on this earth is *not* to be successful, it is to be faithful.

If you are afraid of failure, hear me: We are failing right now.

If you have been struggling for justice and you are discouraged, hear me: You are not alone. Together, we are the body of Christ, the people of the Alpha and Omega, the One who established the foundations of the earth, who set its cornerstone.

If you are afraid of looking foolish: May we all act foolishly and count ourselves among good company. As 1 Corinthians 1:27 (CEB) reminds us, "God chose what the world considers foolish to shame the wise. God chose what the world considers weak to shame the strong."

RE-MEMBERING TO REMEMBER REALITY

The word *religion* traces its roots to a word that means "to bind fast." True religion will bind us fast, reconnect us to our true selves, to each other, to creation, and to God. True religion will re-member us, bring back together what was never meant to be dis-membered, separated.

We have been dis-membered. Throughout this book, Sarah and I have talked about how our economy and culture systemically alienate us from right relationship with ourselves, each other, creation, and Creator. While this alienation is rooted in systems that are roughly five hundred years old, this tendency to see ourselves as separate and superior is much older. As Brazilian Canadian scholar Vanessa Machado de Oliviera says, many Indigenous Peoples see the violence of colonialism as "symptoms of a deeper and older form of violence that happens at ontological and metaphysical realms—the realm of 'being.' This deeper, older sense of violence is the imposed sense of separation between us and the dynamic living land-metabolism that is the planet and beyond, as well as the theological separation between creature and creator." The name of that separation is *human exceptionalism*, or the "belief that humans are a superior species that deserve to conquer, dominate, own, manage, and control the natural environment."[31]

We must re-member who we are. As Sarah describes, the ancient Nuu-chah-nulth guarded against taking the easy way through life using periodic ceremonies for remembering Reality. Umeek writes: "We remember who we are, perched precariously in a balance between creation and destruction." In other words, the Nuu-chah-nulth remember that they are vulnerable beings, part of the web of mutual dependence. They are dependent, like other beings in this web. They are not exceptional nor separate.

The Christian tradition offers some resources that might help us remember Reality. While some of our sacred texts seemingly support human exceptionalism, this is not true of all of them. God's "whirlwind speech" to Job remembers who we are. It restores humans to our proper place within creation.

In the story from the Hebrew Scriptures, Job is living the ancient Hebrew equivalent of the American Dream. He has a big family, health and wealth, and the respect of his peers. But God allows Satan, the Adversary, to test Job and see whether he remains faithful even when everything is taken from him.

Tragedy upon tragedy befalls Job. His world gone, he sits down in the ashes to mourn. Three friends visit him to tell Job why such suffering has come to his house. In long speeches spanning numerous chapters, they parrot the conventional wisdom of that day: God gives prosperity to the righteous and punishes the wicked. Job has surely sinned. He needs to repent so God will bless him again.

Job refuses this conventional wisdom. He has not sinned. He complains of God's crushing unfairness to him and challenges God to tell him what he has done wrong. Finally, God, who has been silent for thirty-seven chapters, speaks out of the whirlwind. At first, this is a deeply sarcastic deity:

> Who is this that darkens counsel by words without
> knowledge?
> Gird up your loins like a man;
> I will question you, and you shall declare to me.
> Where were you when I laid the foundation of the earth?
> Tell me, if you have understanding.
> Who determined its measurements—surely you know!
> Or who stretched the line upon it?
> On what were its bases sunk,
> or who laid its cornerstone
> when the morning stars sang together
> and all the heavenly beings shouted for joy?
> Or who shut in the sea with doors
> when it burst out from the womb,
> when I made the clouds its garment,
> and thick darkness its swaddling band,
> and prescribed bounds for it,
> and set bars and doors,

and said, "Thus far shall you come and no farther,
and here shall your proud waves be stopped"?
(Job 38:2–11)

God continues for four more chapters, questioning the human: "Has the rain a father, or who has fathered the drops of dew? From whose womb did the ice come forth, and who has given birth to the hoarfrost of heaven?" (38:28–30). "Who has let the wild ass go free? Who has loosed the bonds of the swift ass, to which I have given the steppe for its home, the salt land for its dwelling place?" (39:5–6). "Is it by your wisdom that the hawk soars and spreads its wings toward the south?" (39:26).

Job is stunned into silence, as well he should be. God is saying, "I am the Creator; you are a creature. My knowledge is vast, and yours is grass. Get back in your lane, groundling." God counters Job's humancentric worldview. As Bill McKibben writes in his reflection on Job, "Most of the action [in the speech] takes place long before the appearance of humans, and on a scale so powerful and vast that we are small indeed in the picture of things."[32] Instead, God presents a world devoid of us, one that exists for its own sake, with its own meaning.

In these chapters extolling the grandeur of creation, humans make one cameo appearance in Job 38:25–27: "Who has cut a channel for the torrents of rain and a way for the thunderbolt, to bring rain on a land where no one lives, on the desert, which is empty of human life, to satisfy the waste and desolate land, and to make the ground put forth grass?"

God is telling Job about a whole world that knows nothing of human existence. The rain God sends is not for human benefit; it satisfies the needs of the land and the animals that feed on its grasses. We get the sense this world could easily exist without us, even though we could never exist without it. (Which is true. It is Reality.) God clearly delights in this human-free world, exults in it, even. If we humans are the crown of creation, there is no whisper of that here. The God who speaks in Job finds diadems everywhere.

We must re-member and remember. It is so easy for settler Christians to forget. Settler Christians, says biblical scholar David Rensberger, must learn how to move from a "stance of restlessness and agitation, autonomy and control, to a stance of creaturely vulnerability and reliance on God."[33] We must turn to resources within our tradition that help us re-member, like this passage from Job. I also believe we have much to learn from the Amish, one of the few white settler communities who impose religious and cultural limits on industrial technology use and, therefore, production and consumption.[34] We have the most to learn from Indigenous Peoples, who have remembered Reality much better than we have. Together, let's create a true counterculture of holy remembering rooted in this "creaturely vulnerability and reliance on God."

TEN

Choosing Hope and Humility

*The ruling paradigm is the endless frontier and its affiliate my-
thologies. Guided by this paradigm, society continues to throw
science and technology at its accelerating scientific and technological problems and it continues to prescribe more growth
to correct the consequences of previous growth. The technical
recommendations become increasingly ad hoc as the discrep-
ancy between scientific progress and societal welfare widens . . .*
—Daniel Sarewitz, *Frontiers of Illusion*[1]

I (SARAH) RECENTLY listened to an episode of one of my
favorite podcasts that explored two popular approaches to ecological restoration on the Galapagos Islands. The first approach
asserts that "real" restoration requires that we attempt to "go
back" or re-create a state of nature from before human impact.
In this view, the wild needs protection from humans, who are
apparently separate from nature. The second view assumes that
since humans are now the driving force in the global environment, we essentially exist as gods and should thus choose responsibly how our environment should look and function and
manage it accordingly.[2]

These approaches to restoration do not contain the entire discussion about conservation, of course, but I think they are poles familiar to most of us. It occurs to me that both views are humancentric. Is it possible for us to imagine a view of nature more consistent with life? Creation is not static, after all, but a process—it is continually unfolding and constantly in flux. There is no pristine "before" that we can return to. It is also foolish to believe we can control or direct it, given that we barely understand the fundamentals of crucial components like soil ecology. We have classified a mere fraction of microbes that make up the vital life-sustaining soil system.[3] How, then, can we assume we should be the decision-maker for systems we are barely beginning to understand?

Economic and cultural systems also experience constant creation and destruction; I wonder if there is some truth here for human systems as well. The systems we inhabit now are a rather new and aberrant experiment, if we mark the beginning of our current era with universal electrification, which was achieved only after World War II. For simplicity's sake, let's say after 1950 in the United States and Canada. By this measure, we have been fully industrialized for nearly seventy-five years. Globally, the UN forecasts universal access to electricity by 2030. So at a global level, we have not yet reached universal electrification. If we assume that human beings have been pretty much the same—have had the same bodies, intelligence, emotional lives—for the entire time we have had written language, then this span of human history is nearly 5,500 years. Just 1 percent of humanity's time on this earth has been in the fully industrialized era, at least in the West. Put another way: If you drew a line from San Francisco to Paris (5,500 miles) and imagine that this line symbolizes the span of collective human experience as we are now, the portion of if that would make up the industrialized era would be from San Francisco to Sacramento: 1 percent of the distance.

There is nothing "normal" about what we are doing now. What we are doing now is a living experiment.

If we step back from the assumption that our current systems are "just the way things are in the real world," is it possible to imagine different systems? Can we imagine systems that are consistent with the Reality of creation, or systems that meet the needs of everyone within ecological limits?

We can't imagine systems in balance with the life-support systems of earth on our own. We must collaborate with Indigenous systems thinkers to identify the crucial components of systems that comply with the Reality of the earth. While I cannot say with authority that all Indigenous Peoples remember how to live in balance with our natural environment, as complexity researcher Joe Brewer says, systems that *are* in balance have been created and are embodied by Indigenous communities.[4] Let's ask people who have chosen not to be assimilated—chosen not to buy into the allure of perpetual growth paid for by the promise of personal wealth. Perhaps, if Indigenous systems thinkers are willing to share their cosmology with us, we can define the underlying assumptions of a truly sustainable economic system, the desired output, and the desired unit of analysis. We can design the "what."

Once we have done this, we can create a process to build it. We can collaborate with many, many creative thinkers (engineers, artists, writers, mathematicians, and other ordinary and not-so-ordinary folks) to discern the "how"—how to redesign our infrastructure, structure, and superstructure. We can then engage with these changes as they unfold. This would result in second-order change. It would result in a new system, with a new purpose, built upon new assumptions.

Many people say to me, "Sarah, you can't critique the current economic system without providing an alternative."[5] To this charge I respond that the task of imagining and building a new system far exceeds the capacity of one imagination. Building a new system will not be described in a five-step plan. We must co-imagine and co-build something that does not yet exist. As Umeek proposed in his book *Principles of Tsawalk*, we can collectively embark on creating a new sociopolitical system in concert, as siblings.

Living in hope is believing that a different world is possible. Living in humility is understanding that we can't build it alone and must collaborate to find it.

REMOVING BARRIERS TO CREATIVE CHANGE

It is not difficult for those facing oppression to understand the need for change. It can be harder, though, for the beneficiaries of oppression. I describe this difficulty to see Reality as "privilege goggles." Our privilege can cause us to rationalize why things are basically okay or need to change only a little bit. Living with privilege can also cause us to conclude that the rules of the system in place are for our benefit; if we follow the rules, everything will work out.

Many times, over the years, well-meaning people have told me that I can trust the authorities to right the wrongs visited upon Indigenous Peoples poisoned and dispossessed by resource extraction and land-grabbing. The injustice goes on, I have been told, simply because I have not tried the right corrective mechanism yet. I must not have tried the United Nations system, or the United States Treasury, or the Organization of American States human rights mechanisms, or the Inter-American Development Bank's ethical guidelines, or the American Red Cross, or the World Health Organization, or the G-7 . . . Dan and I *have* tried all these mechanisms in seeking justice for a people at risk of total annihilation.

The trouble is *not* that we have lacked creativity, or diligence, or knowledge. The trouble is that the global economic system is doing very well what it was designed to do. There is no mechanism of reform on earth that will make a system designed to extract resources at all costs to do the opposite. But this is nearly impossible for good people to believe. They want to believe the systems that serve them are basically benevolent. Privilege goggles make it easier to believe an easy, complicated story than a simple, hard truth.

Another aspect of being privileged is believing that any problem can be solved using a simple, linear process. This belief is rooted in the habit of being in a position of authority. If you are commonly in control of most things in your life, it is easy to slip into the belief that you can control most things. People offering advice from this perspective tell us to approach primary decision-makers with the correct arguments or to seek better contacts. The basic assumption here is that someone in charge need only learn new information to change their mind, and they, in turn, will adjust the system.

Climate change and ecological overshoot present "wicked" problems, or problems of complexity. There is no one right person who can pull the one right string to change the global economic system or slow perpetual growth. We also cannot assume the role of primary decision-makers—most of us do not have the authority or positional legitimacy or access to power in this system.

Social theorist Doug McAdam suggests that activists are rarely empowered to bring about significant reforms by force of will. Rather, our systems offer openings in what he calls the "political opportunity structure." For example, the death of George Floyd at the hands of police in 2020 galvanized action around an event that activists did not cause or have any way to predict. Because they were well-organized, they were poised to mobilize quickly and effectively across the country. In addition, broad access to phone technology and the internet made it possible for ordinary people to take video and share it quickly. Activists did not create these tools but were poised to make good use of them in advancing their agenda. McAdam argues that activists must recruit and organize so that they are prepared for opportunities that have the power to change the narrative or meaningfully challenge social structures. But privilege goggles hamper effective responses to such opportunities. In times of social upheaval, it is easy to let such opportunities pass by and to rely on the authorities to respond, who often use force and even violence to enforce the status quo. It takes effort for those with privilege to respond as a third public, using our access to power and positional power to challenge systems of oppression. To do this effectively, we must organize. Unconventional tactics are effective for the oppressed, who understand that they do not have the option to meaningfully engage systems levers like public hearings, lawsuits, and lobbying powerful decision-makers. Those in a position of privilege often overvalue the tools they believe will result in meaningful change. In the context of climate change, there are not systems levers that can effect meaningful change. Collective action is what is needed to change the world.

Another barrier to creative change is a fear of failure. In fact, one of the most common reasons I hear for not engaging with the work to dismantle the Doctrine of Discovery is a lack of expertise. Many people of privilege believe that to be effective, one needs to have the right degrees, experience, or contacts. This simply is not true. For collective action to be effective, it takes all of us working together. Good people are afraid they will not have the right answers—when no one can. We find the right answers together.

Several years ago, a friend voiced frustration that he had not achieved the social justice goals he had set for himself in five years' time. He was ready to quit. Don't get me wrong, working for something for five years is the commitment of a lot of life energy. But in the scheme of things, in the scheme of generations, it doesn't make sense to give up after five years. We must plan and organize and work across multiple *generations*. We must be committed to the pursuit of justice regardless of whether we see the outcomes we desire in our lifetimes. Martin Luther King Jr. and his contemporaries in the civil rights movement galvanized a nation because of the generations of activists that came before him.

We cannot fear failure. Recently, a colleague was telling me how demoralized she felt by failure. But all innovation comes at the end of a long line of failures. We cannot give up when we fail. We must try everything, all at once. Our lives, and the lives of our children, depend on it.

We cannot be afraid to act for fear of failure. We are already failing—and doing nothing ensures failure. There is freedom in acknowledging that we haven't succeeded yet. We must keep trying, everything.

BUILDING AN EXPLORATORY PROCESS

We will not identify and build a new system whole cloth. One imagination alone is not capable of conceiving of or building something so complex. Capitalism in Europe was not created by one person or authority, but by many, many people working in concert over generations of time. Capitalism was at one time a system in competition with feudalism and mercantilism (a form of economic nationalism), the economic processes that served European monarchies. It displaced these other systems, which diminished as capitalism matured. Feudalism and mercantilism became obsolete over time. Just as capitalism was not created whole cloth, so we could imagine and build a system that serves us and ultimately displaces an old system that no longer does.

Creative process requires a posture of curiosity or exploration without judgment. In our individualistic culture that favors reductionism, we most often approach innovation with a posture of critique, tearing down new ideas that "can't work." We impose a fallacy of the ideal—where we reject any idea as implausible that cannot be implemented in full immediately. Alternatively, we must experiment and further our knowledge by testing ideas, keeping and improving elements that work, and discarding elements that are not useful.

This process might look something like what we have done in this book. We have invited you to explore ideas, consider suggestions or proposals, and bring your curiosity and imagination. This process often requires suspending disbelief—setting aside biases and avoiding snap judgments like "That's impossible!" When we go to the movies, we willingly suspend disbelief by allowing ourselves to be drawn into the story. If it is a movie about Superman, we don't yell at the screen, "A person can't fly!" We sit back and enjoy the story. In a collaborative, imaginative process, we can work together to build a better story.

Participatory action research (PAR) is an exploratory process where content experts and ordinary people codiscover, codesign, and implement solutions to commonly held problems. It is a community-up approach rather than an authority-down process. I have engaged in this method of problem-solving many times with Indigenous communities, where community members identify the problems they wish to explore, guide data collection, and finally identify potential solutions. We have used an iterative, reflective process together, where we agree to try a potential solution, reflect on our progress, and redirect our work depending on what we find. This methodology is useful in exploring "wicked problems," or very complex problems, where co-participants do not have legitimate power in the system. We have employed creativity, trying many novel approaches, regardless of how counterintuitive they may seem to authorities or so-called experts.

I describe participatory action research as it is described in the language of Western social science. But it has been effective in Indigenous communities whom I have worked with in the Guyana Shield because, at least in part, it replicates those communities' collective decision-making process. The exploratory processes employed by Indigenous communities can help us to imagine and build a system that works for our world and its people. The assumptions and practices of exploration used by Indigenous Peoples can help us to grow beyond the biases of our current paradigm and test ideas we have not yet thought of.

IMAGINING THE RENEWED WORLD

What keeps us from imagining a new world? Maybe it's because we don't know where to begin or despair that a new world is possible. But if our lives really depended on change, we would find a way to begin, wouldn't we? If my son were deathly ill, what would I (Sheri) not do to make sure he was properly diagnosed and given the treatments he needed? I would talk to anyone I could, knock on any doors. I would assemble experts. I would experiment with any treatment I thought might help. I would exhaust all my resources seeking his healing, like the merchant who gave up everything for the pearl of great price (Matthew 13:45).

Since we are not doing this in response to our dire climate situation, I conclude that we don't understand the severity of the problem, or that we are not yet experiencing its severity, or that we've gone numb. For those of us wearing privilege goggles, we may say: "It's not that bad, is it? And surely this or that tweak to the system will solve things, right? At least, I think it will solve it for me and those I care most about." Even after all my work of learning to see with new eyes, I can still find my thoughts going in that direction, like a default setting. Then I know that I am wearing my privilege goggles again. When I notice that happening, I re-member. I remind myself of Reality.

What keeps us from imagining a new world? Maybe it's because we don't like the uncertainty that comes with this imagining. We prefer security and certainty—of course! We don't like to remember that, as Umeek describes, we are "perched precariously in a balance between creation and destruction."[6] By saying that we need to imagine a new world, we acknowledge that the present world is not as secure and certain as our privilege would have us believe—or as our fear wants us to believe.

A few years ago, journalist Rachel Donald started the podcast *Planet: Critical*. She interviewed scientists, economists, academics, activists, politicians, and journalists for a deeper understanding of the climate crisis. Her research revealed a failed system at the intersection of energy, the economy, politics, and our worldview, or the stories we tell ourselves. In a talk summarizing what she has learned, she said:

> How do we begin to tell a story that doesn't yet have an ending? We—our world—is in desperate need of experimentation. But as society becomes increasingly precarious for even the privileged, imagination poses as much of a risk as the system itself. As if feeling its fragility, its vulnerability, people are doubling down on the status quo. They are afraid one wrong move may collapse the structures they've come to depend on. Certainty is sought in authoritarian figures and neofascist regimes; these bare-faced lies promise a return to the past because both the truth of the present and the unknowability of the future are too much to bear.[7]

As society becomes increasingly precarious for even the privileged, imagination poses as much of a risk as the system itself. These words "speak to my condition," as the Quakers say. As much as I think things are bad, as much as I think we need something new, I know that part of me is afraid to imagine because it reminds me of the precarity of this world.

It is an illusion that the world isn't precarious. Permanence is an illusion. Security is an illusion. We know this viscerally when we get the diagnosis, when the pandemic hits, when our car starts skidding off the road, when our loved one takes their last breath. Nothing is guaranteed to us. All is gift. When my son became ill with a mysterious virus in the fifth grade and landed in the hospital in a coma, the tenuousness of his life and sheer gift of the 3,998 days we had had with him became so obvious, so real. During that time, I felt as if I fully understood the gift and fragility of life. When it became apparent he would be okay, I told myself: Don't forget.

One of the things I appreciate about the Amish people I have known is their acceptance of this precariousness. They know they are earthly creatures and that they are not in control. This keeps them humble. When the accident happens, or the fire consumes or, God forbid, the shooter enters the schoolhouse, they grieve and suffer. But they also accept. They are not surprised, because their religion and culture remind them regularly that nothing is guaranteed. Life is a gift from the Creator. All we have is a gift from God.

This is why we need to learn from Indigenous Peoples, who remember better than we do and who have already experienced the end of the world. They have already lived through the apocalypse and have wisdom for us as we face one now.

Sarah recently told me about a metaphor from one of her favorite documentaries, *The Corporation*. When people were first experimenting with flight, they would strap wings onto their back and then jump off cliffs, flapping their wings. For a moment, they felt as if they were flying. But they were free-falling toward the earth. The laws of physics always trump our illusions.

Indigenous people know that the dominant culture is free-falling even though it thinks it is flying high. The laws of ecological reality (including physics) always trump our illusions. Sarah said to me: "Everyone longs for security and permanence. Why wouldn't we? But the amount of resources it takes to maintain that illusion is killing us."

Where does this leave us? It leaves us in the place of imagination, the place of becoming. "Evolution, life itself, is the relationship between things," Rachel Donald said during her talk.

"It is within the in-betweenness that possibility lies and change occurs." In that in-between space, all life is *becoming*, the etymology of which means "to move towards." Life is always in motion, fluid, flowing. We dream of a renewed world, and then we start moving toward it. The point is not to arrive, but to navigate towards that destination. And then, one day, we find change has happened. "The world becomes a new thing by the very truth of possibility, by the very act of experimenting," Donald said. "Yet we suffer from this illusion that the new world order must spring up from the ground fully formed. . . . How can we reimagine uncertainty as the place where possibility emerges?"[8]

I am moved by her words. They speak to the deepest reality I know, which is God. In Exodus 3, God appears before Moses in the burning bush and reveals God's name to Moses. The name is often translated as, "I Am Who I Am," but it can also translated as "I Will Be What I Will Be" or "I Am Becoming What I Am Becoming." God is Being itself, the Ground of our existence, the One in whom we live and move and have our being (Acts 17:28). But God is also Becoming itself. God is evolving, never static, always moving. In almost the last sentence of the Bible, God says, "See, I am making all things new" (Revelation 21:5). Always and everywhere, God is making all things new.

Friends, I am afraid. I am afraid of the world in which my son will come of age and grow up. But I am also hopeful *because* things are uncertain, because things are changing, because I don't know what's going to happen and don't know what to do. I am excited because I am alive at this time of becoming. That uncertainty is where God is moving. That unknowing is where God is moving. That precariousness is where God is moving. That has always been the case. Throughout scripture, God beckons the faithful to step into the unknown, trusting that

God, like a mother eagle, will rise up from underneath them and support them as they take their first fledgling flight into the unknown. Can you feel that with me? Will you, with me, step off the edge and trust that we will be raised up on God's wings?

CELEBRATING THE "FOOLISH"

There are some things I (Sarah) know:

It is possible to be wretched-poor-silenced-forgotten—and to change the world. It is possible to be encumbered-ignored-mediocre-ordinary—and to change the world.

In fact, we—the subjugated and ordinary people—make up most of humanity. We must imagine together the world we want to live in and build it.

If you are discouraged, this reimagined world is for you. If you are tired, this reimagined world is for you. If you do not know your purpose, this reimagined world is for you. If you are demoralized, this reimagined world is for you. If you are hopeful, this reimagined world is for you.

The current systems are failing; they cannot endure, because they were not built to comply with Reality. Divest your heart and your will from longing for failing systems. They are diseased. We must build new ones.

The people who built these failing systems are no more brilliant and special than we are. In fact, they are quite the opposite when we measure the current systems against Reality. We must quit believing that systems leaders (captains of industry, political leaders, the mighty in society) will save us. They will not. We are smart enough to build new systems. We must do this.

We can live on this earth without resource extraction.

We can live on this earth. Without resource extraction. We can live without resource extraction.

We can humble ourselves and call on our Indigenous relatives to explore, with hope and humility, Indigenous cosmology and tools to learn how to live together in balance with the earth—what the Diné call the way of beauty. We can build models in collaboration with these cosmologies, then call on ordinary people to build the systems. You do not have to be a politician, a corporate giant, or a rock star to change the world, to build the kindom of God. You can be you, joining together with other people.

Alone, each of us may feel insignificant: just one life that is easy to dismiss. But together, we are stronger.

What is true cannot be diminished by silencing one voice. Our thirst for the truth is not an insurrection or rebellion. It is an assertion of our dignity. Our dignity cannot be given to us by authorities; it is our birthright and ours to have forever. They can deny it or acknowledge it—but our dignity is not theirs to take away.

Do not live in fear. Walk in certainty, in the nobility of a mighty spirit that is your history and future. It is your birthright to seek out others who are excellent, to work toward a world you imagine, a world where we are free. Our work is not easy but profoundly necessary. The survival of life on Earth depends on our ability to see past the fabricated reality constructed to diminish us and justify the entitled. The bonds essential to this reality cage us all with the logic of greed, selfishness, and determinism: the logic of death. We must find the courage to acknowledge Reality glimmering everywhere around us, embodied by the Creator. And we must have the courage to join together to imagine, create, and construct, with hope and humility, systems that pursue life.

Fourth Vision and Poem

The Remnant (2003)

This vision arrived in 2003, unbidden, as I sat alone in my apartment in Seattle.

I am in South Korea. I travel toward a large, square structure, several stories tall. People from around the world are streaming to the building from all directions. As I enter a large, empty space, I see people greeting each other and chatting excitedly. While I do not know anyone in the crowd, I do not feel anxious or alone. There is a feeling of celebration in the air and an excitement—expectancy. There are representatives from across the territories of Earth assembled, from Asia, Africa, the Americas, Europe, Oceana, the Pacific, and beyond. Many people wear traditional dress, and many are dressed in contemporary clothing. The atmosphere is relaxed, and in time, the people settle into silence.

A group emerges from the assembly and begins to dance in a column of maybe twenty men. Standing two abreast, with pairs falling behind the two that head the column, they begin to sing. The song is a call and response. The song leader tells a story in song, and the rest of the men in the column respond:

I.

    I was at home in my own country
    When my foreign brother called to me
    He said, "While idle were attacked
    By an enemy we cannot hold back
    On strange ships from the North
    Their legions rode in like a storm
    They wasted all in a few weeks
    And what remains is under siege."

    O my God almighty
    Hear us, bring us peace

    We left our fields we left our towns
    And loaded ships with food and arms
    We thousands assembled on the shore
    To kiss our wives then sail for war
    Our hearts heavy, we're men of peace
    But to our brothers we owed allegiance
    And as we sailed a spell was cast
    So now a thousand years had passed.

    O my God almighty
    Hear us in our fast

    Half were delivered to the sea
    A quarter died of disbelief

Half who woke died of despair
Those who remain are numbered here
We raced back home to find our wives
Of our loved ones, none survived
An evil presence filled our lands
The same storm riders who'd slain our friends.

O my God almighty
Hear us, heal our lands

We've crossed the world to find you here
We come with hope and faith held dear
Although we're weary, our numbers small
Our friends long dead, we heed your call
Your children too, gone from this place
Most of them killed, the rest enslaved
The few descendants who remain
Don't remember their true names.

Our wives are dead, our children too
Our descendants slaves to an evil few
Still, we return despite our pain
The remnant here we come to join
Despite all, we lift up praise
We come to serve the one true Name.

O my God almighty
Hear us praise your Name

At the end of their story the column abruptly stopped, and another group, dancing in a column two-by-two, took up the song with their own verse:

II.

In times of peace and of the sword
We've lived on high and served the Lord
Witnessed cities built and razed
For us a lifetime is as a day.

But wails of fear and deep lament
Broke through heavens' firmament
When His people called the Name most high
On wings of flame, we filled the sky

Our charge to heal and to protect
On His behalf our legion sent
But in our task delayed, by war
A thousand years it raged, or more.

The sky turned black, the sea was red
As we fought our brothers to the death
From light to black their hearts had turned
To serve themselves, and creation, burn.

They said, "We've served the Maker since the void
Together, our power exceeds the Lord.
Why serve creation when we are gods
When we are joined to this strange force?"

We fought these beings to the death
Most of our number died with them
We'd never known such death before
We'd never known the loss of war.

We mourn now for our numbered dead
Both dark and light; for all were once friends
There was no victory for us
But despite all, we come at last.

Our wings are battered, our numbers small
Yet we who still live heed your call
The earth is full of evil men
The young ones free from innocence.

In agony we raise the Name
Of Him who covers every shame
We sing together, we hope, we wait
To join the remnant, we celebrate.

When their song ended, they stopped. The assembled remnant, I among them, raised our hands in praise. I knew I would spend the rest of my life joining with the remnant—those of us who can hear the call of the old songs gathering, in resistance. Collectively, as human beings who are guided by the Spirit of Life, we determine the destiny of humanity and even the world.

The Remnant (2013)

Ten years later, I found myself physically in Busan, South Korea, on an Indigenous delegation to the World Council of Churches. While I was alone in my room, I received another vision that was a continuation of the first. As if no time had passed, I found myself in the same large, empty vision space.

I found myself standing quietly among representatives assembled from across the territories of Earth. The two groups of singers had just finished their songs. An air of excitement filled the space, crackling with energy. Drums began sounding with a quick tempo that grew faster and faster. All at once, every woman assembled began dancing in a frenzy, singing the same words.

I danced with them, my body moved to the voices and the drums, the words came from my belly, up through my body, from my lips, words I knew deep within me, spoken for the children and grandchildren I had not yet borne.

"We will carry out this work because we carry the names of our children in our bones."

Doors

There is only one way, and it is the way of Life.
There is only one door to this Way,
    but that door is everywhere.

Still your mind.
Still your body.
Still your breath, and see how, everywhere,
    there are doors.
They are all around you,
    with barely a space between them!
They are within you. You are full of holes!
And they stand open, waiting
    for you to step through.
They will stay open until you do.

Do you see, now, the generosity of doors?
Do you see, now, the inevitability of your arrival?

ACKNOWLEDGMENTS

FROM SARAH

First, I want to acknowledge my husband, Dan Peplow, for years of collaboration: co-thinking, co-writing, and co-labor. The ideas I express here were first explored around the dinner table and on long drives, during untold hours of living and working side by side. Thank you for the careful attention you give to each topic brought forward for discussion, and for your patience talking through the same problems sometimes dozens of times. While my name is on the cover, the ideas I write about here are really a product of a collaboration between the two of us.

The home where we live is a true companion too. It is a privilege to live as a neighbor and guest on the homeland of the Confederated Bands and Tribes of the Yakama Nation. I learn from the beautiful, abundant life here day after day. I am thankful to the elders of this land for carefully stewarding this homeland and its sacred waters. And I want to thank you, Dan, for your labor and nurture of this place that makes it possible for me to be here.

I also want to thank my co-author, Sheri, who has been my conversation partner for the better part of a decade. For many years, we spoke with each other every week at the same time. We spent hundreds of hours learning and exploring together. Once we launched the *Dismantling the Doctrine of Discovery* podcast together in 2021, our conversations spilled beyond our weekly calls into a shared vocation. I am thankful for your patience and wisdom, for your humor and faithfulness. It is wonderful to get to work together.

Members of the Coalition to Dismantle the Doctrine of Discovery have provided community, true solidarity, and friendship to me over many years. Thanks to our co-founder, Anita Amstutz, and long-time chair Jonathan Neufeld. Thanks also to Katerina Gea, Tim Nafziger, Luke Gascho, Carol Rose, John Stoesz, Alison Brookins, Marisa Smucker, Ken Gingerich, Lars Akerson, Manuel May, Hallie Liu Rogers, Sara Gurule, Bizzy Feekes, John Braun, and many others. Individually and collectively, you have heavily influenced my thinking. I owe each of you profound thanks.

Thank you to spiritual leaders Steve Darden and Mark MacDonald for your guidance, wisdom, and friendship over many years. I would not have the courage to write about these things without your example and leadership.

I also want to acknowledge the creative, revolutionary mind of my son, Micah. It is such a privilege to get to talk and learn with you as you critically explore our world. I am thankful that you share your thoughts with me.

Finally, I want to acknowledge the ones that will come after us. My mother-in-law (Etta) will turn 90 this year. My youngest grandson (Ziggy) is under one year old. Side by side, they bookend the lives of four generations, spanning nearly ninety years. These two embody the range in experience from growing up without indoor plumbing to a world shaped by artificial intelligence. Our shared context changes so quickly. My hope is contained in the next four generations, when Ziggy is 89. We must equip him, and the generations that follow his, to imagine and build a world rooted in Reality.

FROM SHERI

Thanks to the good people at Herald Press: Laura Leonard for having the original idea that Sarah Augustine should write a book on climate change; and Sara Versluis, Elisabeth Ivey, and Rachel Martens, who made me sound like a much better writer than I actually am and encouraged us the whole way.

Thanks, Sarah, for inviting me to write this book with you. I had been silently germinating a book like this for years and was delighted and surprised when you proposed that we coauthor the book still forming in my imagination. That the same book existed in both of our brains is indicative of the thousands of hours of conversations we've had together over the years, conversations that I cherish and that have changed my life.

I want to thank the congregation I pastor, First Mennonite Church of San Francisco, for supporting me every step of the way in writing this book. You gave me necessary time, space, and encouragement. Even more so, for almost thirty years you have been the community where I can "see the new world coming, when everyone is free." You are my hope.

I want to thank the leadership of our church's Climate Action Group that served as my first readers—Steve Kusmer, Pat Plude, Helen Stoltzfus, and especially, Jim Lichti. Your thoughtful and encouraging feedback made this book better and helped me know I was on the right track. I also want to thank the members of the "Doom Group," a reading group that focuses on many of the themes mentioned in this book. That group includes Pat, Steve, and Jim, as well as Chris Lotz and Randy Yee.

Thanks to my pastoral colleagues, Pat and Joanna Lawrence Shenk. Pastoring our beloved community with you has been one of the great joys of my life.

Thank you to my ancestors who bequeathed me a "goodly heritage" as well as an injustice needing repair. Both have shaped my life's work. I want to especially thank my most recent ancestors—my beloved parents, Beverly and Lyman. Everything I am has been built on the sure foundation you gave me.

Thank you to my husband and partner of thirty-eight years, Jerome Baggett. Thank you for always asking "Is there anything I can do to help?" as I sat down to write. It was a relief to pass on errands and chores to you when writing dominated my days. But much more than that, your brilliance as a sociologist and thinker have formed how I view the world. Your insights and wisdom are all over this book, even if I didn't attribute them to you.

Finally, thank you to my son, Patrick. It took me years to decide whether or not I should bring a child into this world. Then, a dear friend said to me that perhaps there is a child wanting to be born into just such a time. You are the son of my older age and, like the biblical Sarah, I laughed with joy and wonder when you were born. The joy and wonder remain. You give me courage and hope to fight for the world that must be.

NOTES

Preface

1   We intentionally use "kindom" instead of "kingdom of God" to be gender neutral, to avoid connotations with imperialism and hierarchy, and to reflect the Indigenous understanding that everything in creation is kin to each other.

2   Rebecca Beisler, "Let Us Work Together" *Uniting Church Australia*, August 17, 2020, https://uniting.church/lilla-watson-let-us-work -together/.

3   Mennonites and other Anabaptists have often drawn on Jesus' prayer in John 17, including verse 14: "I have given them your word, and the world has hated them because they do not belong to the world, just as I do not belong to the world."

4   Anthropologist Marvin Harris presents the concept of three societal levels of infrastructure, structure, and superstructure in his 1968 text, *The Rise of Anthropological Theory*.

5   Matthew Davis, "Can Inequality Be Blamed on the Agricultural Revolution?," World Economic Forum, October 25, 2018, https:// www.weforum.org/agenda/2018/10/how-the-agricultural -revolution-made-us-inequal.

6   Grace Pritchard Burson, "The Anthropocene Fall: Agriculture and Genesis 3," *Earth & Altar*, February 26, 2021, https:// earthandaltarmag.com/posts/yhllsd3vzq1otehw1lxexh624ep07x.

7   Aylin Woodward, "European Colonizers Killed So Many Indigenous Americans That the Planet Cooled Down, a Group of Researchers Concluded," Business Insider, February 9, 2019, https://www .businessinsider.com/climate-changed-after-europeans-killed -indigenous-americans-2019-2.

8   Steven Charleston, *The Four Vision Quests of Jesus* (New York: Morehouse, 2015), 36.

9   Charleston, *Four Vision Quests of Jesus*, 39.

10 Charleston, *Four Vision Quests of Jesus*, 39.

11 Brad Plumer, "Earth Is Near the Tipping Point for a Hot Future," *New York Times*, March 21, 2023, https://www.nytimes.com/2023/03/20/climate/global-warming-ipcc-earth.html.

12 For now, let's bracket the disturbing fact that the Promised Land was already inhabited. The supposed conquest of the Promised Land has provided justification for Europeans to conquer and seize land from Indigenous Peoples around the world. I say "supposed" conquest because no archeological evidence exists to suggest the Israelites conquered the cities of Canaan. Instead, the Israelites seemed to have arrived more peacefully over decades. See Israel Finkelstein and Neil Asher Silberman, *The Bible Unearthed: Archeology's New Vision of Ancient Israel and the Origin of Its Sacred Texts* (New York: Free Press, 2001).

Chapter 1

1   Daniel Peplow and Sarah Augustine, "Community-Directed Risk Assessment of Mercury Exposure from Gold Mining in Suriname," *Revista Panamericana de Salud Pública* 22, no. 3 (2007), 202–10.

2   Frank Holmes, "The Race for Copper, the Metal of the Future," *Forbes*, June 1, 2021, https://www.forbes.com/sites/greatspeculations/2021/06/01/the-race-for-copper-the-metal-of-the-future.

3   Settler colonialism is a distinct form of colonization that seeks to replace an Indigenous population with a new settler population, often through genocide and forced assimilation. From Jamila Osman, "What Is Colonialism? A History of Violence, Control and Exploitation," *Teen Vogue*, October 11, 2020, https://www.teenvogue.com/story/colonialism-explained.

4   See "Planetary Dashboard Shows 'Great Acceleration' in Human Activity since 1950," International Geosphere-Biosphere Programme, January 15, 2015, http://www.igbp.net/news/pressreleases/pressreleases/planetarydashboardshowsgreataccelerationinhuman activitysince1950.5.950c2fa1495db7081eb42.html.

5   Larry L. Rasmussen, *Earth-Honoring Faith: Religious Ethics in a New Key* (New York: Oxford University Press, 2015), 58. Also see Tom Murphy, "Death by Hockey Sticks," *Do the Math* (blog), September 13, 2022, https://dothemath.ucsd.edu/2022/09/death-by-hockey-sticks/.

6   Says energy scientist Vaclav Smil of this post–World War II era: "More people now enjoy a higher standard of living, and do so for

many years and in better health, than at any time in history. Yet these beneficiaries are still a minority (only about a fifth) of the world's population, whose total count is approaching 8 billion people." Vaclav Smil, *How the World Really Works: The Science behind How We Got Here and Where We're Going* (New York: Viking, 2022), 1.

7 "Planetary Boundaries," Stockholm Resilience Centre, Stockholm University, September 19, 2012, https://www.stockholmresilience .org/research/planetary-boundaries.html.

8 Purple martin populations are in decline around the world. See Bob Bystrom, "Why Has the Purple Martin Population Tumbled in Minnesota?," Bob Bystrom (*blog*), November 1, 2015, http://bob -bystrom.com/robert_bystrom/Of_Forests,_Fields,_Ponds,_and_ Gardens/Entries/2015/11/1_Why_Has_the_Purple_Martin_ Population_Tumbled_in_Minnesota.html.

9 Joanne Schnurr, "Solving the Mystery of the Declining Purple Martin Population," Ottawa CTV News, updated July 7, 2014, https:// ottawa.ctvnews.ca/solving-the-mystery-of-the-declining-purple -martin-population-1.1902969.

10 "Are Fireflies Disappearing?," *Farmers' Almanac*, March 25, 2021, https://www.farmersalmanac.com/are-fireflies-disappearing-35646.

11 "Living Planet Report 2022," World Wide Fund for Nature, last modified May 10, 2023, https://livingplanet.panda.org/en-US/.

12 Ben Guarino, "'Hyperalarming' Study Shows Massive Insect Loss," *Washington Post*, October 15, 2018, https://www.washingtonpost .com/science/2018/10/15/hyperalarming-study-shows-massive -insect-loss/.

13 Dave Davies, "The World's Insect Population Is in Decline—and That's Bad News for Humans," NPR, February 24, 2022, https:// www.npr.org/sections/goatsandsoda/2022/02/24/1082752634/ the-insect-crisis-oliver-milman.

14 Environmental Defense Fund, "How Will Climate Change Affect the Midwest?," last modified May 9, 2014, https://www.edf.org/sites/ default/files/content/regional_releases_midwest.pdf.

15 Mike Amaranthus and Bruce Allyn, "Healthy Soil Microbes, Healthy People," *Atlantic*, June 11, 2013, https://www.theatlantic.com/ health/archive/2013/06/healthy-soil-microbes-healthy-people/ 276710/.

Chapter 2

1 On the reservation where I (Sarah) live, Washington State regulators do not have environmental jurisdiction—only the federal regulator, the Environmental Protection Agency, does. For this reason, there

is abundant dumping on the reservation that is illegal even a few
counties away. The nitrates in the water table have health impacts on
residents, especially pregnant women and infants, because nitrates
lower the blood's ability to carry oxygen. Kate Prengaman, "Study
Reveals Details on Nitrate Pollution," *Yakima Herald-Republic*,
December 22, 2014, https://www.yakimaherald.com/news/local/
b-study-reveals-details-on-nitrate-pollution-b/article_76ac22b0
-dc2c-571a-8573-7c33ddcabb62.html.

2 Making Caring Common Project, "The Children We Mean to Raise:
The Real Messages Adults Are Sending about Values," Harvard Graduate School of Education, 2014, https://static1.squarespace.com/
static/5b7c56e255b02c683659fe43/t/5bae776da4222ffd8b7508a2/
1538160493964/executive-summary-children-raise.pdf.

3 This and the previous quotations are from Tovia Smith, "For Most
Kids, Nice Finishes Last," NPR, July 14, 2014, https://www.npr.org/
sections/ed/2014/07/14/331346884/for-most-kids-nice-finishes-last.

4 Veneta Lusk, "The Market Crash of 2008 Explained," Wealth
Simple, last modified June 5, 2019, https://www.wealthsimple.com/
en-ca/learn/2008-market-crash.

5 Josephson Institute's 2012 Report Card on the Ethics of American
Youth (Los Angeles: Josephson Institute of Ethics, 2012), quoted in
Richard Weissbourd et al., *Turning the Tide II: How Parents and High
Schools Can Cultivate Ethical Character and Reduce Distress in the
College Admissions Process* (Cambridge: Harvard Graduate School of
Education, 2019).

6 Making Caring Common Project, "Children We Mean to Raise."

7 Making Caring Common Project, "Children We Mean to Raise," 9.

8 Farron Cousins, "Massey Energy Is Not the Only Mountaintop
Removal Mining Villain," DeSmog, June 10, 2011, https://www
.desmog.com/2011/06/10/massey-energy-not-only-mountaintop
-removal-mining-villain/.

9 Although there are recent efforts to create a nonbinary Hebrew to use
in prayers and spoken language, Hebrew is a binary-gendered language.
Adam, which means man/mankind, is a masculine noun and often
refers to humankind in general. The common ending that makes a singular masculine noun into a female noun is "ah." Thus, although there
is no feminine version of *adam*, if there were, it would be *adamah*!

10 "How Is the Human Body Like Planet Earth?" Wonderopolis,
https://wonderopolis.org/wonder/How-Is-the-Human-Body-Like
-Planet-Earth.

11 Bill Moyers, *Genesis: A Living Conversation* (New York: Doubleday,
1996), 12.

12 Interestingly, the word *matter* comes from the same root as *mother* and *matrix*.

13 Aaron von Frank, "Five Amazing Soil Facts That Will Change the Way You View the World," GrowJourney, July 30, 2018, https:// www.growjourney.com/five-amazing-soil-facts-will-change-way-view -world/.

14 Zijun Li, "The Environmental Impacts on the Reversal of the Chicago River," University of Chicago English Language Institute, August 27, 2021, https://voices.uchicago.edu/findingchicago/2021/08/27/ the-environmental-impacts-on-the-reversal-of-the-chicago-river/.

Chapter 3

1 This and the previous quotation are from John Eligon and Lindsey Chutel, "The World Got Gems. A Mining Town Got Buried in the Sludge," *New York Times*, September 23, 2022.

2 Lisa Friedman, "Ten Years After Deepwater Horizon, U.S. Is Still Vulnerable to Catastrophic Spills," *New York Times*, April 19, 2022; John Kelly DeSantis, "Oil Spill in Terrebonne Bay on Opening Day of Shrimp Season Causes Grief for Fishermen," *Houma Courier*, August 20, 2022.

3 Lisa Friedman, "Where the New Climate Law Means More Drilling, Not Less," *New York Times*, September 14, 2022.

4 Jedediah Britton-Purdy, "Humans Have Rapidly Remade the Earth —and Imperiled Its Future," *Washington Post*, March 12, 2021, https://www.washingtonpost.com/outlook/humans-have-rapidly -remade-the-earth--and-imperiled-its-future/2021/03/11/d72163c2 -75fb-11eb-948d-19472e683521_story.html.

5 Tom Murphy, "Finite Feeding Frenzy," Resilience, December 6, 2022, https://www.resilience.org/stories/2022-12-06/finite-feeding -frenzy/.

6 Erik Assadourian, "Raindrops Keep Falling on My Head . . . and They Slide Right Off," Gaian Way, October 10, 2022, https:// gaianism.org/raindrops-keep-falling-on-my-head/.

7 Mark H. Burton, "Invisible Workers, Invisible Systems," Resilience, April 27, 2021, https://www.resilience.org/stories/2021-04-27/ invisible-workers-invisible-systems/.

8 Scholar Michael Lerner defines the polycrisis as a "confluence of environmental, social, technological, financial-economic, natural and other forces" that interact "with ever increasing unpredictability, rapidity and power." Michael Lerner, "Navigating the Polycrisis—Life in Turbulent Times," *Angle of Vision* (blog), April 19, 2023, https:// angleofvision.org/2023/04/19/turbulent-times-2.

9   Della Duncan and Robert Raymond, "14: The Green Transition, Pt. 1—The Problem with Green Capitalism," September 13, 2022, in *Upstream*, podcast, MP3 audio, https://www.upstreampodcast.org/conversations.

10 James B. Nelson, *Embodiment: An Approach to Sexuality and Christian Theology* (Minneapolis: Augsburg Publishing House, 1978), 269.

11 Nelson, *Embodiment*, 50.

12 Nelson, *Embodiment*, 269.

13 Randy S. Woodley, *Indigenous Theology and the Western Worldview: A Decolonized Approach to Christian Doctrine*, Acadia Studies in Bible and Theology (Grand Rapids: Baker Academic, 2022), 73.

14 Andreas Weber, "Nourishing Community in Pandemic Times," *Heinrich Böll Foundation*, April 22, 2020, https://in.boell.org/en/nourishing-community-pandemic-times. Weber borrows the idea of the "Western cognitive empire" from Portuguese sociologist Boaventura de Sousa Santos.

15 Joe Brewer, *The Design Pathway for Regenerating Earth* (Barichara: Earth Regenerators Press, 2021), 51.

16 Robin McKie, "'The Wondrous Map': How Unlocking Human DNA Changed the Course of Science," *Guardian*, June 21, 2020, https://www.theguardian.com/science/2020/jun/21/human-genome-project-unlocking-dna-covid-19-cystic-fibrosis-molecular-scientists.

17 Fritjof Capra and Pier Luigi Luisi, "The Mechanistic View of Life," in *The Systems View of Life: A Unifying Vision* (Cambridge: Cambridge University Press, 2014), 35–44.

18 Woodley, *Indigenous Theology*, 78.

19 Carey Gilliam, "Long-Lasting Health Impacts of DDT Highlighted in New Study," *Sierra*, April 23, 2021, https://www.sierraclub.org/sierra/long-lasting-health-impacts-ddt-highlighted-new-study.

20 Vince Beiser, "Why the World Is Running Out of Sand," BBC, November 17, 2019, https://www.bbc.com/future/article/20191108-why-the-world-is-running-out-of-sand.

21 Hop Hopkins, "Racism Is Killing the Planet," *Sierra*, June 8, 2020, https://www.sierraclub.org/sierra/racism-killing-planet.

22 Saskia Sassen, "The Rise of Extractive Logics," University of California Berkeley Global Urban Humanities, March 13, 2018, https://globalurbanhumanities.berkeley.edu/saskia-sassen.

23 Energy scientist Vaclav Smil points out that "most modern urbanites are . . . disconnected not only from the ways we produce our food but also from the ways we build our machines and devices, and the growing mechanization of all productive activity means that only a very small share of the global population now engages in delivering

civilization's energy and the materials that comprise our modern world." *The Way the World Really Works*, 3. This disconnection from material reality, which is a big change from one hundred or even fifty years ago, contributes to the abstraction of the dominant culture's worldview.

24 Anitra Nelson and Brian Coffey, "What Is 'Ecological Economics' and Why Do We Need to Talk about It?," The Conversation, November 4, 2019, https://theconversation.com/what-is-ecological -economics-and-why-do-we-need-to-talk-about-it-123915.

25 N. J. Hagens, "Economics for the Future—Beyond the Superorganism," *Ecological Economics* 169 (2020), https://www.sciencedirect .com/science/article/pii/S0921800919310067.

26 Naomi Klein, *This Changes Everything: Capitalism vs. the Climate* (New York: Simon and Schuster, 2014), 170.

27 "If you've reached the limit of your stock to make money, you get a derivative on the stock. You go meta, one level of abstraction above the thing and you make money off the financialization." Nate Hagens, "Ep. 36: The Ultimate Exit Strategy," September 14, 2022, in *The Great Simplification*, podcast, MP3 audio, https://www .thegreatsimplification.com/episode/36-douglas-rushkoff.

28 Douglas Rushkoff, "What Zuckerberg's Metaverse Means to Our Humanity," CNN, October 29, 2021, https://www.cnn.com/2021/ 10/28/opinions/zuckerberg-facebook-meta-rushkoff.

29 He explores this in his book *Homo Deus: A Brief History of Tomorrow* (New York: Harper Collins, 2017).

Chapter 4

1 Julian Brave NoiseCat, "John McCain Fought for Native Religious Freedom, Then Sold Sacred Oak Flat," Huffpost, January 6, 2016, https://www.huffpost.com/entry/john-mccain-fought-for-native -religious-freedom-then-he-sold-sacred-oak-flat_n_ 5605990ce4b0768126fd7b70.

2 Dismantling the Doctrine of Discovery Coalition, "Repair Network Call: Protect Oak Flat!," YouTube video, 1:03:05, October 4, 2022, https://youtu.be/nqRMKFfeVW0.

3 See, for example, Carly Wanna, "Replacing US Coal Plants with Solar and Wind Is Cheaper Than Running Them," *Bloomberg News*, January 30, 2023, https://www.bloomberg.com/news/articles/ 2023-01-30/new-us-solar-and-wind-cost-less-than-keeping-coal -power-running.

4 Winne van Woerden, "Green Growth," Resilience, November 1, 2022, https://www.resilience.org/stories/2022-11-01/green-growth.

5   Chris Smaje, "The Three Causes of Global Ecocide," Small Farm Future, April 3, 2020, https://smallfarmfuture.org.uk/?p=1602.

6   Christina Majaski, "What Is the Invisible Hand in Economics?," Investopedia, March 21, 2023, https://www.investopedia.com/terms/i/invisiblehand.asp.

7   Hickel, who is of European descent, grew up in Eswatini, formerly known as Swaziland. I have sometimes wondered if his upbringing in the Global South made him especially mindful of colonization and the injustice of our global economic system. In addition to being a rare academic who can write well for popular audiences, he is one of the few economists looking at ecological issues who incorporates an analysis of historical and ongoing colonization into his work. I have found him to be a clear and ethical guide when confronting the issues addressed in this book. I am especially indebted to his work in this chapter, particularly his historical overview in chapter 1 of *Less Is More: How Degrowth Will Save the World* (New York: Random House, 2020). See also Ian Angus, "Robbing the Soil, 1: Commons and Classes before Capitalism," Resilience, August 11, 2021, https://www.resilience.org/stories/2021-08-11/robbing-the-soil-1-commons-and-classes-before-capitalism/.

8   In a captive market, consumers are severely limited in choosing from whom to purchase.

9   Jason Hickel, "The Age of Imperialism Is Not Over—but We Can End It," *Current Affairs*, December 5, 2021, https://www.currentaffairs.org/2021/12/the-age-of-imperialism-is-not-over-but-we-can-end-it.

10 Oxford University School of Geography and Environment, "How to Save the Planet: Degrowth vs Green Growth?," YouTube video, 1:33:04, September 2, 2022, https://youtu.be/YxJrBR0lg6s.

11 Hickel, *Less Is More*, 48–49.

12 Hickel, *Less Is More*, 58–59.

13 Sarah Augustine, *The Land Is Not Empty: Following Jesus in Dismantling the Doctrine of Discovery* (Harrisonburg: Herald Press, 2021).

14 See Leigh Raymond, *Reclaiming the Atmospheric Commons: The Regional Greenhouse Gas Initiative and a New Model of Emissions Trading* (Cambridge: MIT Press, 2016).

15 Kate Hodal, "One in 200 People Is a Slave. Why?," *The Guardian*, February 25, 2019, https://www.theguardian.com/news/2019/feb/25/modern-slavery-trafficking-persons-one-in-200.

16 Hickel, "Imperialism Is Not Over."

17 Nafeez Ahmed, "White Supremacism and the Earth System," Medium, June 5, 2020, https://medium.com/insurge-intelligence/white-supremacism-and-the-earth-system-fa14e0ea6147.

18 This "outside" can also be within marginalized, "invisible" communities within the core country, such as Indian reservations, Black and Brown urban neighborhoods, and rural, lower income areas such as Appalachia.

19 Hickel, "Imperialism Is Not Over." Here are some definitions that might be helpful: Imperialism has existed for centuries and is most closely associated with the Roman Empire. Imperialism seeks to expand control or domination, both economic and political, over another territory. Colonization is a practice of imperialism where a colonizing country exerts control of a people or area through a combination of military violence, economic and political control, or opening the area to settlers who eventually replace the current population, such as what happened in the United States, Canada, Australia, and South Africa. This latter "method" of colonization is referred to as settler colonialism.

20 Sebastian Partogi, "Medieval Europe's 'Divine Obsession' with Indonesian Spices," *Jakarta Post*, July 20, 2017, https://www .thejakartapost.com/adv/2017/07/21/medieval-europes-divine -obsession-with-indonesian-spices.html.

21 Dutch Mennonites played a significant role in launching the Dutch East India Company—but according to the "standard story" (of which we should be skeptical), they withdrew once the Company started engaging in violence.

22 Olufemi O. Taiwo, "Our Planet Is Heating Up. Why Are Climate Politics Still Frozen?," *New Yorker*, October 25, 2021, https://www .newyorker.com/magazine/2021/11/01/our-planet-is-heating-up -why-are-climate-politics-still-frozen-colonialism-environment.

23 See chapter 7, "Follow the Money," in Augustine, *The Land Is Not Empty*.

24 Jason Hickel, Christian Dorninger, Hanspeter Wieland, and Intan Suwandi, "Imperialist Appropriation in the World Economy: Drain from the Global South through Unequal Exchange, 1990–2015," *Global Environmental Change* 73 (March 2022): 6, https://doi.org/ 10.1016/j.gloenvcha.2022.102467.

25 "EVs vs. Gas Vehicles: What Are Cars Made Out of?," Mining, May 30, 2022, https://www.mining.com/web/evs-vs-gas-vehicles-what -are-cars-made-out-of/. Another report from the United Nation's International Energy Agency says that demand for lithium will increase by 4,200 percent: https://docs.wind-watch.org/IEA-Critical -Minerals.pdf.

26 IEA, "The Role of Critical Minerals in Clean Energy Transitions," https://www.iea.org/reports/the-role-of-critical-minerals-in-clean -energy-transitions/executive-summary.

27 John R. Owen, Deanna Kemp, Alex M. Lechner et al., "Author Correction: Energy Transition Minerals and Their Intersection with Land-Connected Peoples," *Nature*, January 4, 2023, https://doi.org/10.1038/s41893-022-00994-6.

28 Della Duncan and Robert Raymond, "14: The Green Transition, Pt. 1 —The Problem with Green Capitalism."

29 Global Witness, "Last Line of Defence," September 13, 2021, https://www.globalwitness.org/en/campaigns/environmental-activists/last-line-defence/.

30 Nate Hagens, "53: William E. Rees: 'The Fundamental Issue— Overshoot,'" January 11, 2023, in *The Great Simplification*, podcast, MP3 audio, 1:42:32, https://www.thegreatsimplification.com/episode/53-william-rees.

31 Cecilia Jamasmie, "Gates, Bezos-Backed Firm Gets Cash Injection to Find Battery Metals," Mining, February 10, 2022, https://www.mining.com/gates-bezos-backed-firm-gets-cash-injection-to-find-battery-metals/.

32 Editorial Board, "Chile Should Send Its Proposed Constitution Back for a Rewrite," *Washington Post*, August 31, 2022, https://www.washingtonpost.com/opinions/2022/08/31/chile-constitution-vote-reject-rewrite/.

33 Elon Musk, @elonmusk, Twitter post (deleted), July 25, 2020, 4:32 a.m.

34 Ivan Penn and Eric Lipton, "The Lithium Gold Rush: Inside the Race to Power Electric Vehicles," *New York Times*, May 6, 2021, https://www.nytimes.com/2021/05/06/business/lithium-mining-race.html.

35 Hickel, *Less Is More*, 141.

36 Jason Hickel, "Quantifying National Responsibility for Climate Breakdown: An Equality-Based Attribution Approach for Carbon Dioxide Emissions in Excess of the Planetary Boundary," *The Lancet* 4, no. 9 (2020), https://doi.org/10.1016/S2542-5196(20)30196-0.

37 Jason Hickel, Daniel W. O'Neill, Andrew L. Fanning, and Huzaifa Zoomkawala, "National Responsibility for Ecological Breakdown: A Fair-Shares Assessment of Resource Use, 1970–2017," *The Lancet* 6, no. 4 (2022), https://doi.org/10.1016/S2542-5196(22)00044-4. Some argue that 74 percent is too low, as the study only began with the year 1970.

Chapter 5

1 This was a privilege afforded to the first generation of settler colonialists in many areas.

2   Toilet paper was too expensive, so they used pages from old Montgomery Ward catalogs and newspapers, a detail that never failed to impress me as a child.

3   J. Brad DeLong, *Slouching toward Utopia: An Economic History of the Twentieth Century* (New York City: Basic Books, 2022).

4   Sean Illing interview with Brad DeLong, "The Free-Market Century Is Over," in *The Gray Area*, podcast transcript, November 21, 2022, https://docs.google.com/document/d/1OT3R36lDxA_OaNvELK-IUSe_QKyY7Yea9wlw2mJbqEFA/edit. As noted in chapter 1, this wealth was not evenly distributed. Only one-fifth of the world benefited from this productivity explosion, and many suffered because of the extraction necessary to fuel it, as detailed in the previous chapter. DeLong points out, "There are still 500 million people who spend two hours a day or so thinking about how hungry they are and how much they'd like more calories. . . . And half a mile from my extensive Berkeley professor house, there is a man living in a box."

5   Dylan Matthews, "Humanity Was Stagnant for Millennia—Then Something Big Changed 150 Years Ago," Vox, September 7, 2022, https://www.vox.com/future-perfect/2022/9/7/23332699/economic-growth-brad-delong-slouching-utopia.

6   N. J. Hagens, "Economics for the Future—Beyond the Superorganism," *Ecological Economics* 169 (March 2020), https://doi.org/10.1016/j.ecolecon.2019.106520. Hagens also says that a "debt-based financial system cut from physical tethers allowed expansive credit and related consumption to accelerate."

7   In her book *The Land Is Not Empty*, Sarah talks about how Indigenous lands once outside the reach of the global economy have now come into reach largely because of technological advancements. None of this technology would be possible without fossil fuels.

8   "Our Worldview," Institute for the Study of Energy and Our Future, February 1, 2019, https://www.energyandourfuture.org/our-worldview/.

9   Vaclav Smil, *How the World Really Works: The Science behind How We Got Here and Where We're Going* (New York: Viking, 2022), 18.

10 Paul Voosen, "Meet Vaclav Smil, the Man Who Has Quietly Shaped How the World Thinks about Energy," *Science*, March 21, 2018, https://www.science.org/content/article/meet-vaclav-smil-man-who-has-quietly-shaped-how-world-thinks-about-energy.

11 "Share of Electricity in Total Final Energy Consumption," n.d., https://yearbook.enerdata.net/electricity/share-electricity-final-consumption.html.

12 Regenerative agriculture proponents disagree. For example, see Nate Hagens, "46: Vandana Shiva: 'Agroecology and The Great Simplification,'" November 23, 2022, in *The Great Simplification*, podcast, MP3 audio, https://www.thegreatsimplification.com/episode/46 -vandana-shiva.

13 Smil, *How the World Really Works*, 79.

14 Tom Murphy, "Finite Feeding Frenzy," Do the Math, December 5, 2022, https://dothemath.ucsd.edu/2022/12/finite-feeding-frenzy/.

15 This is why energy expert Nate Hagens refers to "rebuildable" energy, not renewable energy. While the inputs from the wind and sun are ever-renewing, the machines that capture these inputs are not.

16 See the work of materials scientist Simon Michaux. Excellent interviews with him can be found at Rachel Donald, "The Unsustainable Green Transition," April 19, 2023, in *Planet: Critical*, podcast, https://www.planetcritical.com/p/the-climate-crisis-and-the-climate# details; and Nate Hagens, "The Great Simplification #19—Simon Michaux," May 18, 2022, in *The Great Simplification*, podcast, https://natehagens.substack.com/p/the-great-simplification-19-simon.

17 Smil, *How the World Really Works*, 102.

18 Ezra Klein, "Ezra Klein Interviews Bill McKibben," in *The Ezra Klein Show*, podcast transcript, November 15, 2022, https://www.nytimes .com/2022/11/15/podcasts/transcript-ezra-klein-interviews-bill -mckibben.html.

19 Here's a startling fact: millionaires will use over 70 percent of the 1.5-degree carbon budget by 2030. From Rachel Donald, "Making Sense of the Crisis," *Planet: Critical*, YouTube video, 53:09, March 28, 2023, https://www.planetcritical.com/p/making-sense-of -the-crisis.

20 Following the math of exponential growth, at a 1 percent annual growth, any quantity doubles in about seventy years; at 2 percent in thirty-five years; at 7 percent in ten years; and so on. To find this number, divide seventy by the annual growth rate. A 2 to 3 percent growth rate, which is considered healthy and normal by mainstream economists, implies a doubling time of roughly twenty-five years. Richard Heinberg, "The Final Doubling," Resilience, November 3, 2022, https://www.resilience.org/stories/2022-11-03/the-final -doubling.

21 Della Duncan and Robert Raymond, "14: The Green Transition, Pt. 1 —The Problem with Green Capitalism."

22 Steve Lundeberg, "Earth Is 'Unequivocally' in Midst of Climate Emergency, Scientists Say," *ScienceDaily*, https:// www.sciencedaily .com/releases/2022/10/221026103215.htm.

23 When the carbon dioxide is used, the technology is referred to as carbon capture utilization and storage, or CCUS.

24 Andrew Nikiforuk, "Tech Won't Save Us. Shrinking Consumption Will," The Tyee, November 3, 2021, https://thetyee.ca/Analysis/2021/11/03/Tech-Will-Not-Save-Us-Shrinking-Consumption-Will/.

25 Bruce Robertson, "Carbon Capture: A Decarbonisation Pipe Dream," Institute for Energy Economics and Financial Analysis, September 1, 2022, https://ieefa.org/articles/carbon-capture-decarbonisation-pipe-dream.

26 Asher Miler, Rob Dietz, and Jason Bradford, "Sucking CO2 and Electrifying Everything: The Climate Movement's Desperate Dependence on Tenuous Technologies," May 10, 2023, in *Crazy Town*, podcast, https://www.resilience.org/stories/2023-05-10/crazy-town-episode-72-dueling-ecomodernists/.

27 David Wallace-Wells, "Vaclav Smil: We Must Leave Growth Behind," *New York Magazine*, September 24, 2019, https://nymag.com/intelligencer/2019/09/vaclav-smil-on-the-need-to-abandon-growth.html.

28 Kate Dooley et al., "The Land Gap Report," Land Gap, November 2022, https://www.landgap.org.

29 "Dutch Scientists Call Crop-Based Biofuels a 'False Solution,'" DutchNews, December 5, 2017, https://www.dutchnews.nl/news/2017/12/dutch-scientists-call-crop-based-biofuels-a-false-solution/.

30 Michael Grunwald, "It's Time to Say 'Put Down That Burger,'" *New York Times*, December 15, 2022.

31 Chris Rhodes, "Architects of Our Future: Energy and the Changing Climate," Resilience, November 7, 2022, https://www.resilience.org/stories/2022-11-07/architects-of-our-future-energy-and-the-changing-climate/.

32 IEA, "Nuclear," updated October 17, 2022, https://www.iea.org/fuels-and-technologies/nuclear.

33 Vijayalaxmi Kinhal, "Nuclear Power Plants by Country," WorldAtlas, March 14, 2019, https://www.worldatlas.com/articles/20-countries-most-dependent-on-nuclear-energy.html.

34 Nate Hagens, "The World's Coming Energy Catastrophe," Modern Wisdom, YouTube video, 1:15:41, August 4, 2021, https://youtu.be/CMqlBI3Zg1M.

35 Jason Hickel, *Less Is More: How Degrowth Will Save the World* (New York: Random House, 2020), 146.

36 Leslie Marmon Silko, *Ceremony* (1977; repr., New York: Penguin Classics, 1986), 135, 138.

37 This occupation began with Juan de Oñate's invasion in 1598.

38 In 1841 the US Exploring Expedition, led by Charles Wilkes, entered the Puget Sound.

39 Chief Seattle, "Chief Seattle's 1854 Oration – ver.1," Suquamish Tribe, n.d., https://suquamish.nsn.us/home/about-us/chief-seattle-speech/.

Chapter 6

1 Joe Brewer, *The Design Pathway for Regenerating Earth* (Barichara: Earth Regenerators Press, 2021), 51.

2 Donella H. Meadows, Jorgen Randers, and Dennis L. Meadows, *Limits to Growth: The 30-Year Update* (White River Junction: Chelsea Green, 2004), xi.

3 Olivia Rosane, "1972 Warning of Civilizational Collapse Was on Point, New Study Finds," EcoWatch, July 26, 2021, https://www.ecowatch.com/climate-crisis-civilization-collapse-mit-2653980183.html.

4 Will Steffen et al., "Planetary Boundaries: Guiding Human Development on a Changing Planet," *Science* 343 no. 6223, January 15, 2015, https://www.science.org/doi/10.1126/science.1259855.

5 Claire Asher, "Scientists: Humans Must Respect These 9 Boundaries to Keep Earth Habitable," *National Catholic Reporter*, April 5, 2021, https://www.ncronline.org/earthbeat/justice/scientists-humans-must-respect-these-9-boundaries-keep-earth-habitable.

6 Asher, "Scientists: Humans Must Respect."

7 Asher, "Scientists: Humans Must Respect."

8 Brewer, *Pathway for Regenerating Earth*, x.

9 Eduardo Brondizio, Sandra Diaz, Josef Settele, and Hien T. Ngo, eds., "Global Assessment Report on Biodiversity and Ecosystem Services of the Intergovernmental Science-Policy Platform on Biodiversity and Ecosystem Services," May 4, 2019, https://ipbes.net/global-assessment.

10 "Living Planet Report 2020," World Wildlife Fund, September 10, 2020, https://www.worldwildlife.org/publications/living-planet-report-2020.

11 Samantha Gross, "Renewables, Land Use, and Local Opposition in the United States," Brookings Institute, January 2020, https://www.brookings.edu/wp-content/uploads/2020/01/FP_20200113_renewables_land_use_local_opposition_gross.pdf. Bill McKibben refutes the ecological devastation of solar and wind in his podcast with Ezra Klein. See note 17 in chapter 5.

12 Asher, "Scientists: Humans Must Respect."

13 Timothée Parrique, "Decoupling Is Dead! Long Live Degrowth!," Resilience, July 26, 2019, https://www.resilience.org/stories/ 2019-07-26/decoupling-is-dead-long-live-degrowth/.

14 David Wallace-Wells, "Beyond Catastrophe: A New Climate Reality Is Coming into View," *New York Times*, October 26, 2022, https:// www.nytimes.com/interactive/2022/10/26/magazine/climate -change-warming-world.html.

15 Richard Heinberg, "Why We Can't Just Do It: The Truth about Our Failure to Curb Carbon Emissions," Resilience, March 23, 2023, https://www.resilience.org/stories/2023-03-23/why-we-cant-just-do -it-the-truth-about-our-failure-to-curb-carbon-emissions/.

16 Jason Hickel, *Less Is More: How Degrowth Will Save the World* (New York: Random House, 2020), 38.

17 Hannah Ritchie, Max Roser, and Pablo Rosado, "Energy," Our World in Data, 2022, https://ourworldindata.org/energy-production -consumption.

18 Richard York and Shannon Elizabeth Bell, "Energy Transitions or Additions?: Why a Transition From Fossil Fuels Requires More Than the Growth of Renewable Energy," *Energy Research and Social Science* 51 (May 2019): 40-43, https://doi.org/10.1016/j.erss.2019.01.008.

19 Calum Chace and Cognitive World, "Review of 'More from Less,' by Andrew McAfee," *Forbes*, December 4, 2019, https://www.forbes .com/sites/cognitiveworld/2019/12/04/review-of-more-from-less-by -andrew-mcafee/.

20 Jason Hickel, "The Myth of America's Green Growth," *Foreign Policy*, June 18, 2020, https://foreignpolicy.com/2020/06/18/more-from- less-green-growth-environment-gdp/. To look at this another way, the average American uses fifty-seven barrel-of-oil equivalents of fossil fuels each year. We use another seventeen barrels to produce the finished products we buy that are made in other countries. Daniel Schmachtenberger, "42: Bend Not Break #4: Modeling the Drivers of the Metacrisis," October 26, 2022, in *The Great Simpli- fication*, podcast, 2:06:08, https://www.thegreatsimplification.com/ episode/42-daniel-schmachtenberger.

21 Hickel, "America's Green Growth."

22 Andrew Nikiforuk, "The Rising Chorus of Renewable Energy Skeptics," The Tyee, April 7, 2023, https://thetyee.ca/Analysis/2023/ 04/07/Rising-Chorus-Renewable-Energy-Skeptics/.

23 James D. Ward et al., "Is Decoupling GDP Growth from Environ- mental Impact Possible?," *PLOS One*, October 14, 2016, https://doi .org/10.1371/journal.pone.0164733.

24 Nafeez Ahmed, "Welcome to the Age of Crappy Oil," *Vice*, August 18, 2016, https://www.vice.com/en/article/vv7pyb/welcome-to-the-age -of-crappy-oil.

25 Peter Rudling, "Wind and Solar Energy Are Neither Renewable nor Sustainable," Energy Education, August 9, 2021, https:// energyeducation.se/wind-and-solar-energy-are-neither-renewable -nor-sustainable/.

26 A 2017 study found that in all fifty-seven cases examined, more efficiency led to more energy usage because of Jevons's paradox. See Christopher L. Magee and Tessaleno C. Devezas, "A Simple Extension of Dematerialization Theory: Incorporation of Technical Progress and the Rebound Effect," *Technological Forecasting and Social Change* 117 (April 2017): 196–205, https://doi.org/10.1016/ j.techfore.2016.12.001.

27 Nate Hagens, "23: The Mordor Economy," January 27, 2023, in *Frankly*, video, 12:52, https://www.thegreatsimplification.com/ frankly-original/23-mordor-economy.

28 Saleemul Huq quoted in Steve Lundeberg, "Earth Is 'Unequivocally' in Midst of Climate Emergency, Scientists Say," *ScienceDaily*, https:// www.sciencedaily.com/releases/2022/10/221026103215.htm.

29 There are many who argue that this juggernaut began with the Agricultural Revolution, and some who locate its genesis even earlier. As a student of deep history, I find these arguments compelling, but I believe there is more merit on focusing on the rise of colonization and capitalism in the modern era.

30 Nate Hagens, "53: William E. Rees: "The Fundamental Issue— Overshoot," January 11, 2023, in *The Great Simplification*, podcast, 1:42:32, https://www.thegreatsimplification.com/episode/53-william -rees; "William Rees—The Dangerous Disconnect between Econom- ics and Ecology," New Economic Thinking, YouTube video, 17:10, June 13, 2011, https://youtu.be/uxfGcwfYlAg. Another example of US overconsumption: the United States consumes fifteen times per capita what the United Nations recommends as sustainable consumption levels. Rachel Donald, "Making Sense of the Crisis," *Planet: Critical*, YouTube video, 53:09, March 28, 2023, https:// www.planetcritical.com/p/making-sense-of-the-crisis.

31 Nate Hagens, "58: Olivia Lazard: Peace and Power in the Mineral Age," February 15, 2023, in *The Great Simplification*, podcast, 1:29:41, https://www.thegreatsimplification.com/episode/58-olivia-lazard.

32 J. R. McNeill and Peter Engelke, *The Great Acceleration: An Environ- mental History of the Anthropocene since 1945* (Cambridge: Harvard University Press, 2014), 5.

33 Reese, "The Fundamental Issue."

34 This phrase comes from the Reverend Michael Dowd.

35 Christopher Ketcham, "Addressing Climate Change Will Not 'Save the Planet,'" December 3, 2022, https://theintercept.com/2022/12/03/climate-biodiversity-green-energy/.

36 Hrangthan Chhungi, M. M. Ekka, and Wati Lonchar, eds., *Doing Indigenous Theology in Asia: Toward New Frontiers* (National Council of Churches in India, Gossner Theological College, and the SCEP-TRE, 2012), 196.

37 Chhungi, Ekka, and Lonchar, 199.

38 Jon Sobrino, *The Principle of Mercy: Taking the Crucified People from the Cross* (Maryknoll: Orbis Books, 1994), 10.

39 Sobrino, *Principle of Mercy*, 17.

Chapter 7

1 Gerald Alfred Taiaiake, "Colonialism and State Dependency," *Journal of Aboriginal Health* 5, no. 2 (2009): 52.

2 This and the previous quotation are from Rishi Sugla, "Again on the Altar: On Climate Solutions and Colonialism," in *Required Reading: Climate Justice, Adaptation and Investing in Indigenous Power*, ed. NDN Collective's Climate Justice Campaign (n.p.: Loam, 2022), 108.

3 Vahakn N. Dadrian, "A Typology of Genocide," *International Review of Modern Sociology* 5, no. 2 (Autumn 1975): 201–12.

4 *Merriam-Webster Dictionary*, s.v. "decolonize," accessed May 16, 2023, https://www.merriam-webster.com/dictionary/decolonize.

5 Aman Sium, Chandni Desai, and Eric Ritskes, "Towards the 'Tangible Unknown': Decolonization and the Indigenous Future," *Decolonization: Indigeneity, Education, and Society* 1, no. 1 (2012): iii.

6 Sium, Desai, and Ritskes, "Towards the 'Tangible Unknown,'" v.

7 Umeek/E. Richard Atleo, *Principles of Tsawalk: An Indigenous Approach to Global Crisis* (Vancouver: University of British Columbia Press, 2011), 164.

8 Jeff Corntassel, "Re-envisioning Resurgence: Indigenous Pathways to Decolonization and Sustainable Self-Determination," *Decolonization: Indigeneity, Education & Society* 1, no. 1 (2012): 96.

9 Vandana Shiva, *Earth Democracy: Justice, Sustainability, and Peace* (Boston: South End Press, 2005).

10 This and the previous quotation are from Corntassel, "Re-envisioning Resurgence," 94–95.

11 Atleo, *Principles of Tsawalk*, 334.

12 Amilcar Cabral, "The Weapon of Theory," address, January 1966, Havana, Marxists Internet Archive, https://www.marxists.org/subject/africa/cabral/1966/weapon-theory.htm.

13 Sium, Desai, and Ritskes, "Towards the 'Tangible Unknown,'" v.

14 For more information about land return, check out the Nuns and Nones Land Justice Project: https://www.nunsandnones.org/land-justice.

15 Nathan Tanner, "Defending ICWA: The Next Fight over Tribal Sovereignty," *Indian Country Today*, November 5, 2022, https://ictnews.org/opinion/defending-icwa-the-next-fight-over-tribal-sovereignty.

16 See Sarah Augustine, "Solidarity and Repair," chapter 8 in *The Land Is Not Empty: Following Jesus in Dismantling the Doctrine of Discovery* (Harrisonburg: Herald Press, 2021).

17 Eve Tuck and K. Wayne Yang, "Decolonization Is Not a Metaphor," *Decolonization: Indigeneity, Education, and Society* 1 no. 1 (2012): 6. Tuck and Yang are cofounders of the Land Relationship Super Collective, which provides a space for building mutual support and strategy sharing for organizations doing land-based work. For more information, see http://www.landrelationships.com/.

18 Sium, Desai, and Ritskes, "Towards the 'Tangible Unknown,'" 8. Emphasis mine.

19 Robert J. Miller, *Native America Discovered and Conquered: Thomas Jefferson, Lewis and Clark, and Manifest Destiny* (Winnipeg: Bison Books, 2008).

20 To read about Indigenous struggles to protect their lands, including the struggle against the Dakota Access Pipeline, see the website of the United South and Eastern Tribes at https://www.usetinc.org/culture-and-heritage/sacred-sites/. See also Isabella Breda, "Human Error Likely Caused Swinomish Reservation Train Derailment, Official Says," Seattle Times, March 23, 2023, https://www.seattletimes.com/seattle-news/environment/human-error-likely-caused-swinomish-reservation-train-derailment-official-says/; Matthew Neisius, "Western Shoshone Nation Opposes Yucca Mountain Nuclear Repository," Commodities, Conflict, and Cooperation (Fall 2016 & Winter 2017), https://sites.evergreen.edu/ccc/warnuclear/shoshone-tribe-opposes-yucca-mountain-nuclear-repository/.

21 Gillian Flaccus, "Pacific Northwest Tribes: Remove Columbia River Dams," AP News, October 15, 2019, https://apnews.com/article/dc9df60df54e46be9b17a3b792df12e1.

22 Heather Hansman, "How a Lack of Water Fueled COVID-19 in Navajo Nation," *Outside Online*, May 12, 2022, https://www.outsideonline.com/outdoor-adventure/environment/navajo-nation-coronavirus-spread-water-rights/; Becky Sullivan, "The Supreme

Court Wrestles with Questions over the Navajo Nation's Water Rights," NPR, March 20, 2023, https://www.npr.org/2023/03/20/1164852475/supreme-court-navajo-nation-water-rights.

23 Louise Morris, "'A Megaproject of Death': Fury as Maya Train Nears Completion in Mexico," *The Guardian*, June 8, 2023, https://www.theguardian.com/global-development/2023/may/23/fury-as-maya-train-nears-completion-mexico.

24 Corntassel, "Re-envisioning Resurgence," 92.

25 General Assembly Resolution 61/295, United Nations Declaration on the Rights of Indigenous Peoples, A/RES/61/295, October 2, 2007, https://www.un.org/en/genocideprevention/documents/atrocity-crimes/Doc.18_declaration rights indigenous peoples.pdf.

26 Wex Definitions Team, s.v. "terra nullius," Legal Information Institute, Cornell Law School, last updated April 2022, https://www.law.cornell.edu/wex/terra_nullius.

27 The OAS charter clearly identifies that the purpose of the institution is an economic one. Articles 34, 39, and 42 state the following goals, all of which are direct quotes from the charter (emphasis mine):

> Substantial and self-sustained *increase of per capita national product*;
>
> *Accelerated and diversified industrialization*, especially of capital and intermediate goods;
>
> *Promotion of private initiative and investment* in harmony with action in the public sector;
>
> Expansion and diversification of exports;
>
> *To speed up the development of the less-developed Member States*;
>
> *Improved conditions for trade in basic commodities*;
>
> Conditions conducive *to increasing the real export earnings of the Member States*;
>
> Establishing a Latin American common market in the shortest possible time.

Organization of American States (OAS), Charter of the Organization of American States, April 30, 1948, https://www.cidh.oas.org/basicos/english/basic22.charter oas.htm

28 "Charter of the OAS,"

29 Michelle Alexander, *The New Jim Crow: Mass Incarceration in the Age of Colorblindness* (New York: The New Press, 2020). See also "Report to the United Nations on Racial Disparities in the U.S. Criminal Justice System," The Sentencing Project, November 2, 2022, https://www.sentencingproject.org/reports/report-to-the-united-nations-on-racial-disparities-in-the-u-s-criminal-justice-system/.

30 Rubén G. Rumbaut, "Reaping What You Sow: Immigration, Youth, and Reactive Ethnicity," *Applied Development Science* 12, no. 2 (2008): 108–11.

31 "Indian tribes are considered by federal law to be 'domestic, dependent nations.' Congress enacted this sovereign authority to protect Indian groups from state authority, and the sovereign authority extends to Indian tribal courts, which adjudicate matters relating to Indian affairs." Federal Bar Association, "Understanding Tribal Sovereignty," September 13, 2022, https://www.fedbar.org/blog/understanding-tribal-sovereignty/. See also US Department of the Interior, Bureau of Indian Affairs: "The Bureau of Indian Affairs' mission is to enhance the quality of life, to promote economic opportunity, and to carry out the responsibility to protect and improve the trust assets of American Indians, Indian tribes and Alaska Natives. "Bureau of Indian Affairs (BIA)," https://www.bia.gov/bia.

32 US Census Bureau, "Facts for Features: American Indian and Alaska Native Heritage Month: November 2022," April 26, 2023, https://www.census.gov/newsroom/facts-for-features/2022/aian-month.html.

33 Of the 535 members of Congress in 2018–2019, the fifty wealthiest members reported between $10.7 million and $259.7 million in net wealth. The median individual wealth held in the 2018 Senate was $1.7 million; the median wealth of those in the House was $500,000. Among the general population, the median *household* income in 2018 was $63,179. Recent data shows that the bottom half of Americans have more debt that wealth. Katie Warren, "One Brutal Sentence Captures What a Disaster Money in America Has Become," *Insider*, May 23, 2019, https://www.businessinsider.com/bottom-half-of-americans-negative-net-worth-2019-5.

34 See Lea Elsässer and Armin Schäfer. "Political Inequality in Rich Democracies." *Annual Review of Political Science* 26 (2023): 469–87; Martin Gilens, "Preference Gaps and Inequality in Representation," PS: Political Science & Politics 42, no. 2 (2009): 335–41; Kristina C. Miler, *Poor Representation: Congress and the Politics of Poverty in the United States* (Cambridge: Cambridge University Press, 2018). Less scholarly articles on the same subject include Liz Essley Whyte and Ryan J. Foley, "Conflicted Interests: State Lawmakers Often Blur the Line between the Public's Business and Their Own," *Center for Public Integrity*, January 28, 2022, https://publicintegrity.org/politics/state-politics/conflicted-interests-state-lawmakers-often-blur-the-line-between-the-publics-business-and-their-own/; Harry Enten, "The GOP Tax Cuts Are Even More Unpopular Than Past Tax Hikes," *FiveThirtyEight*, November 29, 2017, https://fivethirtyeight

.com/features/the-gop-tax-cuts-are-even-more-unpopular-than-past-tax-hikes/; ITEP, "Lawmakers Are Allowing Monied Interests to Trump the Voices of Their Constituents," n.d., https://itep.org/lawmakers-are-allowing-monied-interests-to-trump-the-voices-of-their-constituents/.

35 U.S. Energy Information Administration, "U.S. Energy Facts Explained," last updated June 10, 2022, https://www.eia.gov/energyexplained/us-energy-facts/.

36 World Trade Organization, "Global Trade Growth Loses Momentum as Trade Tensions Persist," World Trade Organization, April 2, 2019, https://www.wto.org/english/news_e/pres19_e/pr837_e.htm.

37 Marc Edelman, "Bringing the Moral Economy Back in . . . to the Study of 21st-Century Transnational Peasant Movements," *American Anthropologist* 107, no. 3 (2005): 331–45.

38 See Articles 2, 12, and 16 in World Health Organization, *International Health Regulations* (2005) (Geneva: WHO, 2008).

39 Pennsylvania Dutch is the dialect of German spoken by the Amish.

40 Leroy Beachy, *Cemetery Directory of the Amish Community in Eastern Holmes and Adjoining Counties in Ohio*, 2nd ed. (self-published, 1975), 75.

41 Walter Brueggemann et al., eds., *Texts for Preaching: A Lectionary Commentary, Based on the NRSV, Vol. 1: Year A* (Louisville: Westminster John Knox, 1995), 379.

Chapter 8

1 Valerie A. Storey, "What Is System Complexity," InfoScipedia, IGI Global Publishing House, accessed May 19, 2023, https://www.igi-global.com/dictionary/system-complexity/68505.

2 Joseph O'Connor and Ian McDermott, *The Art of Systems Thinking: Essential Skills for Creativity and Problem Solving* (London: Thorsons, 1997), 17.

3 Kinza Yasar, "What Is a Computer System?," TechTarget, last updated March 2023, https://www.techtarget.com/searchwindowsserver/definition/system.

4 Tyson Yunkaporta, *Sand Talk: How Indigenous Thinking Can Save the World* (New York: HarperOne, 2020), 17.

5 Yunkaporta, *Sand Talk*, 37.

6 Alexandra Spiliakos, "Tragedy of the Commons: What It Is and 5 Examples," *Business Insights* (blog), Harvard Business School, February 6, 2019, https://online.hbs.edu/blog/post/tragedy-of-the-commons-impact-on-sustainability-issues.

7 "Including Mission in Company's Best Interest Statement," Impact Terms, April 18, 2019, https://www.impactterms.org/best-interest-statement.

8 Lenore Palladino and Kristina Karisson, "Towards Accountable Capitalism: Remaking Corporate Law through Stakeholder Governance," Harvard Law School Forum on Corporate Governance, February 11, 2019, https://corpgov.law.harvard.edu/2019/02/11/towards-accountable-capitalism-remaking-corporate-law-through-stakeholder-governance/.

9 Joi Ito and Jeff Howe, "Emergent Systems Are Changing the Way We Think," *Technology* (blog), Aspen Institute, January 30, 2017, https://www.aspeninstitute.org/blog-posts/emergent-systems-changing-way-think/.

10 "Concepts: Emergence," New England Complex Systems Institute, https://necsi.edu/emergence.

11 "What Are 'Externalized' Costs?" Nature and More, accessed May 19, 2023, https://www.natureandmore.com/en/true-cost-of-food/what-are-externalized-costs.

12 Juliette Jowit, "World's Top Firms Cause $2.2tn of Environmental Damage, Report Estimates," *Guardian*, February 18, 2010, https://www.theguardian.com/environment/2010/feb/18/worlds-top-firms-environmental-damage.

13 United Nations, "New Study Shows Multi-Trillion Dollar Natural Capital Risk Underlining Urgency of Green Economy Transition," April 15, 2013, https://www.unep.org/news-and-stories/press-release/new-study-shows-multi-trillion-dollar-natural-capital-risk.

14 Joanna Macy, "The Great Turning," Ecoliteracy.org, July 24, 2023, https://www.ecoliteracy.org/article/great-turning.

15 Rohini Walker, "The Indigenous Science of Permaculture," KCET, December 23, 2019, https://www.kcet.org/shows/tending-nature/the-indigenous-science-of-permaculture.

16 Anja Bless, "'Regenerative Agriculture' Is All the Rage—but It's Not Going to Fix Our Food System," Resilience, May 16, 2023, https://www.resilience.org/stories/2023-05-16/regenerative-agriculture-is-all-the-rage-but-its-not-going-to-fix-our-food-system.

Chapter 9

1 Patient Education, "Sweet Drinks and Obesity," UCSF Benioff Children's Hospitals, accessed May 23, 2023, https://www.ucsfbenioffchildrens.org/education/sweet-drinks-and-obesity.

2 Steven W. Henderson, "Consumer Spending in World War II: The Forgotten Consumer Expenditure Surveys," *Monthly Labor Review*,

U.S. Bureau of Labor Statistics, August 2015, https://doi.org/10.21916/mlr.2015.29.

3   "Food Prices and Spending," USDA Economic Research Service, last updated February 27, 2023, https://www.ers.usda.gov/data-products/ag-and-food-statistics-charting-the-essentials/food-prices-and-spending/.

4   Mark J. Perry, "When It Comes to Spending on Food as Share of Total Consumer Expenditures, Americans Have the Most Affordable Food on the Planet, and It's Gotten Better over Time," American Enterprise Institute, March 2, 2014, https://www.aei.org/carpe-diem/when-it-comes-to-spending-on-food-as-share-of-total-consumer-expenditures-americans-have-the-most-affordable-food-on-the-planet-and-its-gotten-better-over-time/.

5   Michael Carlson, "Earl Butz: US Politician Brought Down by Racist Remark," *The Guardian*, February 4, 2008, https://www.theguardian.com/world/2008/feb/04/usa.obituaries.

6   Amy Herrera, "America Has the World's Cheapest Food," *Franchesca's Dawn Farm* (blog), August 24, 2019, https://franchescasdawnfarm.com/blog/why-americans-spend-less-money-on-food-than-any-other-nation.

7   Rockefeller Foundation, "The True Cost of Food in the U.S.," last modified November 15, 2021, https://www.rockefellerfoundation.org/report/true-cost-of-food-measuring-what-matters-to-transform-the-u-s-food-system/.

8   Shikha Garg et al., "Hospitalization Rates and Characteristics of Patients Hospitalized with Laboratory-Confirmed Coronavirus Disease 2019—COVID-NET, 14 States, March 1–30, 2020," *Morbidity and Mortality Weekly Report* 69, no. 15 (2020): 458.

9   Rockefeller Foundation, "The True Cost of Food in the U.S.," 24.

10 Rockefeller Foundation, "The True Cost of Food in the U.S.," 24.

11 Anna M. Acosta et al., "Racial and Ethnic Disparities in Rates of COVID-19–Associated Hospitalization, Intensive Care Unit Admission, and In-Hospital Death in the United States from March 2020 to February 2021," *JAMA Network Open* 4, no. 10 (2021): e2130479-e2130479; Don Bambino Geno Tai et al., "Disproportionate Impact of COVID-19 on Racial and Ethnic Minority Groups in the United States: A 2021 Update," *Journal of Racial and Ethnic Health Disparities* (2021): 1–6.

12 Vandana Shiva (@drvandanashiva), Twitter, January 20, 2023, https://twitter.com/drvandanashiva/status/1616674738541309953.

13 "Moderate Obesity Takes Years off Life Expectancy," University of Oxford, March 3, 2009, https://www.ox.ac.uk/news/2009-03-18 -moderate-obesity-takes-years-life-expectancy.

14 Richard Partington, "Is It Time to End Our Fixation with GDP and Growth?," *The Guardian*, June 17, 2019, https://www.theguardian .com/news/2019/jun/17/is-time-to-end-our-fixation-with-gdp-and -growth.

15 Kimberly Amadeo, "Why Trickle-Down Economics Works in Theory but Not in Fact," *The Balance*, updated December 30, 2021, https://www.thebalancemoney.com/trickle-down-economics-theory -effect-does-it-work-3305572.

16 Jason Hickel, "Is the World Poor, or Unjust," *Jason Hickel* (blog), February 22, 2021, https://www.jasonhickel.org/blog/2021/2/21/ is-the-world-poor-or-unjust.

17 Jason Hickel, *Less Is More: How Degrowth Will Save the World* (New York: Random House, 2020), 172.

18 Hickel, *Less Is More*, 175.

19 Hickel, *Less Is More*, 175.

20 Mayo Clinic Staff, "Weight Loss: Gain Control of Emotional Eating," Mayo Clinic, December 2, 2022, https://www.mayoclinic.org/ healthy-lifestyle/weight-loss/in-depth/weight-loss/art-20047342.

21 Quoted in Katie McCallum, "A Dietitian's No-Nonsense Guide to Fighting Emotional Eating," *On Health*, Houston Methodist, December 7, 2020, https://www.houstonmethodist.org/blog/articles/2020/ dec/a-dietitians-no-nonsense-guide-to-fighting-emotional-eating/.

22 Marianne Hayes, "What Is Emotional Spending?," *Personal Finance* (blog), January 18, 2023, https://www.experian.com/blogs/ask -experian/what-is-emotional-spending/.

23 Wayne W. LaMorte, "What Is Culture?," Cultural Awareness, Boston University School of Public Health, last modified May 3, 2016, https://sphweb.bumc.bu.edu/otlt/mph-modules/PH/ CulturalAwareness/CulturalAwareness2.html.

24 Doris Longacre, *More-with-Less Cookbook: Recipes and Suggestions by Mennonites on How to Eat Better and Consume Less of the World's Limited Food Resources* (1976; repr., Scottdale: Herald Press, 2003).

25 Kate Raworth, "What on Earth Is the Doughnut?," *Kate Raworth* (blog), last modified September 30, 2020, https://www.kateraworth .com/doughnut/.

26 Umeek/Eugene Richard Atleo, *Principles of Tsawalk: An Indigenous Approach to Global Crisis* (Vancouver: University of British Columbia Press, 2011), 163–64.

27 Sharifah Rahma Sekalala and Monica Kirya, "Subsidiarity in Global Health Governance: 'Two Publics' and Defiance in the Global Fund's Operations in Uganda," SSRN, last revised August 5, 2013, https://dx.doi.org/10.2139/ssrn.2297753.

28 Jeffrey M. Jones, "U.S. Church Membership Down Sharply in Past Two Decades," Gallup, April 18, 2019, https://news.gallup.com/poll/248837/church-membership-down-sharply-past-two-decades.aspx.

29 Wendy Wang, "The Decline in Church Attendance in COVID America," Institute for Family Studies, January 20, 2022, https://ifstudies.org/blog/the-decline-in-church-attendance-in-covid-america.

30 Noel Moules, "Shalom," in *Nomad*, podcast, February 1, 2020, https://www.nomadpodcast.co.uk/noel-moules-christian-animism-and-the-re-enchantment-of-the-world-n214/

31 Vanessa Machado de Oliveira, *Hospicing Modernity: Facing Humanity's Wrongs and the Implications for Social Activism* (Berkeley: North Atlantic Books, 2021), 19–20.

32 Bill McKibben, *The Comforting Whirlwind: God, Job, and the Scale of Creation* (Boston: Cowley Publications, 2005), 27.

33 David Rensberger, "Whose Land Is It?" *Anabaptist Witness* 7 no. 2 (October 2020): 157, https://www.anabaptistwitness.org/journal_entry/whose-land-is-it/.

34 Writer Wendell Berry says, "What I would call Amish genius has consisted not at all in forswearing industrial technology but in limiting the use of it. So far as I know, theirs is the only community . . . in this country that has done so, or that is capable of doing so." (Obviously, Indigenous communities also do this.) Religiously, Berry says, the Amish accept the biblical acknowledgment that God owns the land. Culturally, many Amish have chosen not to use fossil fuels in farming. Thus, the scale of their farms and manufacturing is "limited by the needs and capacities of living creatures. Amish farmers simply are not going to use technologies that replace their children and their neighbors. That would make it impossible to be Amish." Wendell Berry, preface to David Kline, *The Round of a Country Year: A Farmer's Day Book* (Berkeley: Counterpoint, 2017), xxi.

Chapter 10

1 Daniel Sarewitz, *Frontiers of Illusion: Science, Technology, and the Politics of Progress* (Philadelphia: Temple University Press, 1996).

2 "Galápagos," in *Radiolab*, podcast, June 24, 2022, https://radiolab.org/episodes/galapagos-2206.

3 Manuel Delgado-Baquerizo et al., "A Global Atlas of the Dominant Bacteria Found in Soil," *Science* 359, no. 6373 (January 19, 2018): 320–25, https://doi.org/10.1126/science.aap9516.

4 "Joe Brewer's Bold Quest to Restore a Bioregion," in *Frontiers of Commoning*, podcast, November 30, 2022, https://david-bollier .simplecast.com/episodes/joe-brewers-bold-quest-to-restore-a -bioregion.

5 In Suriname, public health officials told Dan and me, "You can't tell people facing illness and death from mercury intoxication that they are sick if you can't also provide a treatment or a cure." We fundamentally dismissed this premise and provided Indigenous community members with risk assessments and health assessments that documented the impact of mercury on their bodies. We assume that every person has the right to understand her own health and know what is going on in her own body. A person with full information is empowered to decide what the next step should be and how to act. A community with full information is empowered to change the world.

6 Umeek/Eugene Richard Atleo, *Principles of Tsawalk: An Indigenous Approach to Global Crisis* (Vancouver: University of British Columbia Press, 2011), 165.

7 Rachel Donald, "Making Sense of the Crisis," Planet Critical, March 23, 2023, video, 53:08, https://www.planetcritical.com/p/ making-sense-of-the-crisis.

8 Donald, "Making Sense of the Crisis."

THE AUTHORS

SARAH AUGUSTINE, who is a Pueblo (Tewa) descendant, is cofounder and executive director of the Coalition to Dismantle the Doctrine of Discovery. She is also the cofounder of Suriname Indigenous Health Fund (SIHF), where she has worked in relationship with vulnerable Indigenous Peoples since 2005. She has represented the interests of Indigenous community partners to their own governments, the Inter-American Development Bank, the United Nations, the Organization of American States Inter-American Commission on Human Rights, the World Health Organization, and a host of other international actors, including corporate interests. She has taught at Heritage University, Central Washington University, and Goshen College. She is a columnist for *Anabaptist World*, cohosts the *Dismantling the Doctrine of Discovery* podcast with Sheri Hostetler, and is the author of *The Land Is Not Empty: Following Jesus in Dismantling the Doctrine of Discovery*. She serves in a leadership role on multiple boards and commissions to enable vulnerable peoples in Washington State to speak for themselves in advocating for structural change. She and her husband Dan Peplow and their son live in the Yakima Valley of Washington.

SHERI HOSTETLER cofounded the Coalition
to Dismantle the Doctrine of Discovery in
2014 and continues to serve on the steer-
ing committee. She is the cohost of the
Dismantling the Doctrine of Discovery pod-
cast with Sarah Augustine. She was also one of the founders
of what is now called Inclusive Mennonite Pastors, a coalition
of pastoral leaders seeking LGBTQ+ justice in the church. She
has been the lead pastor of First Mennonite Church of San
Francisco since 2000. Her writing has appeared in *Anabaptist
World*, *Mennonite Quarterly Review*, *Leader* magazine, and
more, and her poems appear in *A Cappella: Mennonite Voices in
Poetry*. She is a graduate of Bluffton College and the Episcopal
Divinity School. She is trained as a spiritual director and a per-
maculturist, and lives with her husband Jerome Baggett and
their son Patrick on an island in the San Francisco Bay. She
comes from a long line of Amish and Mennonite settler farmers.